Approaches to Teaching Poe's Prose and Poetry

Approaches to Teaching World Literature

Joseph Gibaldi, series editor

For a complete listing of titles,
see the last pages of this book.

Approaches to Teaching Poe's Prose and Poetry

Edited by

Jeffrey Andrew Weinstock

and

Tony Magistrale

The Modern Language Association of America
New York   2008

For information about obtaining permission to reprint material from MLA book
publications, send your request by mail (see address below), e-mail
(permissions@mla.org), or fax (646 458-0030).

Library of Congress Cataloging-in-Publication Data

Approaches to teaching Poe's prose and poetry /
edited by Jeffrey Andrew Weinstock and Tony Magistrale.
p. cm. — (Approaches to teaching world literature ; 104)
Includes bibliographical references and index.
ISBN 978-1-60329-011-1 (alk. paper) — ISBN 978-1-60329-012-8 (pbk. : alk. paper)
1. Poe, Edgar Allan, 1809–1849—Study and teaching.   2. Poe, Edgar Allan, 1809–1849—
Criticism and interpretation.   3. American literature—Study and teaching (Higher)
I. Weinstock, Jeffrey Andrew.   II. Magistrale, Tony.
PS2638.A66 2008
818'.309—dc22   2008024846

Approaches to Teaching World Literature 104
ISSN 1059-1133

Cover illustration of the paperback edition:
Le corbeau ("The Raven"). By Edouard Manet. 1875. Print collection,
Miriam and Ira D. Wallach Division of Art, Prints, and Photographs,
The New York Public Library, Astor, Lenox and Tilden Foundations

Published by The Modern Language Association of America
26 Broadway, New York, NY 10004-1789
www.mla.org

CONTENTS

PREFACE TO THE SERIES

In *The Art of Teaching* Gilbert Highet wrote, "Bad teaching wastes a great deal of effort, and spoils many lives which might have been full of energy and happiness." All too many teachers have failed in their work, Highet argued, simply "because they have not thought about it." We hope that the Approaches to Teaching World Literature series, sponsored by the Modern Language Association's Publications Committee, will not only improve the craft—as well as the art—of teaching but also encourage serious and continuing discussion of the aims and methods of teaching literature.

The principal objective of the series is to collect within each volume different points of view on teaching a specific literary work, a literary tradition, or a writer widely taught at the undergraduate level. The preparation of each volume begins with a wide-ranging survey of instructors, thus enabling us to include in the volume the philosophies and approaches, thoughts and methods of scores of experienced teachers. The result is a sourcebook of material, information, and ideas on teaching the subject of the volume to undergraduates.

The series is intended to serve nonspecialists as well as specialists, inexperienced as well as experienced teachers, graduate students who wish to learn effective ways of teaching as well as senior professors who wish to compare their own approaches with the approaches of colleagues in other schools. Of course, no volume in the series can ever substitute for erudition, intelligence, creativity, and sensitivity in teaching. We hope merely that each book will point readers in useful directions; at most each will offer only a first step in the long journey to successful teaching.

Joseph Gibaldi
Series Editor

PREFACE TO THE VOLUME

This book is long overdue. Since 1980 the Modern Language Association has published more than one hundred volumes in its Approaches to Teaching series. Although these volumes include a broad representation of American literary texts, it is noteworthy that the works of Edgar Allan Poe, who was the first American writer profound and gifted enough to impress literary Europe, is only now among them. What makes Poe's case interesting, at least in the realm of literary scholarship, for his popular reputation is far less equivocal, is that he remains a controversial artist: his work is as beloved as it is dismissed.

In keeping with the process established by the MLA for the development of volumes to its Approaches to Teaching World Literature series, we began production on this project by soliciting feedback in the form of a questionnaire from those with experience teaching Poe. We requested information about primary and secondary Poe texts taught, topics covered, and difficulties encountered, and the valuable feedback we received helped structure the contents of this volume. However, one response stands out in our minds. When asked about the primary challenge one faces in teaching Poe, the respondent wrote simply, "To overcome the prejudice that Poe was a good writer," and, when asked about specific concerns this volume should cover, the respondent wrote, "Poe is simply not worth much attention."

This surprising (and decidedly critical) response concisely engages issues of perception, quality, and value that are at the heart of literary studies and foregrounds Poe's vexed relation to canonicity, academia, and world literature more generally. Even if we accept that in places throughout his writing Poe was not always "a good writer," his reputation at home and abroad over the past century and a half suggests that he is certainly worthy of much attention. Even withholding any assertions about their quality and value, one could argue that Poe's works are deserving of scrutiny if only because of their academic and cultural ubiquity—that they are so frequently taught in a variety of contexts and in classrooms around the world. Students bring to their study of Poe so many opinions of the man's life and his works that we see operating—for better and for worse—the "Poe phenomenon," a nexus of texts, beliefs, desires, perceptions, misperceptions, anxieties, and associations attached to the name Poe, a name that continues to resonate in popular culture and must be confronted by any teacher who includes his work on a syllabus.

As all respondents to the survey indicated (even the one who made the unflattering appraisal above), any consideration of Poe elicits critical questions. Among these questions are, To what extent does his biography inform his writings? To what extent can one differentiate between the voices of Poe's first-person narrators and his own voice? Is a psychoanalytic approach to Poe's fiction the most effective means to interpreting it? How is it possible that the same creative spirit that produced several of the world's most famous horror stories could also be responsible for inventing the tale of ratiocination and analytic essays on the art of poetry and the short story, the genre he helped define and perfect? Is his writing actually "good," and on what criteria does one base this evaluation? Can an author be a racist and still produce valuable literary contributions? Can one plagiarize and still be original? How did Poe's involvement with the literary magazines of his era shape his career as a writer? How can the historical Poe be situated in relation not only to the politics of publication during his lifetime but also to the philosophical and religious movements of the period? Taken together, these questions and the many others raised by the inclusions in this volume highlight the question of how to teach Poe today.

This collection, like the many others in the MLA's Approaches to Teaching World Literature series, is primarily directed toward beginning or nonspecialist teachers on the undergraduate level. However, we also feel that it has much to offer senior faculty members, Poe experts, graduate students, advanced undergraduates, and those teaching on the secondary level. The volume is divided into two parts: "Materials" and "Approaches." The "Materials" section, written by the editors, gathers together information and suggestions provided by survey respondents. It identifies the most often taught Poe texts and the contexts in which they are most frequently encountered, the editions of Poe's works that are considered most serviceable, recommended secondary reading for both students and teachers, and supplemental aids to the teaching of Poe's works.

Part 2, "Approaches," consists of twenty-six essays. The size of the Poe canon prohibits exhaustive coverage of all texts and topics; with an eye toward being as useful as possible to teachers on all levels, the essays here attend primarily to Poe's most frequently taught texts and have been divided into three sections. Essays in the first section, "Literary, Cultural, and Historical Contexts," explore Poe's works in the light of his historical epoch; essays in the next section, "Theoretical Contexts," offer readings of Poe's works from specific theoretical orientations; and essays in the final section, "Classroom Contexts," examine Poe's works especially in relation to the works of other authors. In each of the essays, the authors discuss Poe with attention to pedagogical concerns: how best to present these specific aspects of Poe in the classroom. Bibliographic information for all the books and articles referenced throughout this volume is presented in the works-cited section.

We are indebted to many for assistance in bringing this book into existence. Especially deserving of thanks are the contributors themselves for their insights and efforts, as well as the participants in the MLA survey. The series editor, Joseph Gibaldi, offered encouragement and sound counsel throughout the process. The MLA commissioned reviews of this volume at various critical phases of its construction; since the reviewers' names were withheld from us, we can only acknowledge their assistance here in helping define, revise, and refine the contents and quality of this publication. The editors would be remiss not to mention those individuals and institutions that afforded help in the preparation of this manuscript. The University of Vermont provided Tony Magistrale with a year-long sabbatical leave that enabled him to compose his chapter and assemble some of the prefatory materials in this volume, as well as to edit the work of many of the contributors selected. As such, this work received important assistance from the staff at the Bailey-Howe Library on the University of Vermont campus. Students at the University of Vermont—graduate and especially undergraduate students enrolled in literary-survey courses—were instrumental in the crafting of Magistrale's essays and are gratefully acknowledged here. Jeffrey Weinstock would like to thank his wife, Astrid, for her unwavering support.

JAW and TM

Part One

MATERIALS

Courses and Texts

Poe's works are taught in an unusually broad array of classroom contexts ranging from high school introductions to literature and survey courses for college freshman to graduate-level seminars. As might be expected, his prose and poetry are most commonly encountered in survey courses of American literature and seminars devoted to nineteenth-century American literature. Poe also frequently finds a home in courses devoted to short fiction, the detective story, science fiction, and the literary gothic.

Because Poe is frequently included in the contexts of American- and world-literature survey courses making use of literary anthologies, the list of most frequently taught Poe texts reflects the Poe works commonly included in such anthologies; indeed, one may argue that the solidification of the Poe canon is directly related to the increasing dominance of anthologies and course readers in undergraduate classrooms. It therefore will come as no surprise to any instructor with even a passing knowledge of Poe that included among his most commonly taught poems and short stories are "Annabel Lee," "The Black Cat," "The Cask of Amontillado," "The Fall of the House of Usher," "Ligeia," "The Murders in the Rue Morgue," "The Purloined Letter," "The Raven," "The Tell-Tale Heart," and "William Wilson." Poe's "The Philosophy of Composition" was the most frequently reported nonfiction inclusion among survey respondents. Also occasionally noted was Poe's review of Nathaniel Hawthorne's *Twice-Told Tales*.

As noted above, Poe's works are most often taught by instructors making use of literary anthologies, including *The Heath Anthology of American Literature*, edited by Paul Lauter and others; *The Norton Anthology of American Literature*, edited by Nina Baym and others; *The Norton Anthology of Short Fiction*, edited by Richard Bausch and R. V. Cassill; *Literature and Its Writers*, edited by Ann Charters; *Literature: An Introduction to Fiction, Poetry, and Drama*, edited by X. J. Kennedy and Dana Gioia; and *Literature for Composition: Essays, Fiction, Poetry, and Drama*, edited by Sylvan Barnet and others. For instructors who wish to focus more fully on Poe or to avoid the use of an anthology, a variety of sources are available. Most often recommended by survey respondents was the Library of America paperback edition of Poe's collected works, *Poetry, Tales, and Selected Essays*, with notes by Patrick F. Quinn and G. R. Thompson. All quotations from works by Poe cited in the essays in this book, unless otherwise indicated, are taken from the Library of America paperback edition. Respondents praised both the volume's inclusiveness and relative inexpensiveness; however, a deficiency of this collection is that it fails to provide a complete table of contents at the start. Rather, the volume includes a separate table of contents for each of its three sections on poetry, tales and sketches, and selected essays, with the latter two inconveniently embedded in the text. Also frequently noted by survey respondents was the Penguin collection edited by Tatiana Rapatzikou and David Galloway, *"The Fall of the House of Usher" and Other Writings: Poems, Tales, Essays, and Reviews*. The volume is inexpensive and provides a representative sampling from each category. Respondents did note, however, that the volume omits certain important selections and is less comprehensive than the Library of America edition. Other collections of Poe's works cited by survey respondents include the Dover Thrift edition, *Tales of Terror and Detection*; the 2004 Norton Critical Edition of *The Selected Writings of Edgar Allan Poe*, edited by G. R. Thompson; Susan Levine and Stuart Levine's *The Short Fiction of Edgar Allan Poe: An Annotated Edition*; and Philip van Doren Stern's *The Portable Edgar Allan Poe*. Leonard Cassuto's edited volume, *Edgar Allan Poe: Literary Theory and Criticism*, contains some of the most important literary essays ("The Philosophy of Composition," "The Poetic Principle") and book reviews Poe penned during his lifetime, including his review of Hawthorne's *Twice-Told Tales*, Rufus W. Griswold's *The Poets and Poetry of America*, and Charles Dickens's The Old Curiosity Shop *and Other Tales*. The Cassuto edition is one of the few places where Poe's critical reviews and essays can be found in a single, moderately priced volume.

While most survey respondents indicated that they taught both Poe's prose and poetry and, therefore, made use of collections of Poe's writings containing both, two collections of Poe's poetry were suggested by respondents: the Dover Thrift edition entitled *"The Raven" and Other Favorite Poems* and the Signet edition of *The Complete Poetry of Edgar Allan Poe*, edited by Jay Parini. Those teaching Poe's *The Narrative of Arthur Gordon Pym of Nantucket* were in the minority of survey respondents but recommended either the version of the text included in *Poetry, Tales, and Selected Essays* or the Oxford paperback Arthur Gordon Pym *and Related Tales*, edited by J. Gerald Kennedy. It should be pointed out here that, while the *Collected Writings of Edgar Allan Poe*, edited by Burton R. Pollin, was not recommended by survey respondents for classroom adoption, it was strongly recommended as a primary source for instructors, especially Pollin's edition of *Pym*, which painstakingly details Poe's reliance on and incorporation of materials from other sources.

Readings for Students

Instructors incorporating Poe into composition courses or literature survey classes generally indicated that they did not assign secondary readings to students. Reasons expressed for this included time constraints and the broad overall objectives of such courses. As might be expected, instructors leading undergraduate and graduate course work and seminars focused explicitly on Poe were more likely to assign secondary reading. However, there was little consistency among respondents concerning assigned secondary readings. Two biographical studies received several recommendations for students: Kenneth Silverman's *Edgar A. Poe: Mournful and Never-ending Remembrance* and

Arthur Hobson Quinn's classic *Edgar Allan Poe: A Critical Biography*. Instructors leading courses including units on literary theory predictably cited the exchange between Jacques Lacan, Jacques Derrida, and Barbara Johnson on Poe's "The Purloined Letter," collected in John P. Muller and William J. Richardson's *The Purloined Poe: Lacan, Derrida, and Psychoanalytic Reading*. In addition, several secondary sources addressing issues of race and gender were cited multiple times by survey respondents: Joan Dayan's "Amorous Bondage: Poe, Ladies, and Slaves"; Teresa Goddu's *Gothic America: Narrative, History, and Nation* (which includes the chapter "The Ghost of Race: Edgar Allan Poe and the Southern Gothic"); and Toni Morrison's *Playing in the Dark: Whiteness and the Literary Imagination* (which includes an analysis of Poe's *Pym*). Survey respondents also suggested many of the essays included in J. Gerald Kennedy and Liliane Weissberg's *Romancing the Shadow: Poe and Race*, which includes contributions from John Carlos Rowe, Terence Whalen, Joan Dayan, and J. Gerald Kennedy (" 'Trust No Man' "), among others.

Readings for Teachers

Reference Works

Indispensable for careful Poe analysis is *The Collected Works of Edgar Allan Poe*, a project begun by Thomas Ollive Mabbott and then continued by Burton R. Pollin under a different title. Mabbott edited volumes 1–3 of *The Collected Works of Edgar Allan Poe*, devoted to Poe's poetry (vol. 1 [1969]) and the tales and sketches (vols. 2 and 3 [1978]). Pollin's *The Collected Writings of Edgar Allan Poe* includes volume 1, *The Imaginary Voyages:* Pym, Hans Pfall, Julius Rodman; volume 2, *The Brevities:* Pinakidia, *Marginialia, and Other Works*; volume 3, *The* Broadway Journal, *Non-fictional Prose, Part I: Text*; volume 4, *The* Broadway Journal, *Non-fictional Prose, Part II: Annotations*; volume 5, *Writings in the* Southern Literary Messenger. These are the definitive editions of Poe's works and contain copious informative annotations. The definitive collection of Poe's letters is the two-volume *The Letters of Edgar Allan Poe*, edited by John Ward Ostrom. A helpful collection of Poe's correspondence, clippings, and early criticism is *John Henry Ingram's Poe Collection at the University of Virginia*, edited by John Carl Miller.

Two academic journals currently cater to Poe scholars. *Poe Studies / Dark Romanticism* was founded in 1986 and is published by Washington State University once a year. The *Edgar Allan Poe Review* is published semiannually by the Poe Studies Association.

The standard bibliography of Poe criticism, which covers materials up to 1967, is *Edgar Allan Poe: A Bibliography of Criticism, 1827–1967*, edited by

J. Lasley Dameron and Irby Cauthen, Jr. This bibliography is annually updated in the periodical *Poe Studies / Dark Romanticism*. James R. Canny and Charles F. Heartman's *A Bibliography of the First Printings of the Writings of Edgar Allan Poe* compiles information on first printings and early reprints of Poe's works. Of related interest is Jana L. Argersinger and Steven Gregg's "Subject Index to 'International Poe Bibliography': Poe Scholarship and Criticism, 1983–1988."

Frederick S. Frank and Anthony Magistrale's *The Poe Encyclopedia* includes over 1,500 entries on topics ranging from Poe's characters and themes to his editors, critics, and influences. It also indexes important bibliographic citations on secondary sources relevant for individual Poe stories and poems.

Background Studies

Survey respondents cited a handful of background studies as especially valuable in situating Poe's writings in relation to their historical context. Most frequently noted was David Reynolds's *Beneath the American Renaissance: The Subversive Imagination in the Age of Emerson and Melville*, which provides insight into religious and reformist discourse, as well as attends to sensationalist literature and popular humor. Several other works mentioned also explicitly treat the nineteenth-century literary marketplace. Meredith L. McGill's *American Literature and the Culture of Reprinting, 1834–1853* focuses on issues of authorship and proprietary control. Lawrence Buell's *New England Literary Culture: From Revolution through Renaissance* provides the backstory, so to speak, to McGill's analysis by studying the development of New England literature and literary institutions from the American revolutionary era to the late nineteenth century. Also frequently noted were Cathy Davidson's *Revolution and the Word: The Rise of the Novel in America*, Leslie Fiedler's *Love and Death in the American Novel*, and Jerome Loving's *Lost in the Customhouse: Authorship in the American Renaissance*.

Although Poe generally is either excluded from considerations of literary transcendentalism or mentioned specifically for his distaste for it, an understanding of literary transcendentalism helps establish the context for Poe's productions. Works attentive to transcendentalism and to the American Renaissance more generally that may be of assistance to instructors include F. O. Matthiessen's seminal study, *American Renaissance: Art and Expression in the Age of Emerson and Whitman*; Buell's *Literary Transcendentalism: Style and Vision in the American Renaissance*; Donald E. Pease's *Visionary Compacts: American Renaissance Writings in Cultural Context*; and Jeffrey Steele's *The Representation of the Self in the American Renaissance*.

Since Poe is frequently situated in relation to the tradition of the gothic, works attentive to the development of this tradition may be of interest to instructors. Most often noted here is Donald Ringe's *American Gothic: Imagi-*

nation and Reason in Nineteenth-Century Fiction. Also mentioned was Louis S. Gross's *Redefining the American Gothic: From* Wieland *to* Day of the Dead. General overviews of the gothic are offered in Linda Bayer-Berenbaum's *The Gothic Imagination: Expansion in Gothic Literature and Art*, William Patrick Day's *In the Circles of Fear and Desire: A Study of Gothic Fantasy*, and Robert F. Geary's *The Supernatural in Gothic Fiction: Horror, Belief, and Literary Change.* One respondent noted that Mark Edmundson's *Nightmare on Main Street: Angels, Sadomasochism, and the Culture of Gothic* was useful for provoking discussion about Poe's continuing influence in contemporary culture.

Another common topic of interest in relation to Poe is his attitude toward racial difference. Studies that can help inform such analyses include Dana Nelson's *The Word in Black and White: Reading "Race" in American Literature, 1638–1867*, Eric Sundquist's *To Wake the Nations: Race in the Making of American Literature*, and Justin D. Edwards's *Gothic Passages: Racial Ambiguity and the American Gothic.*

Biography

According to the Edgar Allan Poe Society of Baltimore's Web site, for over 150 years now, Poe devotees of various stripes have tried repeatedly to pin down the details of Poe's life. However, "[e]verything about him is controversial, literally from the place and date of his birth to the exact location and date of his burial" ("Poe's Problematic Biography"). Individual biographies thus can be at variance with one another over even seemingly basic facts, such as, famously, the cause of his death or even the exact location of his grave.

Recommended biographies for instructors by survey respondents were the same as for students: Silverman's *Edgar A. Poe: Mournful and Never-ending Remembrance* and Arthur Hobson Quinn's *Edgar Allan Poe: A Critical Biography.* While Quinn's biography, despite decades of subsequent Poe scholarship, remains reliable and useful, it should be noted that Silverman's biography is frequently derided by Poe scholars for its surprising bias against Poe, as well as some difficulties in the text with identification of sources. In addition to these biographies, Thomas Dwight and David K. Jackson's *The Poe Log: A Documentary Life of Edgar Allan Poe* provides information about Poe's life in chronological order and is extremely thorough. This invaluable reference source literally traces nearly every day in Poe's life—from what the writer did, wrote, and published to those people with whom he had immediate contact. "Annals" in Mabbott's *The Collected Works of Edgar Allan Poe* features a year-by-year summary of Poe's activities. For those instructors attracted to examinations of psychological themes, Marie Bonaparte's *The Life and Works of Edgar A. Poe: A Psycho-analytic Interpretation* may be of interest.

Criticism

After Poe lived a life where his published work was neglected and scarcely known, his reputation and importance as a writer were rescued from the vicious posthumous lies of his literary executor, Rufus Griswold, by the dedicated efforts of the French symbolist poets, particularly Charles Baudelaire. Poe's impact on nineteenth-century French literature was nothing less than profound and immediate. Baudelaire wrote the first European biography of Poe, *Edgar Allan Poe: Sa vie et ses ouvrages,* and he, Stéphane Mallarmé, and Paul Valéry invested twenty years translating five volumes of Poe tales, literary essays, and prefaces, as well as *Eureka,* into French.

Until well into the twentieth century, the French translations and accompanying literary criticism were the source of Poe's literary reputation in France, throughout the rest of Europe, and around the world. Poe's canon was then rendered into many other languages from these translations. For example, nineteenth-century Russia was highly attentive to French cultural trends, and Poe consequently reached Russia initially through Baudelaire's French. Feodor Dostoevsky and Ivan Turgenev were profoundly influenced by Poe's short fiction, and Dostoevsky's translations of "The Black Cat," "The Tell-Tale Heart," and "The Devil in the Belfry" into Russian in 1861 marked the beginning of a fecund literary influence.

It is clear that Poe's status as a great artist was initially forged abroad, as his reputation among the literati in nineteenth-century America, if it was recognized at all, was primarily that of reviewer and literary critic rather than that of poet and fiction writer. Griswold's efforts to defame Poe, characterizing him as possessing an unstable psychology and as a criminal, a drunkard, a drug addict, and even a pedophile, adversely tainted Poe's reputation—especially at home in America—for more than a century. James Russell Lowell's famous dismissal of Poe as a serious writer in "A Fable for Critics" perhaps best summarizes the American reception: "There comes Poe, with his raven, like Barnaby Rudge, Two-fifths of him genius and three-fifths sheer fudge."

From Baudelaire to Lacan, Poe has always found a critical audience in France for the very reasons that he was dismissed by his American readers (from the nineteenth century right up to T. S. Eliot and Henry James): his melancholic claustrophobia, juvenile posturings, cryptic puzzles, and amoral excesses. Poe did not become recognized as a writer of major importance in his own country until the twentieth century, when his use of symbols and images to suggest rather than state the complex range of psychological conditions and emotions was first appreciated by the modernist and imagist movements. In their general strategic retreat from what they viewed as the puritanism of Victorian sexuality and tradition, early modernists found in Poe a writer who shared many of their own rebellions and perspectives, evident especially in his efforts to externalize an inner vision of reality.

Psychoanalytic readings of Poe's fiction were advanced by D. H. Lawrence in *Studies in Classic American Literature* (1923) and by Bonaparte, author of *The Life and Works of Edgar Poe: A Psycho-analytic Interpretation*. Lawrence was among the first Poe critics to realize that his fiction deals with subconscious urges and that Poe's tales are obsessed with the "disintegration processes" of the human psyche. Love in Poe's tales, according to Lawrence, became the vehicle for portraying all extremes of psychopathological behavior. Bonaparte, a student of Freud, conducted an inquiry into Poe's lifelong fixation on women as mother surrogates. Unable to distinguish Poe from his psychosexually obsessed male narrators, she concluded that Poe was similarly psychotically disturbed and probably sexually impotent. Bonaparte's theories advanced other psychoanalytic readings and opened up a main vein of Poe criticism that continues today.

In 1945, H. P. Lovecraft, himself a master of the fantastic tale, published *Supernatural Horror in Literature*, a volume of literary criticism on the genre that devoted its only single-author chapter to Poe. Lovecraft appreciated Poe as one of the first writers of psychological terror, insisting, "Whatever his limitations, Poe does that which no one else ever did or could have done; and to him we owe the modern horror-story in its final and perfected state" (52–53). In addition to Lovecraft's chapter, mid-twentieth-century Poe criticism is distinguished by three seminal essays: Allen Tate's "Our Cousin, Mr. Poe," Jean-Paul Weber's "Edgar Poe; or, The Theme of the Clock," and Jacques Lacan's "Seminar on 'The Purloined Letter.'" Tate's focus on the particularly "Southern" context of interpreting Poe paved the way for later criticism, such as David Leverenz's "Poe and Gentry Virginia" and Joan Dayan's "Amorous Bondage: Poe, Ladies, and Slaves," aimed at historicizing Poe and particularly at debating his attitude toward the most politically charged issue of his era: slavery. Weber's article, on the other hand, puts its emphasis on Poe's fiction as existing in a solipsistic universe where clocks and clocklike metaphors threaten to disrupt the microcosms of Poe's visionary dreamers. Clocks, representing the outside world—and thus antithetical to the imaginative design of Poe's self-enclosed males—frequently surface in many of his tales. They signal the intrusion of reality, calling attention to the breakdown of the narrative's design and to the psychological fragmentation of the narrator, leading to the total collapse of both. Central to Lacan's reading of Poe's "The Purloined Letter" is the conceptualization of the stolen letter as a signifier, or the obsessive center of the tale around which the characters and action of the story revolve. According to Lacan's view, the letter parallels the human unconscious: the characters who know of its existence are duly influenced by it, and his reading of the tale becomes a parable for his paradigm of psychoanalysis.

While survey respondents were somewhat reticent with suggestions for secondary readings for undergraduates, they were more forthcoming with recommendations for contemporary criticism written about Poe that would be of immediate and practical use for instructors. As noted above, Kennedy and

Weissberg bring together writings on Poe and race from well-established Poe scholars in their *Romancing the Shadow: Poe and Race*. Shawn Rosenheim and Stephen Rachman respond to Patrick F. Quinn's *The French Face of Edgar Poe* with their 1995 collection, *The American Face of Edgar Allan Poe*, which includes the often-cited essay from Dayan, "Amorous Bondage: Poe, Ladies, and Slaves." Also receiving several recommendations was Kevin J. Hayes's *The Cambridge Companion to Edgar Allan Poe*, Kenneth Silverman's *New Essays on Poe's Major Tales*, and Lois Vines's *Poe Abroad: Influence, Reputation, Affinities*. To this list, one must add Eric Carlson's *A Companion to Poe Studies*. The volume's twenty-five essays range widely and include attention to Poe's poetry, fiction, reviews, biography, and reputation.

Single-author monographs most frequently suggested were Whalen's *Edgar Allan Poe and the Masses*, Scott Peeples's *The Afterlife of Edgar Allan Poe*, Jonathan Elmer's *Reading at the Social Limit: Affect, Mass Culture, and Edgar Allan Poe*, G. R. Thompson's *Poe's Fiction: Romantic Irony in the Gothic Tales*, and Daniel Hoffman's *Poe Poe Poe Poe Poe Poe Poe*. Survey respondents also recommended several more general monographs with chapters dedicated to Poe. Special attention was given to Harry Levin's classic *The Power of Blackness: Hawthorne, Poe, Melville*, Perry Miller's equally canonical *The Raven and the Whale: The War of Words and Wits in the Era of Poe and Melville*, and Toni Morrison's *Playing in the Dark: Whiteness and the Literary Imagination*.

Aids to Teaching

TV and Cinema

The most-often-cited nontextual resource referenced by survey respondents was an episode of the animated television program *The Simpsons*, in which the actor James Earl Jones narrates "The Raven." In the episode entitled "Treehouse of Horror," which originally aired on 24 October 1990, during the program's second season, Lisa tells Bart the story of Poe's poem, while Homer imagines himself as the narrator, Bart as the raven, and Marge as Lenore. Respondents also referenced the PBS documentary *Edgar Allan Poe: Terror of the Soul*. Consisting of interviews with Poe scholars including Alfred Kazin, Patrick Quinn, Kenneth Silverman, and Richard Wilbur, as well as an adaptation of "The Cask of Amontillado," this documentary chronicles Poe's life from a number of perspectives.

Cinematic adaptations, while notoriously unfaithful to Poe's actual stories, were suggested by several respondents as entertaining supplements to class discussion. Suggestions here include the Art Babbitt and Ted Parmalee version of "The Tell-Tale Heart," narrated by James Mason; Roger Corman's *House of*

Usher, featuring Vincent Price; and the Federico Fellini film, *Histoires extraordinaires*, which adapts "William Wilson," "Metzengerstein," and "Toby Dammit" and stars Brigitte Bardot, Jane Fonda, and Peter Fonda.

Over ninety films have been produced based on Poe poems and prose narratives, including some of the earliest efforts in cinematic history, such as the lost film rendition of *The Raven* (1915). The most comprehensive source for film adaptation of Poe is Don G. Smith's *The Poe Cinema: A Critical Filmography of Theatrical Releases Based on the Works of Edgar Allan Poe.*

Music and Spoken Word

Poe's aesthetics left lasting impressions on classical as well as popular composers. Sergei Rachmaninoff's choral symphony *The Bells* (1913) was inspired by Poe's famous poem. Claude Debussy, regarded as a leader of the modern school of music in France at the turn of the twentieth century, left substantial sketches for two operas based on Poe stories (*Le diable dans le beffroie* and *La chûte de la maison Usher*). More relevant to contemporary student interest is the work of Alan Parsons, who, with the assistance of two hundred musicians, several electronic synthesizers, and the rock group The Alan Parsons Project produced an album of instrumental performances of several well-known Poe stories and poems entitled *Tales of Mystery and Imagination*, which actually scored a Top 40 hit with "(The System of) Doctor Tarr and Professor Feather."

Next to *The Simpsons*'s version of "The Raven," the most-often-referenced nontextual teaching aid cited by survey respondents was the spoken-word album *Closed on Account of Rabies: Poems and Tales of Edgar Allan Poe.* This album features contemporary pop and film stars narrating Poe's works. For example, Christopher Walken reads "The Raven," Iggy Pop reads "The Tell-Tale Heart," and Diamanda Galas reads "The Black Cat." In addition, the Poe impersonator Norman George has released a double-CD album featuring his readings of favorite Poe stories and poems. And somewhere between spoken word and musical composition is Lou Reed's homage to Poe, *The Raven*, which is available both as a double album and in a condensed one-album form. Readers who wish to explore further the connection between Poe and music should consult Burton R. Pollin's "Music and Edgar Allan Poe: A Second Annotated Checklist."

Web Sites

A *Google* search of "Edgar Allan Poe" yields 2,440,000 hits as of 3 July 2007. Out of this bewildering profusion of Web sites, two were noted most frequently by survey respondents: *The Edgar Allan Poe Society of Baltimore* (www.eapoe .org) and the *Poe Webliography*, developed and maintained by Heyward Ehrlich (http://andromeda.rutgers.edu/~ehrlich/poesites.html). Both are rich and valuable resources for instructors at all levels. *The Edgar Allan Poe Society of Baltimore* Web site contains a wealth of information about Poe, as well as an archive of Poe's written works that often includes multiple variants of Poe's texts. For example, the site makes available seven different variants of Poe's poem "Annabel Lee," all published between 1849 and 1850. Ehrlich's "webliography" characterizes itself as a "critical guide to electronic resources for Poe research on the World Wide Web and CD-ROM, including electronic texts, HTML-encoded texts, hypertexts, secondary works, commentaries, and indexes." The site is extremely well designed and provides many useful links. In addition to these two sites, the *PAL: Perspectives in American Literature* Web page devoted to Poe provides a bibliography of Poe's primary works, a fairly extensive bibliography of selected secondary works, and some minimal attention to Poe's themes and other characteristics (www.csustan.edu/english/reuben/pal/chap3/poe.html).

Images

An excellent collection of images of Poe has been assembled by Michael J. Deas in his *The Portraits and Daguerreotypes of Edgar Allan Poe*. Poe's fiction and poetry have inspired illustrations from artists such as the impressionist painter Edouard Manet's pen-and-ink studies of "The Raven" in the 1870s to contemporary Japanese computer artists and manga. For a bibliographic checklist of illustrative images drawn to accompany Poe's work, consult Pollin's *Images of Poe's Work: A Comprehensive Descriptive Catalogue of Illustrations*.

NOTE

Citations to Poe throughout this volume, unless otherwise indicated, are from *Poetry, Tales, and Selected Essays*.

Part Two

APPROACHES

Introduction

Jeffrey Andrew Weinstock and Tony Magistrale

The essays in this part are divided into three sections. None of these sections contains material that is mutually exclusive; there are, in other words, overlaps among many essays that would allow for their inclusion in different sections. We have split the volume in this way, however, to make it easier for readers to locate and juxtapose essays that share primary pedagogical concerns and contexts.

The first of these sections, "Literary, Cultural, and Historical Contexts," includes essays that address Poe's life, historical and cultural epoch, and conditions under which he wrote and published his work. Too often, Poe is taught as though his fiction and poetry emerged from an ahistorical, nonpolitical vacuum. Recent Poe scholarship (e.g., the edited collections by Rosenheim and Rachman and by J. Kennedy [*Historical Guide*]), however, has tried to redress this misapprehension, since much of the scholarship is deeply concerned with the relation of Poe to the sociopolitical problems of his times, and the essays in this section reflect a similar effort. Of particular note are several essayists who choose to discuss Poe's literary and editorial relation to the magazines of his era. It is important for modern readers of Poe, perhaps accustomed to thinking of the publishing world in terms of giant corporate monoliths and best-seller lists, to understand that in Poe's nineteenth century most writers made their living by publishing in periodicals—primarily newspapers and literary magazines. From 1825 to 1850, there occurred a 600% increase in the number of American periodicals, due in no small measure to new printing technologies, improvements in eyeglasses, diffusion of public education, and a wider distribution network of printed texts.

Therefore it is appropriate for this first section to begin with an essay by Scott Peeples on periodicals. Peeples introduces his students to the 1839 issue of *Burton's Gentleman's Magazine*, which first published several of Poe's earliest fictional narratives. He aims to acquaint students with the magazine world that Poe, of course, came to know empirically as book reviewer, editor, journalist, and contributor of fiction and poetry throughout his career.

Next, Leonard Cassuto's treatment of "Murders in the Rue Morgue" locates Poe as a genre writer in the United States during the 1840s. Cassuto wants his students to understand what makes the narrative a tale of detection and thus representative of writing within generic limits. More significant, however, is his effort to have them consider the story, especially its representations of race and racism, as a "social construction." Reading Poe's narratives of gothic terror as legitimate commentary on their moment in historical time is also the aim of Duncan Faherty's essay on "Usher" and "Ligeia." Both tales are viewed in the context of Jacksonian politics. Andrew Jackson, Martin Van Buren, and other political figures were often lampooned in Poe's early satires, which were written throughout the 1830s. Since "Usher" and "Ligeia" are stories about unstable bloodlines and identities, Faherty argues that students need to read them in the light of Poe's personal misgivings toward the goals of Jacksonian democracy and social mobility. The essay implies that Poe's criticism of mob rule, expressed overtly in the burlesque "Some Words with a Mummy," is also present in Poe's more serious fiction. Historicizing Poe is likewise the intention of Edward Wesp, who deals with satire and democracy in "Some Words with a Mummy." Like Faherty, he exposes students to the antidemocratic position that often resonates through Poe's satires. Further, he locates Poe as a Southern writer in the contentious slavery debates that were occurring during Poe's lifetime.

Marcy J. Dinius explores the relation between Poe and nineteenth-century American print culture. While ostensibly focused on Poe's infrequently taught tale "Hans Pfaall," her discussion of the interrelation among science, culture, and the era of literary periodicals provides an important context for reading other Poe works. Although perhaps not as interested as Dinius in the correspondences that exist between Poe and the magazine world, Jeffrey Andrew Weinstock in his essay on *Pym* traces the topic of plagiarism as it relates to Poe's undocumented borrowings in the novel and other ideas and expectations of nineteenth-century popular culture that were vetted and exacerbated through the magazines and newspapers of Poe's time. The issues Weinstock explores will be of special interest to contemporary students, who often have their own preconceived perspective on Poe as a result of current popular media.

Desirée Henderson's contribution connects several of Poe's "premature burial" narratives to nineteenth-century American representations of fatality and bereavement. Despite Poe's undeniable popularity, many contemporary students struggle to appreciate Poe, dismissing him as morbidly obsessed with death. Henderson posits that this perceived morbidity in Poe's work was actually a response to his time: Poe invoked his epoch's contradictory fear and fascination with death and its representations and was particularly effective in referencing the rituals associated with mourning.

Three essays deal specifically with Poe's poetry, and two of them continue the argument for reading Poe as an elegist obsessed with death and bereavement. Philip Edward Phillips discusses reading "The Raven" and "Annabel Lee" as elegies that participate in the classical tradition of lament and consolation. He connects Poe's poems to student experience with eulogies and contemporary funereal rituals. Benjamin F. Fisher similarly views Poe in the light of the elegiac tradition. His essay centers on "The Sleeper" and considers the poem's affinities to "Lenore," "The Raven," "Ulalume," and "Annabel Lee." Since Fisher is concerned with many of the funeral preparations and services practiced in nineteenth-century America that are alluded to in these poems, readers may also wish to consult Henderson's analogous treatment of these themes.

Concluding this first section is Stephen Rachman's assessment of Poe as an artist whose reputation is trapped between lowbrow and highbrow aesthetics.

Rachman argues that Poe studies embody many postmodern characteristics. Rachman's thesis, similar to Weinstock's, posits that for students to understand Poe's aesthetics accurately, they must recognize that in his time as well as ours there remains a duality to Poe: the highly literate aesthete and the popular commercial merchandiser—the first giving birth to high modernism, the other to the logo for a National Football League franchise. Both these sides of Poe are detailed in Rachman's exegesis of the seldom-taught tale "The Colloquy of Monos and Una."

In the next section, "Theoretical Contexts," essays assume the point of view of particular critical approachs, with the goal of helping teachers apply various critical theories to the meanings of Poe's texts.

Poe stories that feature male-female relationships, in which women are of central, abiding importance, invite a feminist reading. Lesley Ginsberg is interested in providing her students with a feminist reading of "The Black Cat," but she does so through a new-historicist reliance on several obscure primary sources that were published during Poe's lifetime. Ginsberg's students come to recognize the nexus between the patriarchal language used to discuss slavery in these published documents and nineteenth-century constructions of gender and marriage implicit in Poe's short story.

Brian Yothers examines the role the reader plays in deriving meaning from three Poe texts: "Hop-Frog," "How to Write a Blackwood Article," and "The Tell-Tale Heart." Influenced by reader-response theory, Yothers's students compose critical responses to stories examined in class. These responses become a means for deepening student knowledge of individual narratives while also transforming the classroom into an interpretive community that measures the credibility of existing published Poe scholarship—by establishing a criteria for evaluating selected critical interpretations—on the three stories under discussion.

Most of Poe's canon is enriched through psychoanalytic interpretations of his themes and characterization, but the essays by Diane Long Hoeveler and A. Samuel Kimball apply psychoanalytic criticism to help illuminate the detective stories, specifically, "The Purloined Letter." Through the job of explaining and interpreting events that have occurred, Poe's C. Auguste Dupin's role parallels that of the psychoanalyst—piecing together evidence, motivation, and inexplicable human behavior to contain and solve serious problems. Hoeveler is particularly interested in tracing the impact of Jacques Lacan's famous 1955 seminar devoted to this Poe story. Teaching "The Purloined Letter" in relation to Lacan and Freud provides her students the opportunity to interrogate the structure of Poe's "literary formalist devices" and juxtapose them to the methods and purposes of psychoanalysis as an interpretive tool. Breaking down the tale into these two categories in front of the class permits Hoeveler to demonstrate the dynamics that coexist between the characters in the story and readers who project themselves into the narrative's secretive moments of sexual desire, political intrigue, and self-righteous revenge. Kimball likewise focuses on the relation of reader to text, especially since Poe's use of first-person narrative should be seen as a means for characters to disguise self-interest from the reader as well as from themselves. Applying this discussion directly to Poe's Dupin, Kimball reads "The Purloined Letter" not as a triumph of ratiocination but as a deadly game of political vengeance. Moreover, as a teacher guiding students through this complex narrative, he seeks to provoke students into questioning their own first-person illusions as well as those projected in Poe's tale.

Derek Furr applies a "theory of textuality" approach to interpreting the seldom-taught Poe tale "The Visionary" with graduate-level students who are preparing to teach Poe at the high school level. Positing that all literary texts change and accrue meaning over time, he points out that Poe's stories and poems were often significantly revised each time they were republished, as even the title of "The Visionary" was later changed to "The Assignation." Furr requires his students to acquaint themselves with research on hypertext, intertextuality, and reviews in period magazines, and he and his class explore the variances of meaning that attend Poe's constructions of alternative texts.

Studying the language of Poe's stories and how best to present his work to students whose first language is not English are at the heart of Erik Redling's approach to German students reading Poe in English. Using "The Cask of Amontillado" as his subject text, Redling renders Poe's tale as a dramatic performance with students enacting the parts of Fortunato and Montressor.

The third section, "Classroom Contexts," aims to help teachers develop intertextual parallels between Poe and other artists and identify how Poe can best be incorporated into high school and college English classes, especially in American literature survey courses. The essays in this section all undertake various aspects of teaching Poe in a curricular context.

When teachers include Poe in a nineteenth-century survey course of American literature, they must grapple with explaining Poe's death-haunted aesthetics and trauma-driven narratives, written in an age of quaint Romanticism and transcendental optimism. Linking Poe's work to his other literary contemporaries, Herman Melville, Nathaniel Hawthorne, and Washington Irving, is sometimes a fruitful beginning, but Poe arguably shared more with future generations of writers than he did with those of his own era. The importance of reading Poe as a literary figure who influences and dialogues with artists who follow him interests the contributors in this section. Tony Magistrale demonstrates the value of concluding an American literature survey course with a Stephen King novel and juxtaposing it with several Poe tales to highlight the intertextuality between the two authors. While suggesting a list of appropriate texts from each writer to pair on a course syllabus, he focuses on comparing King's novel *The Shining* with Poe's tale "The Masque of the Red Death." Like Magistrale, James Britton is committed to carving out a place for Poe in an American literary survey. Providing a close reading of *Pym* as his primary text, he argues that the novel's problematic representations of race and identity provoke student discussion about far-ranging issues relevant to American literature and culture.

Poe lived in an age when America's literary and national spirit was shaped by Ralph Waldo Emerson and his belief in self-reliance and an expansionist philosophy. Poe referred derisively to the transcendentalists as "Frogpondians" and was severely skeptical of their nebulous metaphysics, democratic spirit, core hopefulness, and trust in the divinity of the self (Poe, *Complete Works* 172). For Poe, the emphasis of the transcendentalists on the individual American as a repository of limitless potential often translated into an arrogant superiority that erased all moral prohibitions against even murder and revenge. Paul Christian Jones explores this contentious dynamic in his essay about teaching Poe's murder tales in the light of transcendental self-reliance. Suggesting that Poe shared with the transcendentalists a similar obsession about the self-reliant individual (although positing very different consequences), Jones offers a methodology for helping students interpret Poe's tales of perversity as a dialogue with the vision of the Enlightenment in Emerson's essays.

In her high school English class, Alison Kelly's American literature students learn to appreciate connections that bring Poe's long nineteenth-century shadow into contact with twentieth-century texts such as *The Great Gatsby*, *Lolita*, and *The Bluest Eye*. In teaching upper-division and graduate-level English-education students who are preparing to become teachers in junior high and high school classrooms, Donelle Ruwe presents a reading of several well-known Poe texts that takes his work beyond the introductory survey course and into the more specialized realm of literary theory and postgraduate education. To acquaint these students with theories associated with gender and cultural studies, Ruwe offers excerpts from teaching plans that serve as starting points for applying several theoretical paradigms to specific Poe texts.

William Etter reads Poe in the highly specialized context of disability studies. Throughout Poe's canon are "nonnormal"—in other words, damaged, grotesque, or ill—human bodies. Poe's gothic fragmentation of these bodies reinforces cultural perceptions of what constitutes normal and legitimate. Teaching the story "The Man That Was Used Up," with its emphasis on prosthetics and the misshapen body of its protagonist, offers students an opportunity to grapple with important issues relevant to disability studies. Although a comic tale, the narrative can also be read as a desperate struggle of a wounded body to make itself appear normal.

Nearly every important writer who followed Poe, representing virtually every national literature, was at least acquainted with him, and those who were not directly persuaded by his vision were forced in some way to acknowledge it, if only in an act of repudiation. Lois Davis Vines introduces the topic of Poe's monumental influence on world literature. Her students engage an aspect of literary scholarship by studying and researching a text by a famous author who was influenced by Poe. Her essay highlights in particular Poe's range as a guiding force on nineteenth-century French writers, including Jules Verne, and Latin American authors.

An impressive aspect of Poe's literary legacy is its enormous breadth of influence on generations of filmmakers, visual artists, dramatists, musicians, and choreographers. Dennis R. Perry moves the discussion from Poe's literary influence to his importance as a figure in film history, specifically the relation between Poe and Alfred Hitchcock. Pairing Hitchcock and Poe in the classroom is appropriate not only because of the director's acknowledgment of Poe's value in shaping his cinematic universe but also because the connection sheds new light on the work of both men. While Perry sees many possible pairings from the canons of both artists, in this essay he provides the example of teaching "Murders in the Rue Morgue" alongside *Psycho*.

No other American artist, with the possible exception of Mark Twain and perhaps the director Steven Spielberg, has managed to bridge the gap between popular culture and highbrow art to the degree that Poe does. If Vines's essay represents Poe's influence as a figure at the center of modernism—a line that stretches from Charles Baudelaire and the symbolist movement to T. S. Eliot and the emergence of twentieth-century Latin American magic realism—then M. Thomas Inge's interest in the illustrated Poe found in comic books, manga art, and the graphic novel recognizes the degree to which Poe's presence has been embraced by popular culture. Inge provides a summary of these comic adaptations—including the popular comic-book periodical *Classics Illustrated*, drawings from cartoonists such as Edward Gorey and Gahan Wilson, and several graphic novels based on Poe's life and works. Inge suggests that teachers share examples of the illustrated Poe with students to help them appreciate what is both gained and lost in any comic book adaptation.

Given that students and their teachers are both overexposed to multiple readings of "The Raven" and "The Philosophy of Composition," Rebecca Jaroff and Domenick Scudera pose an interesting conclusion to the essays in this volume with an innovative pedagogical approach. Using Scudera's play *Poe on Poe* (available at www.ursinus.edu/poeonpoe), as a basis, they stage "The Raven" as a dramatic performance. Poe, who himself is a character in the Scudera play, relies on excerpts from "The Philosophy of Composition" to describe poetic choices he made and those he rejected in crafting the poem. The actors in the play then act out his rejected ideas to give students studying the poem and essay a sense of how different the poem would have been had Poe elected to follow his rejected inclinations.

The essays in this volume, in keeping with the pedagogical design of the MLA Approaches to Teaching series, offer instructors traditional approaches to teaching Poe as well as many original directions for reading his work in new literary, theoretical, and political-historical contexts. Although Poe remains a favorite author for students and teachers alike, his canon is complex and difficult to generalize. Consequently, the art of teaching Poe requires at least a familiarity with the rich range of criticism surrounding his work. Indeed, trying to teach Poe without such an awareness often results in a frustrating pedagogical experience. Thus, in many of the essays in this volume, new scholarship is aligned with fresh pedagogical recommendations. It remains the hope of the editors that this combination will prove to be of interest and value to the neophyte instructor as well as to the seasoned classroom veteran, to the middle school and high school teacher introducing Poe to young readers for the first time as well as to the university professor revisiting Poe in a graduate-level seminar.

Teaching Poe the Magazinist

Scott Peeples

When I teach Poe, I bring to class the 1839 volume of *Burton's Gentleman's Magazine* that includes the first appearances of "The Fall of the House of Usher" and "The Man That Was Used Up," as well as several other tales and poems by Poe. (Luckily for me, my library's special collections happens to own this volume of *Burton's*, and they allow me to take it to class.) I usually begin the class by saying something casually pretentious like, "I thought you might want to see a first edition of 'The Fall of the House of Usher.'" As visual aids go, it is unspectacular, and yet in the age of *PowerPoint*, when images of old things appear regularly in class, the old things themselves can still send a charge through the room. More important than the charge itself, though, is the opportunity that seeing and holding a copy of *Burton's* presents for situating Poe in the publishing world of the 1830s and 1840s. "Why does it matter," I ask, "that this story first shows up here rather than in a book like Poe's collection *Tales of the Grotesque and Arabesque*? What do you notice about the physical appearance of *Burton's*? How is it different from almost any magazine you would see today? What do you notice about the contents?" Together my students and I establish a number of points: that Poe was named as coeditor on the title page; that magazine print was small because paper was expensive; that the engravings are impressive but that there are only a few in each issue; that it is very much a Philadelphia magazine, having a bust of Benjamin Franklin pictured under the title and bylines identifying a number of the authors as Philadelphians; that *Burton's* and many similar magazines imaginatively constructed their audiences in titles that often featured the words "ladies" and "gentlemen" (sometimes separately, sometimes together); that the contents of a monthly magazine seeking a general readership included a wide variety of fiction, non-fiction, poetry, and so on.

I try to assemble some of those observations into a coherent, brief lecture on the publishing environment Poe worked in, a rough outline of which would include the following points. Poe was part of a major cultural development of antebellum America: explaining his career choice, he observed that "the whole energetic, busy spirit of the age tended wholly to the Magazine literature—to the curt, the terse, the well-timed, and the readily diffused, in preference to the old forms of the verbose and ponderous and inaccessible" (*Letters* 1: 268). Indeed, in 1850 there were more than six times as many periodicals other than newspapers as there had been in 1825, and some 4,000 started and folded during the same period (Mott 341–42). These periodicals sought to create a sense of community among strangers populating rapidly growing cities such as New York and Philadelphia—not coincidentally, centers of publishing and the two cities where Poe wrote most of the fiction he is best known for today. In an 1844 letter to Charles Anthon, Poe referred to himself as "essentially a magazinist," and the term fits (*Letters* 1: 270). As Hervey Allen observed long ago, Poe was "the first journalist to conceive of a magazine on a huge modern scale" (328), promoting the medium, theorizing about it, and adapting his art to it. Almost everything he wrote appeared in a magazine before it appeared in a book, and he edited or coedited the *Southern Literary Messenger* in Richmond, *Burton's* and *Graham's* in Philadelphia, and the *Broadway Journal* in New York. In the year he spent coediting *Burton's*, he wrote over eighty book reviews and notices; articles with titles like "A Chapter on Field Sports and Many Pastimes, by an Experienced Practitioner"; an unfinished fictionalized travel narrative ("The Journal of Julius Rodman"); as well as new stories such as "The Fall of the House of Usher," "The Man That Was Used Up," and "The Business Man"; and reprints of other tales and poems. While *Burton's* was "a moderate success" according to the magazine historian Frank Luther Mott (675), with a subscription list of 3,500, William Burton sold his venture to George Graham soon after an acrimonious split with Poe in June 1840; Poe went on to coedit the more widely distributed *Graham's* in 1841–42.

In some ways, then, Poe thrived in this environment of growing cities and periodical publishing, since the medium proved a good match for his skills—tightly weaving short, evocative tales; blurring lines between fiction and nonfiction; bantering with readers through cryptograms and detective fiction. But, at the same time, Poe never made a comfortable living off magazine writing and editing: for instance, the job with *Burton's* paid only ten dollars a week, with additional pay for articles and stories (Mott 674). Poe dramatized the plight of "poor devil authors" (qtd. in Mabbott, *Collected Works* 3: 1207) at the mercy of the owners of magazines in an 1845 sketch entitled "Some Secrets of the Magazine Prison-House." Blaming the lack of an international copyright law (which would have encouraged American writers by forcing publishers to pay royalties to British authors), Poe describes magazine publishers as petty tyrants who "under certain conditions of good conduct, occasional puffs, and decent sub-serviency at all times, make it a point of conscience to encourage the poor devil author with a dollar or two" and illustrates his complaint with a scenario in which an author starves while waiting for his meager payment from the owner of the magazine ("Some Secrets" 1036). While "Some Secrets" was part of a larger campaign for international copyright, Poe's anger at the author's power-lessness reflects not only his frustration as a writer but also his ambition to own and edit his own magazine—a career-long obsession that resulted only in a brief stint as co-owner of the rapidly failing *Broadway Journal* and in extensive plan-ning (mostly hunting for subscribers and contributors) for a never-realized lit-erary magazine first called the *Penn*, later the *Stylus*. At the time of his death, in fact, Poe remained preoccupied with lining up subscriptions and capital for his prospective magazine.

The relevance of this short lecture on Poe as magazinist to the stories and po-ems on the syllabus depends somewhat on the selection of those texts. "The Man of the Crowd" (published in *Graham's* in 1840), perhaps more than any other Poe story, reflects the alienation of modern city life that newspapers and magazines chronicled and sought to ameliorate. In the story, a lone city dweller who desperately seeks "the crowd" is made analogous to a book that will not permit itself to be read, which suggests a link between urban alienation and antebellum print culture; if we think of the story as a piece of magazine journalism—which is how it presents itself—the role of the periodical as urban spectator comes to the forefront. The satire of "The Man That Was Used Up" operates on several levels, but among its concerns is "the rapid march of me-chanical invention" (310), which makes possible both reproducible men like Brevet Brigadier General John A. B. C. Smith and the vast array of printed ma-terials that promote such heroes. But those printed materials could often cut a man down: common tropes for severe literary criticism included "using up" and "tomahawking," and Poe was often referred to as a "tomahawk man" because of the harshness of his reviews. Years later, in a comment that brings to mind Gen-eral Smith, Poe remarked that "[n]ewspaper editors seem to have constitutions closely similar to the deities of 'Walhalla,' who cut each other to pieces every day, and yet got up perfectly sound and fresh each morning" ("Fifty Suggestions" 1299). I mention these stories because their complexity and the range of re-sponses they have received make them strong candidates for inclusion even in a compact survey syllabus. Other tales that are somewhat flatter but more clearly related to the "magazine prison-house" include "How to Write a Blackwood Ar-ticle / A Predicament," "The Balloon Hoax," "The Literary Life of Thingum Bob, Esq.," and "X-ing a Paragrab."

Those last few remain unlikely choices in a fast-moving survey class, but some awareness of the publishing environment Poe worked in can change the way one teaches even the more canonical gothic tales—for instance, "The Fall of the House of Usher" (the one Poe story that I never rotate off the syllabus). Seeing

"Usher" in *Burton's* alongside other popular forms of magazine writing—travel narratives (such as Poe's own "Journal of Julius Rodman"), historical essays ("Usher" is followed by "Discovery of America by the Northmen in the Tenth Century," by Hall Grandgent), and mourning verse (the same issue includes a poem entitled "The Dying Wife," as well as "A Morning's Meditation in a Burial Place," a sketch that concludes with a dirge)—alerts students to the probability that Poe wrote "Usher" and other gothic stories less because he needed a way to exorcise his own spiritual demons than because there was an audience for gothic fiction. Poe was writing not from the fringes of popular culture but right in the mainstream. Imagine a Phildelphia "gentleman" (although "ladies" certainly read "gentleman's" magazines as well) in September 1839 reading *Burton's* by lamplight, in a boardinghouse, perhaps, or a family home. His evening's entertainment is a small bundle of fine print, an orderly but mostly unillustrated mishmash of poems, articles, and reviews. There is no real indication which article titles lead to fiction, much less any certain kind of fiction. Which door will the gentleman enter, and will he stay? Or will he abandon, say, "Sketches from the Log of Old Ironsides" for an essay on Elizabethan theater? Poe thought about this reader, thought about the length of time he invests in reading a magazine story and the choices he makes. What Poe understood, perhaps better than any writer of his time, was how to hold that reader, how to ensure that once he entered the house of Usher, he would remain there until it fell.

With this in mind, I ask students to consider the ways "Usher" is about reading (albeit not necessarily magazine reading) and about the well-worn (even by 1839) conventions of gothicism. Specifically, Poe places a ludicrous (and made-up) gothic romance—"The 'Mad Trist' of Sir Launcelot Canning"—in the hands of his narrator late in the tale, and, on reading this tale aloud to Roderick Usher, the narrator seems to call forth the overwrought gothic elements that simultaneously destroy the House of Usher and bring "The Fall of the House of Usher" to its thrilling climax and sudden close. Creepy old houses, dark family secrets, live burials, dark and stormy nights—as G. R. Thompson points out, with such elements Poe infuses his gothicism with absurdity and satire (*Poe's Fiction* 14, 93). The inclusion of the parodic "Mad Trist" would seem to deflate the suspense and, with it, the serious interest we might have had in "Usher," but instead the trist gives the story intensity. It is as if Poe is saying to his readers, "These crazy gothic stories may be 'uncouth and unimaginative' "—(as the narrator refers to "The Mad Trist" [332])—"but they have an uncanny power over readers." The story concludes with a sentence whose structure and sound, like "the mad trist," evoke the tumult and destruction of the final scene:

> While I gazed, this fissure rapidly widened—there came a fierce breath of the whirlwind—the entire orb of the satellite burst at once upon my sight—my brain reeled as I saw the mighty walls rushing asunder—there

was a long tumultuous shouting sound like the voice of a thousand waters—
and the deep and dank tarn at my feet closed sullenly and silently over the
fragments of the *"House of Usher."*   (335–36)

Poe's italicizing and placing in quotation marks the words "House of Usher" in
the final sentence encourage us to imagine both the house (and the family) and
the story closing, ending, crashing into nothingness as we close our copy of
Burton's Gentleman's Magazine.

Granted, an instructor can emphasize how Poe inscribes the scene of reading
into "Usher" without engaging students in a discussion of magazines, but their
knowing something about the medium Poe worked in enhances their understanding of how the story shows readers being pulled in and manipulated while
pulling us in and manipulating us. And those same ideas of authorial control
and reader response were most famously laid out in—you guessed it—two
magazine essays, the second review of Nathaniel Hawthorne's *Twice-Told Tales*
and "The Philosophy of Composition," both written for *Graham's*. In his review
of *Twice-Told Tales*, the two essential rules Poe establishes for the successful
short story—relative brevity and unity of effect—both serve the larger goal of
maintaining control over the reader: "During the hour of perusal the soul of the
reader is at the writer's control" (572). In "Philosophy," Poe applies the same
principle to poetry, then proceeds to imagine the writing of his most famous
poem as a series of calculations by which to move his readers. The recipe Poe
creates for writing "The Raven" exaggerates the degree to which he relied on
these calculations, but at the same time it conveys an underlying truth: as his
poems and tales appeared amid the crowd of texts that filled antebellum magazines, Poe did come to regard himself as a craftsman whose job it was to first
win and then hold the attention of easily distracted urbanites.

"The Raven" itself demonstrates Poe's ability to make the most of a new
poem's appearance in periodicals. Poe sold "The Raven" to a monthly magazine, the *American Review: A Whig Journal*, but then asked his former em-
ployer Nathaniel Parker Willis to print it in the *Evening Mirror*, a New York
daily, in advance of its appearance in the *Review*. Moreover, while the *American Review* would publish the poem under the pseudonym "Quarles," Willis
would not only reveal the author's name but "puff" (hype) the poem, calling it
"unsurpassed in English poetry for subtle conception, masterly ingenuity of
versification, and consistent sustaining of imaginative lift and 'pokerishness'
[spookiness]. It will stick to the memory of everybody who reads it" (Mabbott,
Collected Works 1: 361). Willis also reprinted the poem in his weekly *New York
Mirror* just after its appearance in the *American Review*; meanwhile, Poe sent
the poem to the magazine where he got his start as an editor, the *Southern Literary Messenger*, which published it in March. By that time, "The Raven" had
appeared in the *New York Express*, the *New York Tribune*, and the *Broadway
Journal*, accumulating more praise that could be used to introduce it to readers.
It is only fitting that a poem that relies heavily on repetition for its effects

should itself be reprinted heavily in the first weeks of its public life and that, after those first weeks, it would continue to be reprinted and parodied countless times both in periodicals and books throughout and well beyond Poe's lifetime.

I have focused on the most standard Poe texts here to make the case that some appreciation of Poe as a magazinist is helpful even in a fast-moving "greatest hits" survey course; but, given time, it is certainly worthwhile having students read not only some of the fiction that deals specifically with publishing and authorship but also selections from Poe's reviews and essays, as well as reviews of his work (and character) by other writers. If enough time is going to be spent on Poe to require a collection of his writing, G. R. Thompson's Norton Critical Edition of Poe (*Selected Writings*) offers a good selection of criticism, including two assessments of Poe written or cowritten by Poe himself. If you are supplementing an American literature anthology (or making one), the *Edgar Allan Poe Society of Baltimore* Web site can provide students with a reliable text of any Poe story or poem and most of his reviews and essays.

As for the visual-aid gimmick, if no actual copies of the *Southern Literary Messenger*, *Burton's*, or *Graham's* are available, the instructor might consider showing what the original texts looked like by gaining access to the Making of America database—the University of Michigan location includes the *Southern Literary Messenger*, where seven early stories and the opening chapters of *The Narrative of Arthur Gordon Pym* first appeared, while the Cornell site includes the *American Whig Review*, which first published "Some Words with a Mummy" and "The Facts of M. Valdemar's Case" (later known as "The Facts in the Case of M. Valdemar"). And there is always the time-honored practice of making photocopies or transparencies from microfilm.

Again, how much use an instructor makes of these resources depends on how a course is structured, but they are most helpful when time is spent observing and commenting on what surrounds the Poe texts in these magazines. For example, "The Man That Was Used Up," whose title character has been chopped to pieces by "Kickapoo" and "Bugaboo" Indians, appears in the same August 1839 issue of *Burton's* as a serialized narrative on the exploration of Indian territory, "The Miami Valley," by "A Pioneer of Ohio"; Poe's political satire "Some Words with a Mummy" appears in the same issue of the *American Whig Review* as an article entitled "The Last Chief Executive," which excoriates the former president John Tyler (from whom Poe had sought a position at the Philadelphia Custom House). These are hardly remarkable coincidences, but they remind us that Poe's tales and poems were a part of the political and social fabric of his times. Even a brief look at a "first edition" of a Poe story can help dispel the notion—still prevalent, despite a long tradition of historicist scholarship on Poe—that he isolated himself from other writers and real-world issues such as slavery, reform movements, and politics generally.

Instructors who prepare a lecture or set of notes on Poe, periodicals, and publishing have a wealth of scholarship from which to draw. Michael Allen's *Poe and the British Magazine Tradition* and Terence Whalen's *Edgar Allan Poe and* the Masses are particularly helpful in elaborating how Poe imagined the possibilities and negotiated the realities of appealing to an audience of magazine readers. *Poe: Journalist and Critic*, by Robert D. Jacobs, provides a narrative overview of Poe's career as a reviewer and nonfiction writer. Sidney P. Moss's *Poe's Literary Battles* tells the stories of Poe's relations with rivals such as Lewis Gaylord Clark and Henry Wadsworth Longfellow, while Sandra M. Tomc's essay "Poe and His Circle" and my "The *Mere* Man of Letters," on Poe and N. P. Willis, also try to better situate Poe in relation to other magazine writers and editors. *American Literature and the Culture of Reprinting, 1834–1853* by Meredith McGill includes two chapters on Poe and his complex response to the widespread practice of reprinting and the copyright controversy. Leon Jackson's essays on Poe's "literary Mohawk" image and on his "semiotics of print" also add much to our understanding of Poe's negotiations with print culture. Finally, the large body of recent scholarship situating Poe in the midst of nineteenth-century popular culture and politics also relates to his career as a magazininst. There are too many relevant titles to list here, but among those that seem closely related to the approach I've outlined are Eliza Richards's *Gender and the Poetics of Reception in Poe's Circle*, Teresa A. Goddu's "Poe, Sensationalism, and Slavery," Lesley Ginsberg's "Slavery and the Gothic Horror of Poe's 'The Black Cat,' " and J. Gerald Kennedy's " 'A Mania for Composition': Poe's Annus Mirabilis and the Violence of Nation-Building."

Poe the Crime Writer:
Historicizing "The Murders in the Rue Morgue"

Leonard Cassuto

Poe would not approve of the way that I teach him. A champion of rigorous formalism and eternal verities, Poe the critic had a strong didactic streak, and he did not hesitate to teach his own work as an example of immutable aesthetic practice. In "The Philosophy of Composition," Poe audaciously presents his own poem ("The Raven") to exemplify pure poetic beauty, floating ethereally above place and time.

I yank Poe out of the firmament and anchor him squarely in his own place and time—and in his professional context. Specifically, I locate him as a genre writer in the United States during the 1840s. Poe was, to be sure, no ordinary genre writer: in the case of the detective story, he receives fair credit for inventing the category. Though detective stories are as old as storytelling (Sophocles's *Oedipus Rex* qualifies as one), they emerged as a literary genre only after Poe established the conventions of the form in his tales of ratiocination. Poe's three stories featuring the eccentric Parisian detective Auguste Dupin, published between 1841 and 1844, became the particular model for later writers of detective fiction.[1] Like so many fictional sleuths after him, Dupin is an odd duck with uncanny powers of observation and deduction. He uses his formidable intellectual endowments to solve crimes, mainly for the pleasure of the exercise. His exploits are duly recorded by his admiring sidekick, an unnamed friend in whom we can clearly see the prototype of Sherlock Holmes's scribe Dr. Watson.

I've been teaching Poe's "The Murders in the Rue Morgue" for the past few years with the idea of showing that much more lurks beneath the surface of crime fiction than a search for whodunit. Specifically, I want students to learn how to historicize even unlikely texts like genre fictions. In doing so, they better understand the relation between literature and society: what purposes stories can serve for groups of people who read them. They also learn to question the boundaries that define and delineate "literary fiction" instead of taking those categories for granted.

The "Rue Morgue" teaching strategy I'm about to describe has proved remarkably adaptable. I've used it with Fordham University students ranging from freshmen to graduate level. The class requires very little customizing; freshmen need a bit more prompting, that's all.

On second thought, maybe Poe would appreciate my teaching of his work. After all, my "Rue Morgue" class is like a mystery story itself, and it features one of the best pedagogical surprise endings I've ever come up with.

The first two parts of my class on "Rue Morgue" follow a conventional format. I begin with a few words about Poe and his literary surroundings. In an introductory minilecture, I describe the rough-and-tumble literary scene of the 1830s and 1840s and Poe's desperate productivity as he sought to make a living and a reputation at the same time. I talk about Poe's editing work as well as his writing, and about his gradual northward migration from job to job, away from his Virginia roots toward the centers of literary power and influence in New York and Boston. This reference to Poe's professional movement across the Mason-Dixon Line to the North glosses the main action of my classroom mystery about "Rue Morgue." It's also a clue to later surprises in store.

After the minilecture comes pointed discussion. To start, I elicit the students' responses to the story, focusing on its unlikely denouement. Students recognize "Rue Morgue" as a conventional detective story of the locked-room variety. The police discover two women murdered in a locked apartment with no obvious means of entry or egress for the murderer. Dupin reads of the killings in the newspaper and decides to solve the case for the sheer pleasure of outwitting the police. The resolution proves surprising, since the murderer turns out to be no one at all—no person, that is. Instead, Dupin deduces that the culprit is an escaped orangutan. This turn of events leads to something of an anticlimax because the detective never confronts the murderer directly with his crimes. He faces off with the orangutan's owner, it's true, and the man confesses readily to his inadvertent complicity. But there can be no admission of guilt by the perpetrator.

Students generally read genre stories very sensitively. They note the lack of a "j'accuse" moment in "Rue Morgue," a moment they have been conditioned to expect through their readings of many other mysteries. They need little prodding to discuss the sheer weirdness of Dupin, who lives in a "time-eaten and grotesque mansion" (400) with the narrator, staying at home all day with curtains drawn and candles flickering before venturing out to the pleasures of the Parisian night. Poe draws Dupin as much more than an alert observer. Conditioned by their own reading in the genre, even college freshmen can see that the grotesqueness of the detective matches the "grotesquerie" (423) of the crime (which is quite graphically described considering the standards of Poe's time).[2] The class engages in this quarrying exercise for a while, piling up relevant observations about the story and the characters.

Then comes the final pivot, which starts when I combine two early quotations from the story. The students have already noticed Poe's emphasis on observation in the story, but I highlight the narrator's important caveat: "The necessary knowledge is that of *what* to observe" (399). Second, I point to Poe's insistence on analysis as a "moral activity" (397). Taken together, these quotations frame a critical question. Given that we are being asked to observe, and given that observation is part of a moral process of analysis for Poe, What is the point of this story? What are we supposed to observe in it?

The class members, so confident in their observations up to now, always have trouble placing their findings into any moral framework. Here especially the unusual ending to "Rue Morgue" flummoxes them. What's moral about catching an escaped ape that commits two murders because it gets scared and doesn't know any better? What can be the moral lesson of a murder story that lacks a nefarious criminal design foiled by the forces of justice? Put simply, how can there be a moral when there is no motive? This is the mystery that the class must solve.

To help my students think about their mystery, I invite them to reflect on literary genres in social context. We talk about how certain stories gain cultural currency because they matter to people. Genres become popular because they respond to collectively held desires. When millions of people buy romances, the genre must be offering them a way of thinking about their own intimate relationships.[3] Crime stories open a window onto shared fears of all kinds. The view may not always be clear; serial killers, for example, represent a lot of different threats to self and society at once.[4] Crime stories channel collective anxieties, so, when we read them, we can see what a culture is worrying about.

"The Murders in the Rue Morgue" is an American crime story from the 1840s. So what fears does Poe's violent, escaped orangutan represent? To answer that question, we would have to know what American readers were worrying about in 1841. Twenty-first-century college students know very little about the 1840s United States and typically refuse to speculate. To unlimber their minds, I hand out a couple of old illustrations of "Murders in the Rue Morgue," including the one reproduced here, by Alfred Kubin (1877–1959), who was known in his time for his striking illustrations of Poe's works (see illustration on next page).

Such depictions of the ape in sexually suggestive and even explicit situations with its female victims shock the students, who point out that the images (such as the Kubin drawing) do not correspond to anything that actually happens in the story. (Poe keeps the women's clothes on even in death, and the ape harbors no apparent sexual curiosity about his victims.) That disjunction is a productive insight. I then ask the students to infer what might lead an illustrator to produce such an image. That is, what anxiety might such a picture be speaking to? Once again, what might American readers have been worrying about in 1841?

The image of the dark ape looming sexually over the white woman lifts the veil for the students. Now the solution to the class mystery starts to coalesce in their view. Americans in Poe's time were worried about slavery. And "Murders in the Rue Morgue" must be a story about race.

This surprise ending unfolds in several stages. Once the main point comes into view, I offer another minilecture, this one on the growing force of the abolitionist movement in the 1840s. American students typically are taught that American slavery in the South was always counterbalanced by abolitionism in the North until the Civil War settled the matter. The actual situation was messier: slavery was not always restricted to the South, and abolitionism did not gain traction in the United States until the 1830s, after which it quickly turned into a juggernaut. Americans had plenty to worry about in 1841, then. Poe wrote "Rue Morgue" at a time when pro- and antislavery positions were polarizing. Sectional tensions were rising, and Nat Turner's slave rebellion ten years earlier had created widespread white fear of the violent potential of rebellious slaves.

Alfred Kubin's illustration of "Murders in the Rue Morgue" for a German edition of Poe's works, *Nebelmeer—mit einer Einleitung von H[anns] H[einz] Ewers* [München: Müller, 1914].

I remind the class that Poe was a Southerner. I inform them of his proslavery position, which is explicit in many of his writings. I also share a persuasive scholarly finding with them. Richard Kopley has researched Poe's reading in Philadelphia at the time he was concocting "Murders in the Rue Morgue." Kopley concludes that Poe was inspired by two separate 1838 newspaper accounts, one of an escaped orangutan and the other of a black man who killed a woman with a razor (*Edgar*). Poe conflates the two into a story of a darkly colored ape who kills white women.

The connection between Africans and apes remains one of the most ideologically potent in American culture. It's also a racial slur that dates back to the early modern period. Just about everyone knows of it, but few know its history. I give students some of the background; it is nicely explicated by Winthrop D. Jordan in his magisterial *White over Black*. Jordan meticulously documents the "tragic happenstance" by which "Englishmen were introduced to the anthropoid apes and to Negroes at the same time and in the same place" (29). The link between African and ape was forged in the sixteenth century. "The animal called 'orang-outang,' " says Jordan, "was native to those parts of western Africa where the slave trade was heavily concentrated" (29).[5] The African-ape association has persisted ever since. By the eighteenth century, it was "usually conceived in sexual terms" and served "as a means of expressing the social distance between the Negro and the white man" (238–39). This evidence makes it clear that Poe's "Ourang-Outang" is not just an ape. The simian murderer in "Murders in the Rue Morgue" stands as a fraught symbol of sexually charged racial anxiety.[6]

Poe's noxious convictions on the most divisive issue of his time prove hard for some students to accept. They think that we read only the good guys. Poe wasn't much of a good guy on race and slavery, but it's still possible to complicate the vision of slavery, savagery, and civilization in his fiction—and doing so can deepen the discussion of race in "The Murders in the Rue Morgue." Consider "The Black Cat," an 1843 tale that I often assign alongside "Rue Morgue" as a different kind of crime story. The story features a presumably white narrator who maintains a benevolent lordship over his pets—until he sadistically tortures and kills his black cat. The perverse white-on-black violence in "The Black Cat" may be read as a warning that slavery corrupts slave owners. Here and elsewhere, Poe does not exempt whites from the "savage" forces that he depicts in blacks (and apes).[7]

Poe created his symbolic ape in "Rue Morgue" at a time when the proslavery beliefs he grew up with had come under unprecedented and growing attack. He was worried about the latent threat that blacks represented, and he was worried about what he called the "Abolition fanatics" whom he thought were underestimating that threat (Rev. of *A Fable* 819). Nor was Poe alone in his concerns—millions of Americans shared them.

Regrettably, millions of Americans still share them. I conclude the discussion of "Murders in the Rue Morgue" by giving out a 2003 newspaper clipping from a New York tabloid. The lead says it all: "A conservative talk-show host was fired for alluding to Rochester's black mayor as an orangutan." According to the article, the radio host, Bob Lonsberry, "played ape sounds and declared a 'monkey's loose up at the zoo again—and he's running for chief executive' " ("Ax").

As a citizen, I deplore this coincidence. As a teacher, I love it. I don't usually go in for a high level of determinism in my classroom since I'm not likely to learn as much as when I improvise during discussion. But the sequence leading from the risqué "Rue Morgue" illustrations to the radio host story is too compelling and effective to resist. It ends with one of those "relevance" moments that make teachers look like magicians.

It feels appropriate to end a class on "Rue Morgue" with a newspaper story. After all, Poe was clearly influenced by his own newspaper reading when he wrote the tale. The newspaper story cements not only the contextual argument that Poe is a man of his time, but, more important, the continuing significance of Poe's time to our own. Lonsberry's employers fired him for "not embracing diversity or the beliefs of the station" ("Ax"), but his firing is almost beside the point; the historical resonance of his racism lingers. Links like the one between Poe and Lonsberry have the potency to create members of the next generation of literary historians. They allow students to see how genre writing merges with "literature" and how literature is bound with the issues of its time. Students learn something of how to read stories that way, and why doing so matters. And they enjoy solving a mystery in the bargain.

NOTES

[1] The three stories are "Murders in the Rue Morgue" (1841), "The Mystery of Marie Roget" (1842–43), and "The Purloined Letter" (1844).

[2] Poe explicitly links Dupin to the murders in the Rue Morgue through the grotesqueness shared by both. Later American crime fiction consistently doubles the detective and the criminal in similar ways; this device remains one of the most durable thematic features of American crime fiction. In Thomas Harris's influential *Red Dragon*, for example, the serial killer Hannibal Lecter says to the FBI agent Will Graham, "The reason you caught me is that we're *just alike*" (67).

[3] The best-selling romance novelist Mary Bly says that the genre is about "that difficult process of living with another person."

[4] For speculation about the meaning of serial-killer stories, see Seltzer; Simpson; and Cassuto (*Hard-boiled Sentimentality*; "Cultural Work").

[5] The animal we now call the orangutan is not native to Africa; the sixteenth- and seventeenth-century accounts cited by Jordan use the name "orang-outang" to refer to the chimpanzee. The terminology had shifted to current usage by the time Poe wrote "Murders in the Rue Morgue"; the "orang-outang" in the story comes from Borneo.

[6] It is worth noting that the orangutan hates "the dreaded whip" of his owner (430).

[7] In "Hop-Frog," for example, the title character bears certain unmistakably racialized signs: he is a dwarf from "some barbarous region" who is compared to a "small monkey" (900). An official fool in the court of a capricious and casually violent king, Hop-Frog lives the life of a royal house slave. When the king violently abuses Hop-Frog and his friend and fellow dwarf, Tripetta (who had "been forcibly carried off" from a home near Hop-Frog's home region [900]), Hop-Frog stages his murderous revenge in the form of a burlesque of "Eight Chained Ourang-Outangs" (904). For a discussion of "Hop-Frog" in relation to the slavery debates, see P. Jones.

"Legitimate Sources" and "Legitimate Results": Surveying the Social Terror of "Usher" and "Ligeia"

Duncan Faherty

"The most conspicuous of the British tourists," Edgar Allan Poe argues in his essay on American scenery, "Morning on the Wissahiccon," "seem to regard our northern and eastern seaboard, comparatively speaking, as all of America." Instead of venturing off the beaten path, "these travellers content themselves with a hasty inspection of the natural *lions* of the land" and boast of completing a survey of the United States. Steaming across the Northeast, they execute a grand tour without straying from the agendas of their guidebooks. Yet, as "Morning on the Wissahiccon" asserts, such a narrow venture is a prosaic approach to the American scene. "The real Edens of the land," Poe declares, "lie far away from" the common "track" (939). Poe's caution against mistaking one region for the entire nation, by extension, implies the need to confront lingering traditions that root American culture exclusively at Plymouth Rock. While this residual figuration is slowly losing currency, it still resonates powerfully with many undergraduates. To confront this lingering paradigm, I assign "Wissahiccon" to underscore how orientation and expectation inform discovery. Instead of simply introducing the masterworks of American literature, my aim is to expose students to less explored uncertainties. As Poe's sketch foregrounds, such a venture yields richer rewards than habitually plodding over well-worn ground.

Toward the end of the sketch, Poe meanders along the Wissahickon Creek in search of an encounter with wildness. Sparked by the sublimity of the "tarns" (943) along the "rivulet" (942), Poe conjures a vision of "the Wissahiccon of ancient days" (943). He imagines the scene "when the Demon of the Engine was not" and "when the red man trod alone," before domestication and mechanization transformed the area, and thereby registers the familiar fantasy of a virgin land (943). While under the sway of this vision, Poe spies a solitary elk and fantasizes about its reactions to "the manifest alterations" rendered by the "utilitarian" settlers (944). Poe's musings are short-lived, as an advancing "negro" emerges "from the thicket" to secure the elk—"a *pet* of great age and very domestic habits"—and return him to a nearby "villa" (944). The ominous signs of bondage and enclosure quickly expunge the "romance" of the scene, effectively foreclosing the possibility that North America was ever free from the complexities of race, colonization, and capital (944). "Wissahiccon" concludes, like so many of Poe's works, with beauty eclipsed by instability. In effect, the sketch complicates preconceptions of cultural development as Poe moves from casting an illusion of an unspoiled wilderness to revealing the scene as a frontier with political, cultural, racial, and commercial dimensions.[1]

From the outset of a survey course, I want the students to reckon with (as Poe discovers he must in the sketch) the multivalent histories of the terrain under examination. The protean landscape of early American literature, suggestively unsettled by the profusion of rediscovered texts, can make crafting a survey a difficult task. Yet, perhaps, even more challenging than plotting the syllabus is the issue of introducing the subject of the course itself. One of my goals is a recalibration of the students' conceptions of American cultural development. Most undergraduates understand American history as a rising tide of progressive inclusion, as a narrative of increasing surety and national cohesion. Accustomed to thinking of the Civil War as the only chaotic moment in the nation's early history, they often are shocked by the precariousness of antebellum life. Teaching against the grain, I want the students to become critical of their assumptions about cultural development. Similarly, I want to reacquaint them with Poe by challenging their preconceptions of his work. Of all the authors we will read, the students are most cognizant of Poe; yet the Poe they are accustomed to is the Poe of Halloween and Vincent Price movies. Most students are surprised by the idea that Poe was concerned with issues of race, landscape, and property. A discussion of "Wissahiccon" disrupts their expectations, since it makes the familiar seem strange. I hope that students, by reading "Wissahiccon" as an opening frame, are better prepared to discover tensions where they expect to find seamlessness. By drawing the students' attention to the complexities of American settlement, "Wissahiccon" effectively inaugurates a broader discussion of the social dimensions of more canonical works (like Poe's tales of terror) that might at first glance seem unrelated to larger cultural trends.

Most traditional studies of American literature—and thus most undergraduate surveys—depict Poe as an anomaly in the development of United States literary history. Such practice is a miscalculation, for Poe's works (as even a cursory analysis of "Wissahiccon" suggests) reflect and encode the variegated nature of early-nineteenth-century culture. Poe's tales are not disassociated from the swirl of Jacksonian life; rather, they exhibit the impact of the market revolution on individual and national identity formation. The challenge of teaching Poe mirrors the challenge of teaching "America" in a survey course: both tasks require troubling received notions by exploring the tangled dimensions of the subject in question. By figuring Poe as a writer of social texts, we can direct our students to engage in the messy, probing, and ultimately productive work of active reading and thick description. As the students evaluate Poe as a writer occupied with more than just the macabre, they see his work as multivalent and gain increased exposure to the tumultuous dynamics of American cultural development. Across a survey, I supplement the brief historical overviews of our anthology with occasional lectures to mark how literary texts might serve as registers of cultural practices. Still, for students really to grapple with the complexities of national development they need more sustained access to historical information. During the middle portion of my course, I assign Louis Masur's

insightful and expansive microhistory *1831: Year of Eclipse*. Focusing on such
key themes as slavery, Native American autonomy, the interplay between religion and politics, the simmering tensions of state's rights and national union,
Masur artfully portrays the complex unfolding of the Jacksonian era. The text is
a wonderful resource to use with undergraduate students; it is deeply informative and thoroughly readable. With a firmer grounding in the period's dominant
issues, the students are ready to engage literary texts as historically informed
artifacts.

The Jacksonian period was one of unusual uncertainty for American society,
characterized by rampant economic change, social mobility, racial violence, and
underlying fears of mobocracy and rootlessness. Andrew Jackson's election in
1828 created seismic shifts in American culture, leaving almost no corner of national life undisturbed by the rush to embrace change. This constant social revolution created an atmosphere of uncertainty, clouding the predominant faith
in progress with palpable fears over disunion and dissolution. This unease only
increased across the 1830s. Angry over never inheriting John Allan's vast fortune, disheartened by endless financially driven relocations, fueled by Southern
antebellum attitudes toward race and class, and disdainful of the tyranny of the
majority, Poe—more so than any of his contemporaries—embodies the under-
pinnings of Jacksonian life. Instead of presenting Poe as divested from dominant modes of cultural development, we should recast him as central to any
meaningful survey. By registering how Poe's fictions explore the fissures of his
social world, we can direct our students to question how Jacksonianism dramatically altered national mores. In particular, two commonly anthologized tales,
"The Fall of the House of Usher" and "Ligeia," frame the issues of disunion and
dissolution in intriguing ways. Approaching these tales after reading "Wissahiccon" and discussing Masur's book, my students find these tales to be emblematic of Jacksonian uncertainties.

Many of the popularly anthologized Poe stories, including "Ligeia" and "The
Fall of the House of Usher," were first collected in *Tales of the Grotesque and
the Arabesque* (1840), a volume that explicitly announces its concerns with the
"legitimate" terrors of the Jacksonian era (Preface 129). Since this was an original context for the tales, we begin our study of Poe by reading his preface. After
introducing students to the arguments of Poe's preface, they can weigh how
these works address tensions in national myths. "If in many of my productions
terror has been the thesis," Poe maintains in the preface, "that terror is not of
Germany, but of the soul." Poe argues that he has "deduced this terror only
from its legitimate sources, and urged it only to its legitimate results." In effect,
Poe implies that his tales do not have "features of . . . pseudo-horror" about external evil but reflections of contemporary conditions (129). In displaying how
the most commonly anthologized pieces of *Grotesque and the Arabesque* address real-world questions, I aim to exhibit the "legitimate results" of presenting Poe's sensational tales, which evolved from "legitimate sources." As we
discuss the preface, I have the students catalog the possible "legitimate" terrors

of Poe's era, asking them to recall the types of cultural and social issues that *1831* argued were hallmarks of the period. Subsequent discussions lead us to think about what kinds of submerged cultural fears Poe might have had in mind when he argued for the legitimacy of his tales. Such a sustained critical approach will empower students to investigate how even the familiar unworldly tales of Poe represent cultural structures of thought and feeling. If students attend to the cultural implications of Poe's works, they will be wary of confining the strangeness of his tales to abstract psychological schema and move toward developing more nuanced reading and writing practices.

The mysterious cause of the collapse of the House of Usher has been a constant source of energetic speculation. As the "deep and dark tarn" engulfs "the fragments of the '*House of Usher*'" (336), the "time-honored"—yet branchless—Ushers fade from existence (318). Poe's fascination with the blurring association of a family without "collateral issue" and an antiquated house suggests a context for "Usher" too often neglected in classroom discussions (319). Written during the wildfires of Jacksonian social mobility, the "legitimate" terror of "Usher" resides in its depiction of the collapse of patrician privilege and power. The surge of nationalism spawned by Jackson's populism generated a fervor to democratize all aspects of national life by eradicating any semblance of class-based distinctions. Instead of functioning as a site of cultural order, the pseudoaristocratic house of Usher fails to extend any issue beyond the boundaries of its own unstable foundation. Haunted by the mute ghosts of the past, the Ushers are rendered obsolete by a society rapidly redrawing its boundaries and ceaselessly redefining its systems of identity construction.

In *Grotesque and the Arabesque*, "Usher" followed "The Man That Was Used Up," a satiric portrait of a famous war hero turned politician whose distaste for the past is surpassed only by his insatiable desire for change. At its heart, "The Man That Was Used Up" lampoons Jacksonian politics by ridiculing the false promise of continual reinvention. Just as "The Man That Was Used Up" exposes the hollowness of mechanized progress, "Usher" reveals the barrenness of myths of privilege as anchors for cultural growth. Roderick Usher declares himself "the last of the ancient race of the Ushers," and his prophecy conveys alarming reverberations for more than just Poe's tale (323).[2] Fears over a vanishing sense of privilege and position were a by-product of the rampant alterations occurring in the nation. As the social space was reconfigured, so too were geographic conceptions of economics, politics, and cultural centers. By the mid-1830s, with Manhattan as the epicenter of the market revolution, speculation and credit replaced production and cultivation as the watchwords of the day. Simultaneously, increased western migration altered political power in the country, so much so that by 1840 Ohio (admitted to the Union in 1803) surpassed Virginia both in total population and in the size of its congressional delegation. These shifts displaced historic patterns of economic and political authority. By sketching the time-worn claustrophobia of Roderick's environment, Poe also delineates how the social leveling of Jacksonian democracy diluted ancestral and geographic privileges. As students think about these shifting demographics, we can challenge them to note the multiple ways in which expansion affected development. Given just a handful of data, they can hypothesize about the cultural implications of the emergence of western states as rivals to older eastern centers of power. Even a quick consideration of the era's social flux allows students to see how "Usher" might be more at home in the 1830s than they initially imagined.[3]

In introducing students to Jacksonian America, I also have them consider the relevant facts about Jackson's life and rise to power. Born in a backwoods settlement in the Carolinas, Jackson was the first president not native to either Virginia or Massachusetts. Popularly admired as the paradigmatic self-made man, Jackson was feverishly embraced by Americans of all stripes. As such, his ascension evinced how the national map had been redrawn by the late 1820s. While Jackson was, in the words of Alexis de Tocqueville, "a man of violent character, and middling capacity," his frontier origins established him as symbolic of the unending possibilities of social mobility (265). Tocqueville's figuration of Jackson as "middling" poignantly captures the Janus-like status of Jackson in the 1830s: for his supporters, Jackson's rise from the middle embodied the promise of democracy; for his detractors, it proved that social leveling led only to declension and mediocrity. Vowing to bend everything from the Bank of the United States to the Cherokee to the will of the "majority," Jackson reinvigorated national conceptions of self-fashioning. Through his relentless promotion of self-determination as an inalienable right, the enigmatic Jackson was associated with the forces of unbridled change. In view of our discussions of Jacksonianism, students can recognize how the listless Ushers exemplify the class eclipsed by Jackson's iconoclastic remaking of the social order.[4]

As we discuss "Usher" in class, I give the students printouts of census data displaying population demographics across the first five decades of the nineteenth century. These charts allow them quickly to understand how the rapid westward expansion recast political and social power. Mastering the intricate realities of national expansion is a difficult task, and I do not want to overwhelm students with facts and figures. However, I think it is important to find shorthand ways of reminding them that the country did not gently evolve from thirteen colonies to fifty states overnight. My aim is to push them to keep in mind how what we read interacts with an unfolding—and decidedly not ever stable—sense of national identity. To underscore the precariousness of national expansion, we examine some short selections from Tocqueville's *Democracy in America* that catalog the restless stops and starts of Jacksonian society. One of the most prescient quotations vividly captures just how out of place the House of Usher is in such a climate of perpetual motion:

> In the United States, a man carefully builds a dwelling in which to pass his declining years, and he sells it while the roof is being laid; he plants a garden

and rents it out just as he was going to taste its fruits, he clears a field and
he leaves to others the care of harvesting its crops.   (512)

Only hereditary custom links Roderick Usher to his house; none of its inte-
rior or exterior designs exhibits his personal vision. As testament to this ossifi-
cation of identity, the narrator remarks that the surrounding "peasantry" have
redefined the "House of Usher" as an interchangeable signifier for "both the
family and the family mansion" (319). This conflation of inhabitants and structure compromises Roderick's identity. Denied, architecturally, the possibility of
independence, the burdens of history prevent Roderick from making the House
of Usher into Usher's house. As the nation overindulged on the idea of regeneration through mobility, static pseudoaristocratic houses became untenable
spaces. Roderick's devotion to a myth of a purity of blood, of a single undeviat-
ing line of succession, was heretical in a culture hastening to redraw all the
tenets of national life. Circling back to Tocqueville's figuration of Americans as
ardently restless, we examine how the House of Usher appears destined to be
engulfed by the eruptions of Jacksonian change.

Whereas "The Fall of the House of Usher" postulates the implausibility of
maintaining privileged inheritance, "Ligeia" further troubles the insecurity of
identity during the Jacksonian era. As the sickly Rowena attempts to fortify herself by drinking some "light wine," the narrator notices "three or four large
drops of brilliant and ruby colored fluid" staining the otherwise transparent liquid (273). "[I]mmediately" after "the fall of the ruby-drops, a rapid change"
overcomes Rowena. As he watches over her, the narrator detects a "barely no-
ticeable tinge of color" flush across Rowena's cheeks only to observe it ebb and
flow until she dies (274). When the corpse walks toward him, he is paralyzed with
terror as "the fair-haired, the blue-eyed Lady Rowena Trevanion of Tremaine"
transforms into Ligeia with her ebony "wild eyes" and hair "*blacker than the
wings of the midnight!*" (277). Seemingly, a handful of "ruby" drops convert the
wellborn Lady Rowena into a body without a discernible "paternal name"
(262).

Completely unaware of Ligeia's origins, the narrator confesses that she "came
and departed as a shadow" (263). While he suggests that her family must be "of
a remotely ancient date" (262), he cannot recall any pertinent details about her
except the "strangeness" of her beauty (263). Noting how her "gazelle"-like eyes
seem "far larger than the ordinary eyes of our race," the narrator catalogs numerous coded details about Ligeia's features that collectively raise the issue of
miscegenation (264). Arguably, I suggest to the students, if the narrator had recalled meeting Ligeia in an "old, decaying city" along the Mississippi instead of
one "near the Rhine," we might assume they had met in an octoroon ball in
New Orleans (262). Describing how some "idolatrous" god of "Egypt"
"presided" over their "ill-omened" marriage (262), the narrator leaves little
doubt about the complexity of Ligeia's racial identity. As we discuss Poe's presentation of Ligeia, I speak about antebellum conceptions of Egypt, summariz-

ing how Scott Trafton and Bruce Dain have uncovered the intertwining of representations of Egypt with cultural constructions of racial identities. As our discussion unfolds, I ask the students to probe the implications of having no "paternal name" and to reflect on the meaning of the catalyst—the few drops of staining liquid—of Rowena's transformation. By registering the popularity of the "tragic mulatto" in antebellum culture, we can demonstrate how Poe's figuration of Ligeia embeds a consideration of systems of racial categorization in a narrative that questions the limits of willful self-determination.

Confronting the complexity of systems of racial classification is a difficult challenge, especially for students who typically divide the nation along reductive geographic lines, which they have been conditioned to presume separate a proslavery South from an abolitionist North. This oversimplification of history prohibits the students from fruitfully navigating the tangled banks of national development. I trouble their prejudices about the antebellum period by underscoring the contradictory ways in which the entire nation debated the consequences of slavery and citizenship. In so doing, I highlight the arguments of Teresa Zackodnik's discerning article "Fixing the Color Line: The Mulatto, Southern Courts, and Racial Identity." By registering "the corporal challenge" that " 'mulattos' posed to a social system built upon" a "racial binary," Zackodnik demonstrates how society was forced to "marshal contradictory notions of race in order to silence and subsume such threats" (422). Uncovering how shifting legal debates fueled a constant unease over identity, Zackodnik records the feverish struggle to pigeonhole the ungraspable. When students are exposed to this historical perspective, they can judge how the end of "Ligeia" might register a rampant nervousness over the instability of the color line. By considering how the tale obscures the seemingly stable binary of color, the students gain a vivid insight into the confusion of antebellum America.

The intermingling of identities that composes the tale's end reflects the nebulous state of personal identity during the Jacksonian era. Even the minutest drop of blood could modify a paragon of whiteness like Rowena into the shadowy figure of Ligeia. Yet the transubstantiation of the tale's conclusion is not as startling as it might seem. More than simply expressing fear over the unreadable legacies of miscegenation, the tale interrogates the commodification of all forms of identity construction. Pointedly, the narrator expresses confusion over why Rowena's "haughty family" allowed their "thirst of gold" to export their "beloved" "maiden" (270). Overpowered by a desire for profit, Rowena's parents sell her as chattel; even the lady with an aristocratic pedigree becomes a commodity. By implying that the marketplace has infected all areas of social interaction, Poe confuses the identities of Ligeia and Rowena even before the strange reanimation. In depicting the consequences of inhabiting a world without any stability, the tale strikes an ominous note for a culture speeding to redefine its notions of self-determination.

To help the students further understand the social implications of Poe's tale, I assign Joan Dayan's essay "Poe, Persons, and Property." Dayan argues that

Poe complicates "the issues of human servitude" by portraying "the slippage between degrees of color, gradations of personhood, and the bounds of civility and savagery" (109). Dayan's insight into how a variety of Poe's tales encode the tensions between notions of "unpolluted, legitimate pedigree" and "the inerad-icable stain, the drop that could not be seen but must be feared" empowers the students to question the social horror of "Ligeia" (119). Instructed by Dayan's analysis, they begin to comprehend how—under the sway of the Jacksonian market revolution—the racial identities of Ligeia and Rowena are indistin-guishable. The barbaric traffic lurking beneath the surface of "Ligeia" involves more than just racial injustices; rather the "legitimate" horror of the story in-criminates all types of social intercourse. Jacksonian social mobility raised the possibility of unending flux, causing the nation to risk the prospect of drowning in the riptides of change. In "Ligeia," the binaries of black and white, rich and poor, and even dead and alive become hopelessly blurred beyond recognition. While it would be reductive to equate an arranged marriage with the inhuman-ities of slavery, the tale does seem purposely to confuse the boundaries be-tween Rowena and Ligeia to broadcast the incessant horrors of indeterminacy.

Trafton has argued that "Poe is a theorist of the anxieties of Manifest Des-tiny" (98). By debating the manifold meanings of manifest destiny, we can begin to register Poe's apprehensions over the state of Jacksonian culture. The press westward engendered the prospect of never-ending social mobility, fostering limitless possibilities for self-fashioning. In such a climate, residual patterns of identity construction offered no stable foundation for cultural order. If all iden-tities were subject to utilitarian revision, then they were also always contingent. Manifest destiny, with all its implications for American culture, is born from the synergy of Jacksonianism. Perhaps the most profound critique of 1830s Amer-ica is Tocqueville's *Democracy in America*, a text marked by a determination to discern, as the title of one of his chapters asks, "why the Americans show them-selves so restive in the midst of their well-being" (511). Throughout *Democracy in America*, Tocqueville deploys the phrase "in the midst" to describe the un-certainties he witnesses around him, wondering how "in the midst of an uncer-tain future" and how "in the midst of the universal movement of society" the nation managed to keep from fracturing apart (394, 170). Poe's tales explore the ramifications of life "in the midst" of Jacksonianism, tracing the darker side of Tocqueville's equivocations. As such, Poe's speculations about the legitimate terror of unstable identities are interrogations of the cultural implications of a blind devotion to unending and unregulated change.

In reading Poe's tales against the cultural contexts of late Jacksonian democ-racy in the classroom, we can register the connections between the legitimate "terror of the soul" and the flux of identify that ensued from the unremitting permutations of the period. In so doing, we open up areas of inquiry for our students. We may have become accustomed, when plotting America's literary past, to repeating what Poe's detective Dupin calls "the gross but common error of confounding the unusual with the abstruse" ("Murders" 414). By refashioning our relation with Poe's work, we can revise the distorted shape of ahistorical literary surveys. We should ask undergraduates to read "Ligeia" and contemplate the commodification of identity, to examine the widespread fears over mobocracy and social unrest embedded in "The Man That Was Used Up," to explore the collapse of class privilege embedded in "The Fall of the House of Usher," and to query the limits of fantasies about a virgin land by analyzing "Morning on the Wissahiccon." If we do so, our students will encounter the uncertainties of the past and the intricacies of academic readings as well.

NOTES

I am grateful to Bill Kelly for teaching me to think of Poe's works as social texts and to Kim Engber, David Humphries, Wayne Moreland, and John Weir for their thoughtful readings of drafts of this essay.

[1] Poe's use of both a solitary Native American and a solitary animal to represent a pre-Anglo-American past are consistent with the tropes of the Hudson River School painters, who interchangeably employed both figures to mark an area as a wilderness. In " 'Ut Pictura Poe': Literary Politics in 'The Island of the Fay' and 'Morning on the Wissahiccon," Louis Renza provides an informative analysis of the ways in which "Wissahiccon" explores the relationship between literary production and nationalism. While my conclusions about Poe's intent at the end of the sketch differ from Renza's, his work is an extremely rich resource for anyone considering teaching "Wissahiccon."

[2] While Eric Sundquist's suggestive book *Home as Found* does not analyze Poe, his arguments about how James Fenimore Cooper turns to incest as a solution to the Jacksonian crisis of authority is similar to the argument that I am making about "Usher."

[3] For more information on the cultural ramifications of the Jacksonian market revolution, see Charles Sellers, *The Market Revolution: Jacksonian America, 1815–1846*; Marvin Meyers, *The Jacksonian Persuasion*; and Sean Wilentz, *Chants Democratic*.

[4] The best recent works on the cultural effects of Jacksonian politics are Louis Masur's *1831: Year of Eclipse* and Ted Widmer's biography of Martin Van Buren.

"Some Words with a Mummy": Teaching Satire and the Democratic Threat in Poe's Fiction

Edward Wesp

A persistent challenge of teaching the fiction of Edgar Allan Poe is to find a way to help students read his work in the context of a broad American literature course whose readings are situated in antebellum social and political concerns. One way to achieve this is through an investigation of a wide range of Poe's fiction that emphasizes Poe's participation in Southern critiques of Northern democracy; this focus acts as a counterpart to approaches that foreground race as the primary term of debate. Through a brief detour outside the core Poe canon, students can be exposed to a way of understanding narrative techniques central to Poe's work as a contribution to the American debate on the terms of slavery, democracy, and freedom.

To introduce this way of understanding Poe's work, I begin by showing students that Poe's fiction does, on occasion, explicitly address issues of American democracy and the political and intellectual-historical context of that institution. In "Some Words with a Mummy," probably the clearest example of this satirical mode, Poe mounts a none-too-subtle critique of American democracy as a self-deluded intellectual project.[1] The story details a conversation between an ancient mummy and a group of modern gentlemen who have managed to revive the mummy from his rest by way of electrical stimulation. The exchange between the mummy and his contemporary interlocutors primarily presents the mummy's bemused reaction to a variety of modern advancements, reflecting at one point, for instance, on the very concept of progress, noting "as for Progress, it was at one time quite a nuisance, but it never progressed" (820). In "Some Words with a Mummy," democracy gets a similar treatment. After listening patiently to the narrator's praise of American democracy, the mummy

> seemed not a little amused. When we had done, he said that, a great while ago, there had occurred something of a very similar sort. Thirteen Egyptian provinces determined all at once to be free, and so set a magnificent example to the rest of mankind. They assembled their wise men, and concocted the most ingenious constitution it is possible to conceive. For a while they managed remarkably well; only their habit of bragging was prodigious. The thing ended, however, in the consolidation of the thirteen states, with some fifteen or twenty others, in the most odious and insupportable despotism that ever was heard of upon the face of the Earth.
>
> I asked what was the name of the usurping tyrant.
>
> As well as the Count could recollect, it was *Mob*. (820)

There is an advantage to the clarity of Poe's satire here, as students are presented with an unequivocal, if unexpected, view of Poe as taking a politically legible position. Especially in the context of an early American literature survey, this mocking of the foundational American project of democracy is bound to resonate.

Another effective example of Poe's engagement with the trappings of American democracy is the story "The System of Doctor Tarr and Professor Fether," which describes a trip to an insane asylum in which the narrator fails, until the climactic and chaotic end of the story, to realize that the patients have overthrown the doctors and taken their place. While the story attests to Poe's widespread preoccupation with insanity, the specifics of the "system of soothing" used to treat the patients (713)—which proves to be entirely ineffective—is certainly legible as a stand-in for the optimistic principles inspiring democratic liberty. This connection is made clear when the final scene of mayhem in the asylum is accompanied by an orchestra playing "Yankee Doodle Dandy." Especially when the story is taught alongside "Some Words with a Mummy," students will get the joke as American patriotic music provides the background for the revelation that the inmates are literally running the asylum.

Taking advantage of the opportunity these stories present means helping bridge the gap between their satirical tone and the feel of Poe's better-known and more respected fiction. Without this connection, reading the satire stories could reinforce the sense that the psychological tales are divorced from social or political concerns. The next step, therefore, is to identify elements of Poe's narrative form that can be linked back to the more apparently antidemocratic positions adopted in Poe's satires. Such identification is valuable even in texts that seem to avoid such concerns for abstract aesthetic or theoretical psychological contemplation.

To do this, I ask students to lay out a timeline of the narrative in each story, thinking especially about the differences between what the reader, narrator, and other characters know and what is actually true at any given point during the fictional period described by the tale. As this exercise unfolds, students are able to see, first, that the two stories share a narrative structure in which the narrator comes to realize that he has misunderstood the basic situation in the fictional world the story describes. Additionally, in the surprise ending of "The System of Doctor Tarr and Professor Fether," students recognize a very familiar pattern of Poe's fictional technique in which the narrator spends the bulk of the story patting himself on the back, only to realize his mistake in the midst of a violent and frightening final revelation.

To reinforce this point, a quick review of the narrative structure of some other more frequently assigned and anthologized Poe texts can buttress the students' sense of connection. Narrative timelines for other stories can be prepared by small groups of students and then assembled on the board so that the class can see the formal continuity between Poe's psychological and satirical fiction.

Almost any of Poe's popular stories—for example, the guilt-ridden revelations at the end of "The Black Cat" or "The Tell-Tale Heart" or the shocking return from the grave in buried-alive stories like "The Fall of the House of Usher" or "Berenice"—allow for this connection to be drawn.

Once the class becomes comfortable with the idea that there is reason to read the satire stories as connected formally to Poe's overall body of work, students are in a position to consider thematic connections as well. It is worth pointing out that in "Some Words with a Mummy" Poe's structure of surprising reversal plays out at two levels. On one level, the mummy's historical report dramatically upends the modern men's understanding of the world around them. On the other, the mummy reveals that the failure of the ancient experiment with democracy also unfolded over a recognizably Poe-esque time frame that students can see at work in both the horror and the satire stories. Democracy institutes itself by way of intellectual decree, the formulation of "the most ingenious constitution it is possible to conceive" (820). Democratic society then proceeds—like many of Poe's protagonists—with much self-congratulation, unable to see its forthcoming demise. But, in the end, it falls victim to a force (the destructive violence of the mob) to which it was blind. Moreover, if the mummy is to be believed, the contemporary American project of democracy is presumably heading unwittingly toward a similar fate.

Pulling all this together, it is possible to help students understand what they have experienced narratively as a surprise ending can be seen thematically and culturally as a deep and consistent skepticism in Poe's writing. One defining element that comes out of the project of analyzing the narrative timelines is not only that the narrators of the story did not know the actual situation but also that they did not know that they did not know. It is their lack of skepticism as much as their lack of awareness that leads to their downfall.

At the level of the individual, the rational skepticism encouraged by the experiences of Poe's narrators is at the heart of Poe's presentation of a psychologically decentered subjectivity. Viewed with an eye toward Poe's treatment of democracy, however, that skepticism also generates a political critique of ideas basic to American self-imagination. This point is made explicitly in "Some Words with a Mummy" and by analogy in "The System of Doctor Tarr and Professor Fether." Finally students can be asked to think about the connection between psychological and political skepticism. One way to raise this question is to have students consider the familiar characters of Poe's fiction in a different context (now that it is clear that Poe has raised the issue himself): how do we think differently about democracy if the citizens afforded democratic power are like the characters in horror tales? In this way, students can begin to imagine the social and political implications suggested by the very private narrative world Poe's fiction creates. Considered in this context, it is fairly clear that Poe's destabilizing narrative construction presents readers with an account of human experience that is incompatible with the assumptions made about self-governing democratic citizens. Put bluntly, if people work like Poe says they do, then giving them more freedom suddenly seems to be a disturbing prospect.

There are many benefits to providing Poe's political satire as context for his more familiar work, the first of which is simply to provide a more full and rewarding range of interpretive directions for students. While students are commonly enthusiastic about reading Poe's fiction for its representation of individual psychology, it can be exciting—for me and for students—to help them develop interpretations of his work that add to this initial set of interpretive expectations.

Instructors, by showing students that that psychological analysis is connected to theories of political and social imagination, can help students see more of what is at stake in Poe's work. In ways that can profitably recall the theorization of democracy in revolutionary-era readings, Poe's work makes clear a link between assumptions about individual human subjectivity and the kinds of society in which such people might reasonably be imagined to participate. Making this connection works well in a survey course, since doing so integrates Poe into the semester-long consideration of how American literature reflects and shapes both authors' and readers' understanding of American national identity. Additionally, once students can recognize that even apparently nonpolitical texts like Poe's horror fiction do in fact contribute to an understanding of the assumptions underlying social understanding, it is easy to ask them to look to other texts in order to consider alternative or competing literary representations of individual subjectivity. How, for example, does the ambiguity surrounding the end of Nathaniel Hawthorne's *The Scarlet Letter* or "Young Goodman Brown" differ in its implications about the relation between the individual and social structures? How does the internal first-person narration of Charlotte Perkins Gilman's "The Yellow Wall-Paper"—which students often initially identify as similar in style to Poe's first-person narratives of madness—manage to provide a different view of the link between social order and individual experience? Whatever links turn out to be most appropriate for a given syllabus, it is at the very least beneficial for students to see that the revolutionary-era contemplation of human nature and democracy did not settle the issue once and for all.

One potentially fascinating way to make use of the political implications of subjectivity in Poe's work is as a part of a unit—or course—on the debate over slavery that preceded the Civil War. It is possible to use students' politically situated understanding of Poe's skepticism of human rationality as a bridge to a body of antebellum Southern writing that is becoming a more available and indispensable part of approaching this period of American social and political history through literature. The availability of this writing has made it more feasible to present Poe to students in a useful manner as a Southern writer, at least in the context of the slavery debate. As I noted earlier, specific selections of Poe's writing could support readings focused on the subject of race and servitude, but a sequence of readings that uses political-satire texts to clarify Poe's use of rationality as a political and personal term is more appropriate to another approach. In particular, by unearthing a more politically minded Poe, teachers can draw students in to a compact but meaningful presentation of antebellum southern critiques of democracy and capitalism.

The most readily available texts to pair with Poe in this regard come from the self-styled Southern historian George Fitzhugh, whose work now appears in at least two important anthologies as a representative of Southern proslavery apologists.[2] The most intriguing link with Poe is that Fitzhugh's writing is often less concerned with an active defense of slavery than it is with a critique of the very foundation of democratic society. In journal articles, books like *Cannibals All!*, and his ambitious Northern lecture tour, Fitzhugh presented a rejection of democracy and capitalism that, in my experience, will remind students of Poe's mummy. In Fitzhugh's view, America's historical self-definition as a new nation founded on democratic principles represents a deeply naive misunderstanding of human nature. While the revolutionary-era writings of Thomas Jefferson and Thomas Paine focus on the rational construction of a systematic social order of individuals, Fitzhugh asserts that these writers have missed an inherent hierarchical tendency in humankind. In a succinct statement of his position, Fitzhugh writes:

> [T]he vain attempts to define liberty in theory, or to secure its enjoyment in practice, proceed from the fact that man is naturally a social and gregarious animal, subject, not by contract or agreement, as Locke and his followers assume, but by birth and nature.   (*Cannibals* 71)

These essential elements of "birth and nature" are the origin of Fitzhugh's history. From this perspective, the inauguration of the American democracy indeed makes little sense, since it simply compounds the long history of errors Fitzhugh traces back to the emancipation of the serfs in Europe. The self-conscious announcement of a new social order stands little chance of success in the face of man's "social and gregarious" innate tendencies, and his account of the American nation's self-deluded reliance on the "ignus fatuus" of democracy portends a very Poe-like fall.

Poe and Fitzhugh can be a complementary set of readings to give students a glimpse at this oppositional voice in American literary and cultural thought both because of their parallels and because of the productive tension that can be generated by reading between them. Students, by reading these texts together, are encouraged to interact critically with texts that, for different reasons, they might otherwise tend to cast aside. In the case of Fitzhugh's history, the goal of parallel reading is of course not to argue for the plausibility of his position. Indeed no responsible presentation of his writing would allow students to read past the fabrications and inaccuracies that in the end betray his critique of the North as a self-serving distraction from the slavery system he was supporting. At the same time, for the reading to be valuable it is necessary to have students move beyond an entirely dismissive reaction so that they can engage with the material in a way that allows them to develop a sense of the social-rhetorical scheme on which the critique of democracy rests. To help students find that engagement, I have asked them to compare the picture of human nature presented in Fitzhugh with the one they have come to see in Poe's writing. This allows students to think about the ways in which Poe's narrative provides individual examples of the more abstract premise that democracy is a misguided rationalist fantasy.

While this continuity gives students a feel for a Southern position in the debate on slavery that they must reckon with, it is equally important in helping them see the way that Poe's work broadens the narrow version of democratic critique marshaled as a defense of slavery. Poe's skepticism clears the way for recognizing the contested field in which the terms of American democracy are debated and challenged elsewhere in the reading students will do during a course that covers the early period of American literature. So, while a comparison with Fitzhugh may present students with one unfavorable version of the extrapolation of Poe's critique of rationalism and social order, getting students to recognize the political stakes of Poe's skepticism can be a good way to help them avoid an overly simplistic version of the period in which the South is the repository of all social ill and the North is the realization of perfect social equality. In a way that a writer like Fitzhugh could never do, Poe can work as a point of crossover, registering a critique of assumptions closely associated with the American democratic project that falls somewhere between the outright rejection of other Southern writers and the more constructive internal critiques of authors whose work is intended to move American culture toward the democratic ideal it has set for itself. After Poe, for instance, the critique of Herman Melville's "Bartleby" resonates more deeply, beyond the particularity of burgeoning office culture to larger problems of managing freedom and restriction, and the critical undertones of Harriet Jacobs's account of life in the North present themselves with even more troubling force. While it is true that the work of few of the other authors students encounter in an American literature class are likely to offer such direct critiques of the principles of democracy, Poe's work can remind students that American literature is not simply a reflection of the idea of democratic freedom but a subtle and complex history of contesting ideas about what *American* means and what it means to be American.

NOTES

[1] For a valuable consideration of Poe's place as a Southern critic of democratic rationalism, see R. Gray.

[2] Fitzhugh has become a common point of reference for literary scholars interested in the tradition of Southern proslavery conservatism. The prominence of Fitzhugh as a representative of this tradition, for example, his inclusion in recent editions of the *Heath Anthology of American Literature* and *The American Intellectual Tradition*, has been accompanied by justifiable questions about how representative his work really is. It is

certainly true that some of Fitzhugh's positions departed from the mainstream of the proslavery argument, most notably his suggestion that slavery was such a fundamentally superior system of social order that he could justify the prospect of whites enslaving other whites. Much more representative are Fitzhugh's historical rejection of democracy as progressive and his emphasis on hierarchized, patriarchal institutions as the basis of social order.

Teaching the Mechanics of Deception: "Hans Pfaall," Science Fiction, and Hoaxing in Antebellum Print Culture

Marcy J. Dinius

While "The Unparalleled Adventure of One Hans Pfaall" and its debatable status as one of Poe's hoaxes have sustained literary critical interest over the years, the tale has been all but forgotten in the classroom. In my teaching experience, I have found that this interesting example of Poe's science fiction and equally remarkable details about its cultural context offer twenty-first-century students unique insights into the shifting status of art and science in nineteenth-century America, the chaotic world of antebellum print, and the uncertainties of truth, knowledge, and reality in an age of rapid technological and social change. While it may never make it onto an American literature survey syllabus, "Hans Pfaall" can work quite well in upper-division seminars on nineteenth-century American print culture, literary nationalism, literature and science, and, of course, Poe's works. In addition, "Hans Pfaall" provides the advantages of being shorter than *The Narrative of Arthur Gordon Pym of Nantucket* in courses with a crowded syllabus, more accessible than *Eureka*, and surprisingly relevant to the themes of such diverse works as "The Raven," "The Philosophy of Composition," and "The Purloined Letter."

To get at some of the big issues in "Hans Pfaall," it is helpful both to introduce a range of important literary and historical contexts into discussion and to provide students with guided research assignments outside the classroom to enrich their sense of the culture in which the story was written and read. This contextual approach encourages students to read the story with some of the following questions in mind: What is this story about? Is it an example of science fiction? What is science fiction? What is the relation of these two terms in the story, in the society that we see depicted in the story, and in the society whose members first read this story? Does "Hans Pfaall" have a moral? If so, what is it?

Literary and Historical Contexts

Our students live in an age in which the disciplinary boundaries between the sciences and the humanities are fairly firmly drawn—or, at least, in which each discipline is firmly established. They tend to find it difficult to imagine times in which science existed not as something to be practiced by scientists in the quest for facts and truth but rather as a part of broader fields of inquiry dabbled in by gentlemen, holy men, philosophers, and amateurs. Accordingly, they are often surprised to learn that it was in Poe's lifetime that what previously was known as natural philosophy narrowed significantly as research in biology, chemistry, and physics became the work primarily of professionals newly designated as scientists.[1] This modern notion of science came about in part, we can suggest, as a result of shifting cultural values. An overview of this shift might include some of the following observations.

In American society, the significance of scientific inquiry officially was established with the Constitution, which created patent laws to "promote the progress of science and useful arts" (art. 1, sec. 8). This early connection between scientific value and the written word grew even stronger during the nineteenth century through a vibrant print culture that served as the primary vehicle for conveying the results of scientific inquiry to the public.[2] In the same moment, calls for a national literature representative of the intellectual, political, and natural potential of America were circulating widely. Despite such appeals, the nascent literary profession promised most American writers little more than a meager income in return for ample frustration. These frustrations largely resulted from publication practices that strongly favored novels by British and other foreign authors over native literary production. Consequently, American authors had to rely on periodical publications to bring their works before the public. Yet if some writers became successful by publishing in periodicals, most remained at the mercy of predatory editors. Few magazines had fixed, much less generous, rates for paying their contributors; despite copyright laws, stories and poems were frequently published without attribution. Moreover, editors commonly reserved the right to alter works to suit their length requirements or tastes, and newspapers and magazines in exchange partnerships with other periodicals reprinted pieces without remuneration or restraint.[3] In competing with scientific writing for column space in popular periodicals and thus for the public's attention, writers such as Poe increasingly viewed scientific fact as a rival of the literary imagination.

This brief survey of antebellum science and literature can be enriched by an assignment that sends students to the archives to discover firsthand the place of each in nineteenth-century print culture. Students can be asked to browse through antebellum periodicals to locate one example of scientific writing and one of literary writing and to give attention to the context in which each originally appeared. Fortunately, students with access to the Internet now can complete such an assignment as readily as those with access to a research library's special collections by browsing in electronic archives such as Cornell University's and the University of Michigan's *The Making of America*. In a written summary of their findings, students would respond to the following questions:

> In which periodicals did you find your examples?
> What kinds of articles precede and follow those that you chose?
> For the scientific example, how technical would the language or description seem to be to the general reader?
> What is the most important information that the writer seeks to convey?
> For the literary example, is the author named?

Are you familiar with this author?
What is the subject of the story or poem?
Can you determine if the story or poem was printed elsewhere (in another periodical, in or as a book)?
More broadly, what were your impressions of the periodicals in which you found these writings?
Who might their target audiences have been?
Do you imagine that they were read primarily for entertainment, information, or both?
How do they resemble publications that we read today?

Such an assignment, especially when shared in class in brief presentations, offers students a deeper, broader understanding of nineteenth-century American science, literature, and culture through their expression in print.

Poe was particularly well positioned both to observe and to participate in the rivalry of literature and science in antebellum print through his work as magazine editor and as a poet and short story writer. Given his own difficulties as an artist in gaining public recognition and sustained approbation, he personally experienced the vicissitudes of these changing cultural dynamics. In support of these observations and as part of the literary context of "Hans Pfaall," we can introduce into our discussion of literature and science two brief examples of Poe's views on their relation, easily reproduced on a handout. The poem "Sonnet—To Science," one of Poe's earliest poetic works, was published first in 1829; then in 1831; and, after the publication of "Hans Pfaall," twice again in 1836 and 1845—without significant modifications from the original version.[4] In reading through and discussing the poem, we can ask students to consider how its tone, its view of the relation between literature and science, and the relevance of biographical information (such as Poe's youth, his interest in science, his status as a poet) enter into our reading. A passage from an 1836 book review in which Poe laments, "When *shall* the artist assume his proper situation in society—in a society of thinking beings?" would also be relevant to this discussion (Rev. of *Conti* 164). As a prelude to a discussion of the same topics in "Hans Pfaall," students can consider how the view expressed in this quotation relates to that in "Sonnet—To Science." They can then explore the relation of both views with their own discoveries in the archives about how antebellum society perceived science and the arts and how Poe regarded his society.

Adventures in "Hans Pfaall"

Most of "Hans Pfaall" is a fantastic account of a Rotterdam bellows mender's balloon voyage to the moon, filled with scientific and pseudoscientific details that make the story at once informative and imaginative, humorous and earnest. Students will be amused, if not occasionally appalled, by Pfaall's experiments on the cat and kittens on board, by his description of the effects of the voyage on his body, and by nineteenth-century imaginings of the sights and experiences of space travel. During our first day of discussing "Hans Pfaall," I ask my students to consider not only what happens in the story but also how the story is written in a session that begins to explore the relation of form and content. We talk about what effects the story's mixing of genres (from travel narrative and scientific treatise to newspaper story and imaginative tale) have on the plot and characters and on the reader. As a means of focusing our reading as discussion evolves, I direct students' attention to the conclusion of Pfaall's letter and that of the story. In thinking about "Hans Pfaall" as a story within a story and how the narrative's structure relates to its content, I begin by asking:

> What are Pfaall's demands at the end of his letter? What does he promise in return? How do these demands affect the account of his voyage in the rest of the letter?
>
> How do the recipients of the letter react? What is the reasoning behind each of their reactions? What light do Poe's earlier writings about science shed on Professor Rub-a-dub's response to Pfaall's letter? What can we make of Superbus von Underduk's and Professor Rub-a-dub's humorous names?
>
> What is the public response to Pfaall's letter when it is published? Why do the people of Rotterdam react as they do? What is the narrator's attitude toward the public? What is his attitude toward Hans Pfaall?
>
> Given its conclusion, what is "Hans Pfaall" finally a story about? Does it seem to have a moral? If so, what is it?
>
> What connections can we draw among the characters, events, and settings of this story and what we have learned about nineteenth-century America and its print culture?
>
> What does this story have to say about the relation between authors and readers in general, the economic and social value of artistic creation and scientific information, and the relation of facts and the imagination?

This set of questions begins to get at some of the more interesting, if not confounding, publication and reception histories of both Hans Pfaall's letter and "Hans Pfaall" itself.

The Note

In completing their earlier archival assignment and discussing the story's conclusion, students will have begun to consider the significance of the circumstances of a text's original publication to how it is read thereafter. In taking up these details with respect to "Hans Pfaall" in a second day of discussion, students gain some insight into the mysterious note that they encountered at the end of the story and into subsequent and ongoing literary critical debates about whether

"Hans Pfaall" should be considered a hoax. At this point we can explain that the story was first published as "Hans Phaall—A Tale" in the June 1835 number of the *Southern Literary Messenger* and ask students to consider the differences between the two titles and what readers might expect of the story from the different titles. As a means of getting at the issue of whether "Hans Pfaall" should be considered a tale or a hoax, we can also share with students the original editorial introduction to the story. This introduction declared that " 'Mr. Poe's story of *'Hans Phaall*,' will add much to his reputation as an imaginative writer" and praised the "impossibilities of the story" that the writer "details . . . with a minuteness so much like truth, that they seem quite probable" ("Editorial"). We can then ask them to consider important differences between the two genres in the light of this initial response to the story.

These considerations help ground a class session that addresses a reading of the concluding note that Poe first added to "Hans Pfaall" when he republished it in *Tales of the Grotesque and Arabesque* in 1840; a survey of major nineteenth-century hoaxes; and, more broadly, a discussion about plagiarism. In advance of this session, students can be asked to prepare brief presentations on such relevant topics as the Great Moon Hoax, nineteenth-century penny newspapers, Poe's career as an editor, accusations of plagiarism against Poe, and Poe's own "Balloon-Hoax."[5] With the important contextual information gained from these reports, students should be well prepared to consider the following questions toward drawing important conclusions about "Hans Pfaall," early science fiction, and antebellum print culture:

> Why did Poe add this note at the end of "Hans Pfaall"? What does it argue? What is the tone of the note? How does and/or doesn't it sound like the story?
>
> In what ways is it relevant to the story? More specifically, how does Poe's classification of the story as a hoax relate to the discussion of hoaxing in the story itself?
>
> What more does the note tell us about Poe's view of the relation between literature and science?
>
> How does the note affect our conclusions about the story? How might you have read the story differently if you had read the note first?

Through such a guided contextual reading of "The Unparalleled Adventure of One Hans Pfaall," students ultimately begin to understand how early science fiction, by presenting itself as scientific information rather than literary invention, borrowed on the growing popular credibility of science to gain the attention and endorsement of a culture that was increasingly encouraged to value science at the expense of literature. Perpetrated in print—the modern marketplace for determining the value of new and different knowledge—scientific hoaxes succeeded in deceiving the public by exploiting the indeterminacy of authority that was an inevitable effect of the chaotic print culture of the mid–

nineteenth century. In revisiting this era that positioned the arts and sciences as rivals for popular attention and that allowed the free circulation of texts without concern for their authorship or authenticity, students learn how the hoax and early science fiction such as "Hans Pfaall" proved to be genres that shrewd writers like Poe could exploit to their advantage. If American society would not assign the artist "his proper situation in society" (Poe, Rev. of *Conti* 164), we may conclude with our students, then science-minded fiction writers were left to assign it to themselves, by the most effective means available to them.

NOTES

Limited portions of the argument in this essay are adapted from my article "Poe's Moon Shot: 'Hans Phaall' and the Art and Science of Antebellum Print Culture, *Poe Studies / Dark Romanticism* 37 (2004): 1–10.

[1] As Daniels explains, this specialization of natural philosophy resulted in "the creation in the early nineteenth century of an esoteric body of knowledge called 'science.' As one would expect, the term 'scientist' was also coined at this time to refer to those who had previously been designated 'natural philosophers' " (38). Zochert elaborates on the causes and effects of this shift: "The traditional orientation of science toward the natural world and the naming of its parts was being challenged by a specialization which placed theoretical considerations above simple description; the gentleman philosopher able to combine leisure with the pursuit of science (and often with considerable literary grace) was being superseded by a more disciplined class of scientists with distinct claims of professionalism" (7).

[2] For the seminal study of the national significance of periodical publications, see Mott.

[3] For studies of the dynamics of antebellum print culture particularly with respect to Poe, see Elmer (*Reading*); McGill (*American Literature*); Moss; Rachman; and Whalen (*Edgar*).

[4] For a list of textual variants in different versions of "Sonnet—To Science," see Mabbott's note in the *Complete Poems* (90). Fisher discusses the significance of science in Poe's works more broadly ("That").

[5] For information about the Great Moon Hoax and nineteenth-century penny newspapers, students can be directed to Locke; F. O'Brien; Poe's letter to Kennedy; and the section on Locke in Poe's "The Literati of New York." For discussions of Poe and plagiarism, students can consult Dameron; Elmer (*Reading*); McGill (*American Literature*); Moss; and Rachman. On Poe's work as an editor, see Jacobs; Marvin; McGill (*American Literature*); and Moss.

What Difference Does It Make?
Pym, Plagiarism, and Pop Culture
Jeffrey Andrew Weinstock

My students *know* Poe.

They arrive on the first day of my survey course in American literature or my seminar on the Romantic period or my course on the American gothic with all sorts of ideas about Poe—not just about his writings, but about him, the guy with the quill (they always visualize him with a quill), the prominent forehead, and the neat moustache, who looks more than a little like Gomez Addams. Few of my students have ever heard of, for example, Philip Freneau or Charles Brockden Brown or Catharine Maria Sedgwick, so they lack preconceived notions regarding these authors. And while most have read something by Nathaniel Hawthorne—usually *The Scarlet Letter*—and perhaps a handful could pick Mark Twain out of a lineup, almost none of them would presume to know these authors personally or to be able to identify important events in their lives. But students are convinced they know Poe—who he was and what he was like. They know, for example, that he was a drug addict, a misanthrope, and a loner. They know that he was an erratic genius whose works spilled forth upon a midnight dreary (while, of course, he pondered). Some are convinced that he participated in the ghoulish acts he describes in his fiction. Those in my survey course who *have* taken the time to read the Norton biographical headnote or who have a legitimate interest in Poe enjoy sharing that he married his wife, Virginia, when she was thirteen and that he was an alcoholic—which serves to confirm their general impressions of Poe's deviancy. And, occasionally, one of my students will absolutely know how he died: opium overdose, suicide, or—my favorite so far—killed in a duel.[1] Poe, in short, is for my students the quintessential Romantic genius writing in a garret, half mad, starving, and alienated from the society that scorned his dark vision—a strange synthesis of *The X-Files*'s Fox Mulder and *Silence of the Lambs*'s Hannibal Lecter.

Students think they know Poe for a variety of reasons and, to a certain extent, it is because they do. Most have read Poe—often "The Raven" and "The Tell-Tale Heart"—in primary or secondary school, and for many he was a refreshing break from what they perceived to be the drier and dourer content of the rest of the curriculum. Outside the classroom, Poe remains ubiquitous in American society: from the caricature of him that adorns Barnes and Noble shopping bags to *The Simpsons*'s Halloween rendition of "The Raven" to the *Closed on Account of Rabies* CD featuring among others Christopher Walken, Iggy Pop, and Jeff Buckley performing renditions of Poe's poetry and prose, Poe, perhaps more so than any other nineteenth-century author, pervades American culture.[2] He pops up so regularly that, as with many celebrities, we feel we know him. Then, of course, there are Poe's familiar first-person narrators that invite less experienced readers to associate the speaking voice with Poe himself. Whatever the reasons for students' perceptions of intimacy with Poe, these assumptions allow for a valuable pedagogical intervention that brings to the fore ideas about the nature of authorship, genius, and literary value. While in my opinion these issues can be addressed with just about any of Poe's texts, his *Narrative of Arthur Gordon Pym of Nantucket* (1838) works especially well because it is rollicking, sloppy, an example of plagiarism, and thoroughly invested in antebellum popular culture and publishing practices. In short, it undercuts student perceptions of Poe's alienation, originality, and compositional technique and instead creates a picture of an author who was a nineteenth-century American pop-culture muncher who capitalized on topical issues and literary trends (Lenz 30).

Pym is a wonderfully teachable book and works especially well in my seminar on American Romanticism; it is short for a novel, extremely readable by modern standards (students find the language more accessible than Brown's *Wieland* for instance), exemplary of Romanticism's rejection of the Enlightenment emphasis on reason, and it introduces issues of interpretation and reliability from the first paragraph that make for engaging classroom discussion.[3] Beyond this, it's just *so* outrageous: from living interment (twice) to mutiny to cannibalism to the endlessly debated white figure at the story's conclusion, the work reads as an engaging excursion into the realm of the imagination unbounded that grips those students with a penchant for tales of adventure, fantasy, and science fiction. Everything about the book initially confirms student impressions of Poe as a wildly original and imaginative author whose solitary genius produced dark visions "in which the whole world is haunted and mysterious" (Barker). Because the work fosters these impressions, it is therefore productive to raise the following questions: To what extent does it matter that Poe freely borrowed (plundered is more apt) from a variety of sources in composing *Pym*? How does one's appreciation of the novel and of Poe's genius change if the narrative is considered in the light of (famously) its apparent racism, as well as its investment in nineteenth-century beliefs regarding the earth as hollow and fads such as Egyptology?[4] This line of questioning builds toward interrogation of the commonplace banality that "great literature" is "timeless." Attentiveness to Poe's compositional practices and incorporation into *Pym* of nineteenth-century pop-culture fads raises the vexing question: What difference does it make that Poe's imaginative narrative is not somehow above or apart from the culture in which he lived—and in which he struggled to make a living—but is imbued from start to finish with the ideas, beliefs, and attitudes particular to his times?

Plagiarism

In these days of *Turnitin.com* and heightened awareness of intellectual property rights on academic campuses, provocative questions for classroom discussion include

To what extent is "genius" associated with or dependent on "originality"?
When is something "original"?
When is something plagiarized?
Can a genius plagiarize? Is an author still a genius if she or he does so?
Is a work still "valuable" or worthy of "canonization" if it is the product of
    marked appropriation from other sources?
More specifically, if Poe is shown to be a plagiarist, does he still deserve a
    place in the canon of American letters?

Poe's writing and especially *Pym* provide perfect test cases for these questions
because, where plagiarism was concerned, Poe was a hypocrite. According to
Stephen Rachman, Poe had a "lifelong obsession with 'detecting' plagiarisms"
and famously accused both Henry Wadsworth Longfellow and Hawthorne,
among others, of having plagiarized from *him* (51).[5] However, as Daniel Hoffman observes, although Poe "revelled in showing up the plagiarisms of others"
(97), he often concealed his own liberal borrowings from the texts of others.
Nowhere is this more evident than in *Pym*.

    An important component of what William E. Lenz has called the "industry"
of *Pym* scholarship (37n2) has been identifying Poe's sources and isolating the
moments in the text when Poe alludes to, borrows from, or explicitly plagiarizes
other texts. According to Burton R. Pollin, *Pym* incorporates more source material than any other Poe work, excepting his unfinished "Journal of Julias Rodman." Pollin contends, "Of [*Pym*'s] two hundred pages, perhaps one-fifth
represents texts either copied loosely or closely paraphrased from other writings, while perhaps one-third to one-quarter of its 328 paragraphs show distinct
traces of his readings" ("Poe's Life" 93), and both J. O. Bailey and Pollin provide extensive analyses of Poe's source material. Poe lifted whole sections from
Jeremiah N. Reynolds's "Address" (1836), in which Reynolds vigorously petitioned Congress to establish an exploratory venture to the South Seas, and from
Benjamin Morrell's *Narrative of Four Voyages* (1832), a ghostwritten account
of Morrell's South Seas adventures. Indeed, material from Morrell dominates
chapters 14 and 15 of *Pym*, in which a Pym vastly more experienced and mature than the one who starts the novel discourses knowledgeably on nautical
navigation as well as South Seas flora and fauna, and virtually all of chapter 16,
which provides an overview to South Seas exploration, is incorporated verbatim
from Reynolds's address.[6] Pollin's invaluable annotated version of *Pym* provides
an extensive catalog of Poe's sources and painstakingly identifies his borrowings
throughout the text. It is pedagogically useful to assign relevant pages from
Pollin—or from the original sources—and to read them alongside Poe's incorporation of the materials.

    Students likely will find this revelation of Poe's "indebtedness" to other
sources intriguing and potentially troubling, and this discrepancy between their
expectations concerning literary genius and the reality of Poe's plagiarism can

serve as a productive starting point for a conversation concerning canonicity and literary merit. In particular, students may be asked:

> Does any author create free from outside influences? If not, what constitutes originality and how valuable is it?
> When and under what conditions is "borrowing" from other sources acceptable in a work of fiction?
> How does Poe's plagiarism affect your assessment of *Pym* and Poe as an author? Can an author be both canonical and a plagiarist?

Instructors may also wish to ask students whether they agree with the apology for Poe's plagiarism given by Pollin: "[I]t is unjust to censure borrowings in a book which was satirical in its parodic aims and whimsical or playful in its general technique" (Introduction 17). This conversation can then lead into a general discussion of the nature of authorship, and the ambitious instructor may wish to assign Michel Foucault's famous essay "What Is an Author?," readings from Harold Bloom's *The Anxiety of Influence*, as well as Rachman's essay "*Es Lässt Sich Nicht Schreiben*: Plagiarism and 'The Man of the Crowd,'" in which Rachman proposes that Poe's variety of "creative plagiarism" has the potential to become "a subversive, quasi-justifiable literary strategy to devalue, revalue, or realign our ambivalence toward 'originality' in literature" (52). What this attention to the plagiarism issue in relation to *Pym* helps students realize is that Poe's imaginative literary productions are not (or are not just) the solitary speculations of an alienated genius, but works that engage in a dialogue with other texts and the larger field of literary production during Poe's lifetime.

Popular Culture

The other important part of this conversation about Poe's compositional practices is how they reflect nineteenth-century ideas, attitudes, and expectations. The particular value of Foucault's essay is that it argues that ideas of authorship—of what constitutes an author and a text—are not universal and invariable but have changed over time. While students can certainly debate the impact of Poe's plagiarism on their assessment of him and his texts in the present, they also need to bear in mind that compositional practices and ideas of authorship in the antebellum United States varied from our contemporary understandings. As Rachman notes, "Eighteenth- and nineteenth-century literary gentility was conveyed through a liberality of quotation bespeaking a classical education" (64). Furthermore, Poe was writing at a time when, in the absence of an international copyright law, American periodicals routinely pirated and reprinted British publications.[7] Of particular value for discussing the literary marketplace during Poe's period of publication is Meredith McGill's *American Literature and the Culture of Reprinting, 1834–1853*.

However, Poe's reliance on and incorporation of source materials into *Pym* goes beyond a narrow focus on questions of plagiarism and testifies to his awareness and manipulation of American popular culture trends and attitudes. As Lenz observes, critical attention to Poe's depictions of extreme states of consciousness frequently obscures his success at exploiting "contemporary cultural attitudes and popular literary conventions" (30). Although students tend to think of Poe as an alienated and solitary genius who crafted universal and timeless tales, this perception is belied by the fact that Poe acted as a "cultural weather vane and barometer of American attitudes" (Lenz 33) whose fascination with topics like phrenology, mesmerism, Egyptology, and certain forms of occultism reflected popular American fads of his lifetime. As part of my course on American Romanticism, I assign students topics for five-to-ten-minute presentations with which we start each class. Topics I have used include polar and South Seas exploration, mesmerism, phrenology, Egyptology, sensationalist literature, sentimental literature, Spiritualism, travel writing, westward expansion and Native American policy, aspects of slavery and abolitionism, and whaling. The topic of plagiarism in *Pym* converges with nineteenth-century interest in South Seas exploration, and I assign one student to present on the controversy surrounding the hollow-earth theory ardently supported by John Cleves Symmes, popularly referred to as Symmes's Hole.[8]

Students, particularly those familiar with sensationalist supermarket checkout-line reading like the *Weekly World News*, will be amused to learn of Symmes's unshakable conviction that the earth was "hollow, and habitable within" (qtd. in Kafton-Minkel 61). On at least nine occasions, Symmes brought petitions before Congress requesting funding for an expedition to explore the North Pole and the lands he proposed were beyond it. He was "determined to be the leader of the first journey from the outer to the inner world, and to conquer the inner world for the United States" (Kafton-Minkel 56). As Peter Fitting's anthology *Subterranean Worlds* demonstrates, the idea of a hollow earth was by no means Symmes's invention. However, Symmes and his followers' vocal support for this theory, combined with the publication in 1820 of *Symzonia*, a "proto-science fiction" work that was ostensibly published by Adam Seaborn but often attributed to Symmes himself and that details an expedition to the inner world (Fitting 97), popularized this idea to the point that, according to one commentator, " 'Symmes's Hole' was a phrase more or less . . . on everybody's tongue; the papers in the decade between 1820 and 1830 were more or less full of Symmes's Hole" (qtd. in Kafton-Minkel 61).[9]

Symmes failed in his appeals to Congress and did not live to see his vision of polar exploration realized. However, his supporter Jeremiah Reynolds—the same Reynolds from which Poe "borrowed" material for *Pym*—eventually did have better luck. Reynolds himself organized an aborted expedition to the South Pole in 1829, notable primarily for the article that came out of it called "Mocha Dick; or, The White Whale of the Pacific," published by Reynolds in the *Knickerbocker* in 1839 and read with interest by Herman Melville. Then, in

1836—two years before the publication of Poe's polar adventure—Reynolds again petitioned Congress to fund a South Seas exploratory venture and was successful (in part because he distanced himself from Symmes's hollow-earth theory and emphasized instead the political and economic benefits of exploration [Whalen, *Edgar* 153]). On 14 May 1836, the House of Representatives appropriated $300,000 to finance a South Seas venture, and in 1838 the United States Exploring Expedition sailed under the leadership of Charles Wilkes (Whalen, *Edgar* 153).[10]

The idea of Symmes's Hole of course seems incredible to us today. However, as Lenz observes, in the early nineteenth century, "science and pseudoscience shared one bed. Phrenology, mesmerism, and religious enthusiasm were woven into the fabric of American society" (32). Poe, we might add to this, was one of those doing the weaving:

> Having before him the palpable idea of the United States Exploring Expedition . . . , the inflamed rhetorical pleas of Reynolds, the bizarre theory of Symmes, and literary antecedents in Coleridge's *Rime of the Ancient Mariner* and Mary Shelley's *Frankenstein*, Poe imagines the Antarctic in the symbolic terms of the Gothic.   (Lenz 33)

In particular, the end of *Pym*, in which the Antarctic waters warm and the current flowing southward gets progressively stronger, takes on new meaning when it is read in the light of antebellum fantasies about polar exploration. In *Pym*, Poe, in characteristic fashion, appropriates, manipulates, and redeploys ideas already circulating in American culture. Calling attention to the popular fascination with the idea of Symmes's Hole and its relevancy to *Pym* foregrounds Poe's embeddedness in his historical context and problematizes presumptions concerning his alienation from mainstream culture or his universality.

Emphasis on Poe's relation to American culture of the 1830s also raises interesting questions about literary value. Students may be asked questions like the following:

> What does background knowledge about Symmes's Hole (or other antebellum fads and pseudosciences such as Egyptology, mesmerism, and phrenology) add to a reading of *Pym*?
>
> Does this background information allow for a "correct" interpretation of the text?
>
> If this information is required to interpret the text, is the text "universal"? Is it "timeless"?
>
> If Poe in suggesting the idea of a hollow earth is in *Pym* capitalizing on a preoccupation of his time period, rather than inventing this idea, does this undermine claims to his originality?
>
> Is Poe's text in any way devalued by demonstrating its embeddedness in its historical context?

I approach *Pym* through Poe's plagiarism and incorporation of popular culture both to ask my students to appreciate the text as an original literary production that is simultaneously marked by literary and American history (in the way that all texts invariably are) and to raise larger questions about canonicity and literary value. Because *Pym* is extreme in many ways—and because the realities surrounding the text and Poe's compositional practices often run contrary to students' assumptions about Poe—the work explicitly provokes questions that may only be implicit in other works and can be used to stimulate productive discussion about the relation of the author to his or her culture and about understandings of the nature of authorship in general.

NOTES

[1] I have had a lot of fun asking students to write down how they think Poe died. Besides being entertaining, the results speak to their understandings of Poe based on their backgrounds in literature and American popular culture. Simply asking this question can serve as an interesting starting point for a conversation about biographical criticism.

[2] For more on Poe and pop culture, see Neimeyer and Peeples (*Afterlife*) as starting points. It is important to point out that misconceptions about Poe are not unique to contemporary students. Many of them can be traced all the way back to Rufus Wilmot Griswold's slanderous account of Poe's life, in which he "cleverly manipulated and invented details of Poe's life for the least favorable account he could create" ("Poe and Griswold" 4). For an excellent account of the Poe-Griswold relationship and extensive bibliography of academic work on it, see the *Edgar Allan Poe Society of Baltimore* Web page ("Poe and Griswold").

[3] In many respects, it is difficult to find a more perfect example of Romanticism than *Pym*—it has just about every characteristic associated with Romanticism, including freedom from verisimilitude; a tendency toward the mythic and allegorical; a focus on radical forms of alienation, contradiction, and disorder; emphasis on extreme states of consciousness and the unconscious; a willingness to abandon moral questions; and Poe's characteristic gothic themes and devices. Richard Chase's *The American Novel and Its Tradition* and Michael Davitt Bell's *The Development of the American Romance* remain excellent starting points for discussions of American Romanticism. For a synopsis of the variety of critical responses to *Pym* engendered by the novel's ambiguities, see Whalen (*Edgar* 157–58).

[4] On Poe's alleged racism, see Dayan ("Amorous Bondage") and Rowe ("Edgar"), with Whalen's *Edgar Allan Poe* as a careful corrective. On Egyptology, see Irwin ("American Hieroglyphics").

[5] Hoffman also refers to Poe as "obsessed" with detecting plagiarisms (98). Poe's 1842 review of Hawthorne's *Twice-Told Tales* and his review of Longfellow's *Ballads and Other Poems*, which initiated what has come to be known as Poe's "little Longfellow war," are both contained in *Edgar Allan Poe*, edited by G. R. Thompson, and make appropriate supplementary texts for a discussion of Poe and plagiarism. Other sources that address Poe's plagiarism include Dameron; Ljungquist; Elmer ("Poe"); and Hulsey.

[6] Other critics who explore Poe's sources in *Pym* include Beegel; Mead; and Moldenhauer. For comparison purposes, students could be provided with Poe's review of this

address, printed in the *Southern Literary Messenger* in January of 1837, in which Poe quotes sections of the address (included in Thompson, *Edgar Allan Poe*) and pages from Pollin's annotated version in *Collected Writings*, in which he provides Morrell's and Reynolds's original text.

[7] McGill fascinatingly recounts the publication history of several of Poe's own works, including "The Fall of the House of Usher," which she reports was reprinted anonymously in London's *Bentley's Miscellany* six months after its appearance in Poe's *Tales of the Grotesque and Arabesque*, and then in the *Boston Notion* under a heading that suggested British authorship ("Poe" 282).

[8] In some instances, I ask students to summarize particular texts or chapters of texts. For example, as concerns *Pym*, I direct one student to summarize Toni Morrison's position in *Playing in the Dark* and one to summarize Terence Whalen's rich discussion in chapter 6 of *Edgar Allan Poe and the Masses*.

[9] Symmes's ideas are summarized in Kafton-Minkel. Selections from *Symzonia* are included in Fitting. Both make for interesting supplementary texts for a study of *Pym*. It is also worth nothing that Thoreau references Symmes's Hole in the concluding chapter to his *Walden*, when he writes, "It is not worth the while to go round the world to count the cats in Zanzibar. Yet do this even till you can do better, and you may perhaps find some "Symmes' Hole" by which to get at the inside at last" ([ed. Baym] 1975).

[10] This expedition is exhaustively summarized in Stanton.

Understanding the Fear and Love of Death in Three Premature-Burial Stories: "The Premature Burial," "Morella," and "The Fall of the House of Usher"

Desirée Henderson

That Poe wrote about death in both terrifying and picturesque ways comes as no surprise to any informed reader, but to appreciate Poe's representations of death, it is important to situate them in the widespread fascination with death that dominated nineteenth-century America. This cultural phenomenon is typically viewed as two opposing trends, the sensational and the sentimental, which alternately depicted death as horrific, violent, and senseless or as beautiful, peaceful, and meaningful. While apparently dichotomous, the two styles of representation thrived simultaneously and were evident in many venues of nineteenth-century life: art, advertising, funeral and memorial practices, religious ideology, as well as literature. Understanding this context can help dispel the belief that many students have that Poe had a perverse morbid streak; rather, they can see that he was influenced by a unique historical moment. An introduction to these forms of representation also reveals that one of the defining characteristics of Poe's work is his combination of sensational and sentimental styles, nowhere more evident than in narratives of premature burial that link the horror of death with the desire (often sexual) for the dead or dying.

Most students begin their experience with Poe either with a gleeful embrace of his grotesque violence (reminiscent of their favorite horror films) or a shuddering dismissal of his morbidity (censuring him as pathological). It is possible to move students beyond these initial responses by introducing them to the nineteenth-century context. I ask students to consider the fact that at the beginning of the century death occurred in private homes and that the dead were prepared for burial by family members before being interred in local graveyards near their homes or churches. In contrast, by the end of the century, death increasingly occurred in hospitals, and the dead were prepared by a new professional class of undertakers and embalmers before they were interred in large cemeteries in city suburbs (if not on Civil War battlefields) or were even cremated. The technological developments in the treatment and disposal of the dead reflect a growing distance between the living and the dead that created a widespread anxiety about the practice of mourning and the meaning of death itself.[1]

The prominence of death in nineteenth-century culture was a reaction to the increasing alienation between the living and the dead. Certain practices of the age exemplify this preoccupation: some of the most popular tourist destinations of the mid-century were rural cemeteries like Boston's Mount Auburn or New York's Greenwood Cemetery. These parklike cemeteries (predecessors to the lawn cemeteries common today) combined graveside monuments with picturesque landscape design, and Americans visited them for picnics, carriage rides, and romantic strolls. At the same time, department stores in major cities developed specially designated sections devoted to the accoutrements necessary for proper mourning: black clothing, ribbons, and crepe; black-trimmed handkerchiefs, fans, and veils; and black wreaths, feathers, and drapery for decorating the home of the bereaved. Finally, memento mori proliferated: it was common to collect funeral rings or brooches decorated with locks of hair from the deceased. Even deathbed photographs became common after the development of photography during the middle of the century. These practices reveal not a morbid obsession with death but an attempt to grapple with the place of death in an increasingly modern, capitalist, and industrialized society. Nineteenth-century Americans sought to make sense of their grief by establishing new rituals that allowed them to preserve their relationships with the dead, even as the physical realities of death became distanced and impersonal.

One particular expression of the changing place of death in America was a cultural paranoia regarding the possibility of premature burial. As the diagnosis of death was increasingly handled outside the family unit and was often based on unscientific criteria, Americans feared the potential of a comatose or impaired individual being buried alive. "True life" accounts of these occurrences, complete with shocking images of contorted corpses or coffins torn apart from the inside, fueled the anxiety. Entrepreneurs profited from the fear by constructing and selling creative apparatuses such as so-called safety coffins, equipped with speaking tubes, bells, flags, or fireworks to signal life or stocked with rations to keep the individual alive. Poe was not only aware of this mania but is often credited with contributing to it, since premature burial is one of the most common themes in his writing.[2]

Literature, especially popular literature of the period, was not immune to these social disruptions and anxieties and was inundated with representations of and reactions to death. The two divergent styles, sensational and sentimental, flourished during the middle of the century as the print revolution gave rise to mass-market literary forms such as the story paper, penny press, and dime novel. Helping students understand the basic characteristics of the sensational and sentimental styles, as well as their massive popular appeal, provides a background for appreciating the ways that Poe utilizes and adapts them.

Sensational literature can be defined by its desire to provoke a powerful, sensory reaction, or sensation, in the reader—one of horror, revulsion, shock, or titillation. Nineteenth-century sensational literature was designed to appeal to and be accessible to a working-class audience, and it recounted in detail experiences like rape, torture, murder, incest, cannibalism, and satanism. Not surprisingly, sensational depictions of death focused on death as the result of violence, emphasizing the grisly physicality of the event and stressing that the dead do not rest easily but return to torment the living as ghosts or avenging spirits.

Like the true-crime writing or horror fiction of today, sensational literature delighted in presenting readers with a portrait of the underbelly of society, providing a cathartic release by allowing them to briefly delve into horror before returning to their ordinary lives.[3]

Sentimental literature can also be defined by its desire to provoke a powerful reaction in the reader, a sentiment or heightened expression of genteel emotion. It sought to appeal to a middle-class audience and generally depicted individuals who overcame obstacles such as orphanhood, poverty, loss of love, or grief in order to gain a deeper appreciation of life, family, or God. Death was a favorite subject in sentimental fiction: characters languished under mysterious illnesses, died slowly but elegantly, and were mourned by loved ones who wept incessantly over their deathbeds and gravesites. Similar to today's romance novels, "chick lit," or self-help literature, sentimental literature depicted suffering as the prerequisite to self-fulfillment; the tender feeling of grief was one of the idealized mechanisms by which one affirmed the beauty of life.[4]

To introduce students to these two divergent forms of writing and, in particular, their depictions of death, instructors have several options. For a brief introduction, I rely on images such as the frontispiece to an early American true-crime pamphlet, *The Horrible Murder of Mrs. Ellen Lynch* (see illus.). While not as graphic as many similar illustrations, this image handily communicates the sensational emphasis on the physical violence of death and the reader's position as a voyeuristic witness. By contrast, the 1853 illustrated edition of Harriet Beecher Stowe's *Uncle Tom's Cabin* portrays the picturesque death of Little Eva, one of the iconic images of the century (Stowe, *Uncle Tom's Cabin*). As depicted in these illustrations, the death of Eva is as beautiful and beneficial as it is tragic.[5]

Alternatively, instructors may provide examples from sensational and sentimental texts that capture the divergent styles of depicting death. Many standard works of sentimental literature are available; I direct my students to poems by Lydia Sigourney, specifically her "Death of an Infant" (1827), or to the extended scene of Eva's death in chapter 26 of *Uncle Tom's Cabin* (1852). These texts exemplify the treatment of death as a transcendent experience in which the physical shell is traded for an angelic existence, an event that benefits those that witness and commemorate it. Students will readily grasp that these texts deflect the reader's attention away from the physical suffering of death toward its spiritual promise, particularly for the living. Indeed, these texts demonstrate that, in a sentimental aesthetic, the response of the living determines the value and meaning of the death itself.

Examples of sensational literature are more challenging to locate. A few notable sensation texts have been reissued, including novels like George Lippard's *Quaker City* (1845) and E. D. E. N. Southworth's *Hidden Hand* (1859), and several collections of Louisa May Alcott's "blood and thunder" writing. For a broad introduction, I have students browse a sampler of nineteenth-century

The frontispiece to *The Horrible Murder of Mrs. Ellen Lynch* (1853) captures the voyeuristic horror of the sensational genre. Courtesy of the American Antiquarian Society.

sensation novels by Lippard, Laughton Osborne, William Gilmore Simms, and John Neal available online through *Wright American Fiction*. Or I have students read an excerpt from David Reynolds's *Beneath the American Renaissance*, such as his description in chapter six of dark adventure or subversive fiction, which includes summaries of numerous sensational works. These texts can communicate to students the graphic and shocking nature of sensational fiction. Death in these novels is meaningful only as a source of horror or titillation for the reader; questions of spirituality or the afterlife are eschewed in favor of a detailed rendering of murder, torture, or dismemberment.

    Once the basic poles of the two styles of representation have been established, it is possible to begin a discussion of the ways and reasons that Poe combines

them. One of the things that makes Poe a remarkable writer of his era is his ability to straddle the two divergent styles. Like his fellow sensational and sentimental writers, Poe is a product of his time and reflects the nineteenth-century
cultural interest in death. But, unlike most, Poe dramatizes how the living are simultaneously repulsed by and drawn toward death.[6] The practice of combining
sensational and sentimental stylistic elements is particularly evident in his depiction of the experience of being buried alive. Premature burial evokes the fear of
death, a revulsion from charnel objects and spaces, a desire to flee from the
brink of death. Yet it also relies on a curiosity about death, an acceptance of
death's inevitability, even a feeling of love or the desire to draw close to the mystery of death. (Students can be asked to consider the continuing appeal, in television and movies, of the undead, especially vampires, as romantic or sexual
partners as an expression of the desire to intimately know death.) Poe focuses on
the experience of premature burial as an enactment of the fragile boundary between the living and the dead. Indeed, what is compelling about the experience
is the way that categories are perversely blurred, as the living and the dead become one.

Grouping together a set of stories linked by the experience of premature
burial underscores the prevalence of this theme in Poe's writing while allowing
students to see the variations in it. Instructors can begin with the seemingly
straightforward premature-burial story, aptly titled "Premature Burial," and the
following questions: How does Poe seek to provoke sensation in his readers?
What techniques does he use to place the reader in the experience of premature burial, and are they successful? Students will appreciate Poe's ability
to dramatize the feelings of claustrophobia and confusion that strike the main
character. They will also perceive the change of tone at the story's conclusion,
which promotes the moral that a "close call" with death results in a greater appreciation of life. Students can be asked to identify this shift, namely, how Poe
is moving from a sensational to a sentimental register. In what ways does this
redirection require the reader to rethink the preceding moment of terror?
Many students will criticize this "trite" ending, so it is worthwhile to encourage
them to interrogate the purpose behind Poe's deliberate introduction of a sentimental aesthetic.

A discussion of the story "Morella" should commence with these questions:
Is this a premature-burial story? In what ways can Morella be understood to
have been buried prematurely? This gets to the heart of the motivation behind Morella's reincarnation or reanimation: What was she unable to achieve
in her lifetime? Does she intend to regain her husband's love or to exercise
revenge against him? (Comparisons can be made here between Morella and
the title character in "Ligeia.") Ask students to consider whether Morella is a
sentimental heroine or a sensational antagonist or, more specifically, why Poe
employs both tropes in his depiction of this character. By penetrating the
characterization of Morella, students are prepared to interpret the reaction
of the husband. It will be clear to them that the return to life is, at least

initially, successful and that the husband loves the daughter in a way that he was unable to love Morella. Why, then, is this filial relationship doomed? Discuss how the perverse blurring of boundaries between father and daughter, and the hint of incest, mirrors the perversion of the living dead. How does the shocking conclusion of this story compare with the conclusion of "Premature Burial," particularly since "Morella" appears to undercut the sentimental moral of "Premature Burial"?

In addition, students should examine Poe's most famous premature-burial story, "The Fall of the House of Usher." Because the gothic and sensational tropes of the story predominate, it can be useful to begin by asking students to identify the less obvious but equally important sentimental themes; specifically, have them analyze Usher's reaction to Madeline's death as an expression of the sentimental memorial practices common in the nineteenth century. This context adds a layer to Usher's character that is necessary to deepen the shocking effect of the story's sensational revelation. In other words, is it precisely because Usher is capable of a sentimental response to his sister's death that his decision to keep his sister buried alive is horrific? This question will raise the issue of Usher's motivations and will suggest a third possibility, beyond insanity or incest: Could Usher's act of burying Madeline alive have been an act of love? What legitimate reasons could Usher have believed he had? The use of sentimentality to highlight the depths of sensational horror can also be a starting point in a discussion of the narrator: Why is this "normal," outside observer necessary to Poe's narration, and why does he survive? Can the narrator be seen as escaping his own death, his own temporary exposure to the spaces and corruptions of death?

These queries lead to an overarching set of issues that can provide a writing prompt for analyzing these three premature-burial stories, as well as the others in Poe's oeuvre. Ask students to examine the idea of premature burial as a metaphoric rather than literal state and to consider the following question, What character(s) are metaphorically buried and by or under what? Students may gain insight into the complexities of Poe's gothic narrative if they shift their analysis from the spectacle of literal entombment to the state of virtual confinement. This move also prompts them to analyze the confusion of identity enacted by the living dead as a metaphor for individual characters' identities or for social relations in general.

In sum, an analysis of these three premature-burial stories indicates how Poe provokes sensation in the reader to capture the desire of the living to flee from death, even to deny the reality of death altogether. Poe also, however, elicits sentiment to reveal the desire of the living to be close to the dead, even to inhabit the experience of death for a moment. These complex and contradictory impulses are a reflection of the full spectrum of nineteenth-century America's responses to death—the expression of a culture's fear and love of death.

NOTES

[1] The accounts of death in nineteenth-century America in this and the next paragraph are condensed from several important and detailed studies. For a general history of death in America, see Laderman. On cemetery tourism, see Sears, chapter 5. On the commercialization of mourning, see Haltunnen, *Confidence Men*, chapter 5. On memento mori, see Pike and Armstrong.

[2] For more on premature-burial paranoia, see Bondeson.

[3] The best accounts of nineteenth-century sensational literature and culture are Denning; Reynolds; and Streeby.

[4] Nineteenth-century sentimental literature and culture has been examined by numerous scholars but notably Kete; Samuels; and Tompkins.

[5] The illustrated edition of *Uncle Tom's Cabin* is available online at Stephen Railton's site Uncle Tom's Cabin *and American Culture*; see specifically the images in chapters 25–27. Additional frontispieces or illustrations capturing the flavor of sensational popular fiction can be found in Reynolds.

[6] The complex relation between Poe and popular literary forms, including the sensational and sentimental, has been explored in greater depth than is possible here by numerous scholars, including Elmer, *Reading*; Reynolds; and Whalen, *Edgar*.

Teaching Poe's "The Raven" and "Annabel Lee" as Elegies

Philip Edward Phillips

In "The Philosophy of Composition," Edgar Allan Poe famously concludes that "the death, then, of a beautiful woman is, unquestionably, the most poetical topic in the world—and equally is it beyond doubt that the lips best suited for such topic are those of a bereaved lover" (1379). Discussing the composition of his most famous poem, "The Raven," Poe was simultaneously promoting the poem that gained him entrée into the New York literary circles after its publication in 1845 and attempting to establish his own poetic program, whose principal aim was the creation of Beauty, which is best achieved by poetry that moves or elevates the soul.

Poe was well acquainted with the loss of loved ones (e.g., Eliza Poe, Mrs. Stanard, Henry Poe, Frances Allan, and Virginia Poe), and his aesthetic principles may, on some level, reflect his own experiences of such loss. In lyric poetry, the form conventionally used to express loss, bereavement, and comfort is the elegy. This essay, therefore, offers an approach to teaching two of Poe's most famous poems, "The Raven" and "Annabel Lee," as elegies that participate in and radically subvert the classical traditions of lament and consolation. This approach to teaching "The Raven" and "Annabel Lee" is intended to benefit English teachers at all levels, from high school American literature teachers to community college or university instructors who wish to include selections of Poe's poetry in an introduction to literature course or to discuss matters of form and tradition in a survey of American literature.

Many of my undergraduate students at Middle Tennessee State University read Poe in high school, and most of them recall having read and enjoyed "The Raven" and "Annabel Lee." In fact, several students have told me over the years that it was because of Poe that they became interested in reading literature for pleasure. Others have said that they enjoy reading Poe because they can relate to his melancholy tone and his explorations of the feeling of loss. When I was giving a lecture on Poe and nineteenth-century American poetry at Soongsil University in Seoul, South Korea, I learned that students of English literature in Korea share a similar interest in Poe's writings, especially "Annabel Lee," whose universal and even fairy-tale representation of love and loss strikes a chord with them. So, what accounts for this transcultural fascination, and how can teachers of Poe use this interest to lead students to read and appreciate Poe's poetry within the contexts of world literature and of the elegiac tradition, particularly in an age in which people increasingly shy away from reading poetry? We can begin to answer these questions by acknowledging that Poe is a poet whose writing does not intimidate students but rather appeals to their personal experiences of love, loss, and memory—experiences with which they can and do readily identify.

Both "The Raven" and "Annabel Lee" participate in the elegiac tradition, albeit in unusual and even unsettling ways. In the broadest sense of the term, an elegy is a mournful, contemplative lyric poem, treating the death of a beloved from the perspective of a living mourner. Both of Poe's poems lament the loss of the speaker's beloved, and both search for consolation in the midst of despair. An avid student of ancient and modern literature, Poe was keenly aware of the elegy and its venerable tradition, from the pastoral elegies of Theocritus, Moschus, and Bion to the funeral elegies of Thomas Carew, John Cleveland, Alexander Pope, and Samuel Johnson; the "graveyard school" of poetry, including the poems of Oliver Goldsmith and Thomas Gray; and the English pastoral elegies of Edmund Spenser, John Milton, and Percy Bysshe Shelley. Although Walt Whitman's pastoral elegy for President Abraham Lincoln, "When Lilacs Last in the Dooryard Bloom'd," would become the first "modern" pastoral elegy in American literature, with the procession of mourners reversed as the body of Lincoln passes by train through the throngs of mourners, Poe's haunting elegies were among the first major elegiac poems in American literature.

For students to appreciate more fully Poe's place within the elegiac tradition, a review of the conventions of the form and how those conventions are used or modified in the poems is useful. From the start, I usually emphasize to students that the elegy form and its "conventions" emerged from the very real human experience of loss. To that end, I often begin my discussions of the elegy by drawing on my students' own experiences of losing someone close to them and perhaps attending funerals of loved ones. One way for students to understand the elegiac form is to relate it to its prose counterpart, the eulogy, which is customarily delivered at funerals to remember the deceased and to place the loss of the deceased within a larger, often spiritual context that provides some measure of comfort to the living. When students recognize that eulogies are for the living as much as for the dead, then they can begin to appreciate elegies not as conventional poetic exercises but as attempts to lament the loss of someone and to find consolation for the living and the dead.

The elegy has its roots in the Greco-Roman traditions of lament, which gives vent to the emotions, and of consolation, which applies reason to the loss experienced. When beginning a discussion of elegy, I ask students to think of a time when they attended a funeral or a memorial service and to reflect on the kinds of things that were said about the deceased and the things that were said for the benefit of the living. Students are usually willing to share aspects of their own experiences and quick to see the connection between funeral rites and the conventions of the elegy. I may then ask students to form small groups and to address the following questions in preparation for our discussion of the poems: To what extent are funerals for the dead, and to what extent are they for the living? What type of praise is normally offered at a funeral? In what ways do funeral rites attempt to strike a balance between mourning for the deceased and offering comfort to the living? What kinds of consolations are offered at funerals? Students often respond to these or similar questions by generating a useful list of details derived from funerals that they have attended that can be applied to the elegies being studied. Building on the list developed by the students, I can then put the responses on the board and proceed to introduce students to the ancient literary tradition of writing elegies.

In *Classical Genres and English Poetry*, William H. Race enumerates seven topics of lament, some or all of which, he demonstrates, may be found in lamentations: a list of mourners, often summoned in a "call"; the disfigurement of mourners or the corpse itself; praise of the deceased; a contrast between past and present; a description of the deceased's final day; a reminder of the finality of death; and complaints questioning the purpose of life or the justice in the deceased's death (92). These topics clearly focus the audience's attention on the deceased, heighten the feelings of loss, and emphasize the reality and finality of that loss. Students will easily see the similarities between the classical topics and their own list of topics. According to Race, the classical authors often responded poetically to the topics of lament through consolations, which took various forms according to the particular method of assuaging grief: the "manly consolation," which argues that death is common, grief is futile, time will cure, and one must simply endure; consolation through "commemoration," in which the poet includes funeral rites and a tomb or commemoration through poetry; and apotheosis through ascent to heaven (or to the Elysian fields) or through deification, in which a hero like Hercules becomes a constellation (104). While almost all elegies contain elements of lament and consolation, such as Milton's "Lycidas," Matthew Arnold's "Thyrsis," and Whitman's "Lilacs," others may consist of pure lament with no apparent consolation, such as William Carlos Williams's "The Widow's Lament in Springtime" and Poe's "The Raven." It is often instructive to compare Poe's elegies with those of other writers, such as Milton's "Lycidas," which contains virtually all the major elements of lament and consolation as well as a pagan and a Christian consolation in the treatment of the death of Edward King, called Lycidas in this pastoral elegy.

Having discussed Poe's life and literary career in a previous class, students should read and come prepared to discuss "The Raven" and "Annabel Lee." At the beginning of many classes, we discuss the conventions of funerals, and, in this class, I provide my students with a handout on the topics of lament and consolation, based on Race's discussion of these Greco-Roman literary traditions. I first establish that these topics derive from funeral rites with which my students are likely familiar, and then I ask them to identify lament in the poems. We then turn to consolation, taking note of the different approaches Poe takes toward expressing and assuaging grief.

In "The Raven," Poe creates a pure lament, in which the narrator's desperation and dejection are heightened with the effective use of the refrain, "nevermore," which is given in response to the narrator's own repeated and increasingly self-destructive questions (bordering on Poe's notion of the "perverse") about whether he will ever again see his "lost Lenore." The speaker himself is the sole mourner, whose utterances echo through the darkness. His cries are repeated, and this repetition is characteristic of elegiac verse. There is no procession of mourners, but the poem's universality incorporates the reading audience in the narrator's lament. While there is no disfigurement of the corpse, the reader observes the speaker's disfigurement; the speaker is "weak and weary" (line 1), "nearly napping" (3), and his soul is "burning" (30) for his lost Lenore. In the final line of the poem, the speaker's soul, beneath the shadow of the ominous raven, "shall be lifted—nevermore!" The speaker praises the deceased explicitly and implicitly throughout the entire poem; indeed, the speaker's love "[for] the rare and radiant maiden whom the angels name Lenore" (11) provides the impetus for the elegy itself, and the angels' imagined opinion confirms for the speaker the celestial quality of her beauty and their love. The speaker expresses his loss most poignantly by contrasting their past happiness with his present despair. Using subtle and even suggestively sensuous language, the narrator pines in stanza 13 that "[s]he shall press, ah, nevermore!" the "cushion's velvet lining" on which the mourning speaker rests his head. The repetition of the word "nevermore" further reinforces the finality of death. Characteristic of Poe's ethereal maidens, Lenore's final day is never described; the focus is instead on the speaker and his dialogue with the raven, whose rote responses of the word "nevermore" serve as the poem's refrain and reiterate the poem's theme of *"Mournful and Never-ending Remembrance"* discussed by Poe in "The Philosophy of Composition" (1385).

One reason this poem reaches so many students worldwide is that the speaker's overt and implicit complaints and questions concerning the justice of his loss go unanswered, except for the raven's unsatisfactory reply of "nevermore," which resounds as a death knell in the speaker's ears, "perversely" confirming the finality of Lenore's death. In the end, "The Raven" achieves Poe's desired effect—to "[excite] the sensitive soul to tears" and to attain the "Beauty" that he describes in his "Philosophy of Composition" (1377). However, the poem offers the narrator no consolation or comfort; the raven becomes "emblematical of *Mournful and Never-ending Remembrance*" (1385).

"Annabel Lee," published in 1849, often prompts comparisons between the speaker's lost love, Annabel Lee, and the poet's deceased wife, Virginia. Whether read with this autobiographical emphasis or not, Poe's "Annabel Lee" remains one of his greatest literary achievements for its simplicity, symbolism, sound, and dark beauty. The poem, in commemoration of its namesake, taps into love and loss, whose delicacy of expression is appreciated internationally. "Annabel Lee" contains all the principal topics of lament but, unlike "The Raven," provides some degree of consolation—the speaker's memory brings dreams of Annabel Lee, who undergoes a kind of apotheosis into the heavens by the end of the poem.

If for no other reason than its length, "Annabel Lee" is a more approachable text for many students. More significant, though, the poem naturally appeals to students, who can read the beloved, Annabel Lee, as anyone whom they themselves have loved and lost, either to death or to disapproving parents. As with

"The Raven," I ask my students to identify lament and consolation in this poem. It is often effective to read or recite this poem to students before beginning discussion, since Poe's use of sound and, in particular, of end rhyme reinforces the name of the beloved, Annabel Lee, a subtle but not insignificant part of the poem's consolation. Students take note of the speaker's passionate praise of Annabel Lee's beauty and her love for the speaker—despite the apparent opposition of her "high-born kinsmen" (line 17). The speaker is the sole mourner in the poem, but the kinsmen populating Annabel Lee's funeral procession "bore her away" (18) from the grieving speaker, who has now come to join her "[i]n her sepulchre there by the sea" (40). Students often note the contrast between past—"many and many a year ago" (1), when the speaker and his beloved were together, when "she was a child and I was a child, / In this kingdom by the sea" (7–8)—and present, when the speaker is reminded by the moon and the stars in the sky of the "bright eyes" of his Annabel Lee despite the reality of her interment in the tomb (36). The speaker dramatizes Annabel Lee's final day, arguing that the envious seraphs of heaven coveted the purity of his and Annabel Lee's love and thus chilled and killed her. Their love transcends the comprehension of both earthly and heavenly observers, and "that was the reason" (23), the speaker complains, why his Annabel Lee was taken away by death and put "in her tomb by the side of the sea" (41).

Unlike "The Raven," "Annabel Lee" provides some measure of consolation in the forms of commemoration in verse and apotheosis, but this consolation is at best subtle and subject to interpretation. Because their love "was stronger by far than the love / Of those who were older than we— / Of many far wiser than we" (27–29), the speaker asserts that "neither the angels in Heaven above / Nor the demons down under the sea / Can ever dissever my soul from the soul / Of the beautiful Annabel Lee" (30–33). The moonbeams bring "dreams" of his Annabel Lee, while the rising stars recall her "bright eyes." The speaker metaphorically joins his beloved in her tomb in the final stanza. Just as the greater part of Hercules was believed to have been translated into the heavens as a constellation and just as a Christian might find comfort in a loved one's ascension to an eternal life in heaven, so too does Annabel Lee find an eternal resting place in the poet's elegy, in the speaker's memory, in the lines of verse, and in the audience's imagination.

This approach to teaching Poe's "The Raven" and "Annabel Lee" as elegies is not meant to be exhaustive by any means. Students no doubt will discover other elements of lament and consolation or formulate their own unique approaches to these works. Introducing students to the formal topics of lament and consolation will simply provide readers of these poems with a useful means by which to read and appreciate Poe's careful craftsmanship and deliberate artistry. Drawing on students' own experiences with love and loss can significantly enhance the level of engagement with the poems in class and, ideally, leave the students with a lasting appreciation of the beauty of Poe's poetry.

Mourning and Eve(ning): Teaching Poe's Poetry

Benjamin F. Fisher

Death as a recurrent theme in Poe's poems is no new topic; however, several poems merit reconsideration of that theme. Students often wish to discuss the role of the speakers in these poems, along with the funeral customs and mourning observances in which Poe's male narrators (and they are chiefly male) are involved. So I focus on form as well as context in "The Sleeper," then turn to "Lenore," "The Raven," "Ulalume," and "Annabel Lee." Few critiques center on form in poems encompassing Poe's oft-repeated dictum—that the death of a beautiful woman constitutes the most poetic of all themes.

I try to dispel the myth of Poe as a disoriented little man dressed in black, alcoholic beverage in hand, a raven on one shoulder, black cat on the other, contemplating his next debauching of a young woman, all the while spinning tuneful but meaningless verse. Instead, I stress that we confront a Poe whose superb creative imagination underlies all that seems sensational and that Poe, well aware of the contrasts, uses the sensational for mere thrill effect. Recurrent death themes in Poe's works reflect the popular, often extreme, attention that Anglo-American culture gave to death during the nineteenth century. I refer those wanting additional knowledge of such circumstances to relevant secondary materials.[1]

"The Sleeper," entitled "Irenë" when it originally appeared in Poe's *Poems* (1831), is the earliest among the poems named above, which foreground a bereaved lover. These poems number among those typically selected for anthologies, from Rufus Griswold's widely read and acclaimed *The Poets and Poetry of America* (1842) to recent texts for academic use, although "The Sleeper" has elicited repeated misunderstandings. The final version demonstrates Poe's modifying what were mawkish or lurid excesses into sophisticated literary art, as he tended to do in revising his creative works. I mention in class Poe's own high estimates of "The Sleeper," including that he ranked it superior to "The Raven" in "the higher qualities of poetry" (*Letters* 2: 332).[2]

I give classes two influential, if divergent, opinions regarding "The Sleeper." First, Arthur Hobson Quinn, in his long-standard biography of Poe, who, while acclaiming certain passages, deplores the line, "Soft may the worms about her creep!" as an image "for which no defense can be made" (185). I believe that Quinn and others who follow his lead misread the implication in this line.[3] I next mention Edward H. Davidson's statement that the poem is "modeled rather closely on the burial ritual in the *Book of Common Prayer*" (108), a surprise for those who suppose that all Poe's situations and characters were concocted from his own warped psyche.

Read objectively, "The Sleeper" becomes less a work by an author bent on shocking readers than one, to cite Davidson again, in which "Poe provided his age with a handbook on how the upper middle class should take care of its dead" (108). Death probably caught the attention of Poe's early readers because of the brief life expectancy in the Western world during the early nineteenth century and because funeral preparations and services generally took place in the deceased's home, often followed by elaborate processions to the grave, rather than in a funeral home as we know it.

Many students seem puzzled by the opening seventeen lines in "The Sleeper," so we discuss how the pictorial effects form a descent from the moon and vapors emanating from it down over the mountain into the valley, onward across a graveyard and ruined building (enveloped in fog), extending finally to the lake—the whole reminiscent of diffuse paintings by J. W. M. Turner or Robert Weir, whose misty scenes directly inspired "Ulalume." This kaleidoscopic imagery dovetails perfectly with the overwrought mind of the speaker, whose initial irrationality is understandable. He has evidently stepped outdoors for relief from what to him are the oppressive confines of the house containing the corpse of his beloved. Replying to student questions about the man's crazed state, I note that, in these lines, Poe may also incorporate folklore of moon madness (lunacy). Though the man seeks momentary respite from the nearby realities of death, the moon's influences on life and death call up a progression from life to death as the hazy moonlight weirdly illuminates a grave and a ruin that resembles a robed ghost, all linked to pervasive drowsiness, even in the apparently slumbering lake. There, water, the most elemental source of life, sleeps silent and motionless, just as the corpse "sleeps" close by. The survivor may also be overtired, and thus his own half-sleeping, half-waking state is mirrored in what he sees—or thinks he sees.

Next, he moves inside, where the corpse, prepared for burial, lies on its bed (in colloquial phrasing, is "laid out"). I lecture to familiarize students with the burial custom involved, which highlights Poe's realistic rendering of nineteenth-century practices. In the second stanza of "The Sleeper," Poe's speaker remains in denial, choosing to deem the lady sleeping, not dead—although the transition from the "bright" lady (line 18) and the breezes blowing through the open window that move the bed canopy "fitfully" and "fearfully" (25) to ghostly shadows and the unusual pallor, garb, and loosened hair of the lady interject a note of foreboding. In Poe's time, many believed that night air was poisonous; therefore, the lady's seeming unawareness of potential danger disturbs the speaker. From this background information, students readily accept the reality in Poe's depiction of character and custom.

That the lady's soul slumbers beneath the "closed" eyelids may subtly reveal the necessity that someone press shut the eyelids of a corpse (26). Similarly, the lady's pallor might initially suggest a long-held Western-world aim of maintaining a fair, not a tanned or weathered, complexion. Pallor is, of course, frequently characteristic in corpses. The "dress" seems unusual to the speaker because it is probably the lady's shroud (34), a garment designed especially for a corpse. Here, I offer students a variation on burying a lady in her wedding dress from William Faulkner's As I Lay Dying (1936), in which, to avoid wrinkling the flared skirt of Addie Bundren's wedding dress, her corpse is placed in the coffin with its head at the narrow end and feet at the wider end. What to students seems an uncommon arrangement of the body was no grotesquerie but a commonplace. I also relate that loosening the long hair (when women usually did not cut their hair) on a female corpse intertwined beliefs that a woman's long hair had erotic appeal and that hair on a corpse's head continued to grow after death so that keeping it confined would be unnatural. Students thus grasp another bit of realism related to burials in Poe's day.

To allay what some find repulsive in the two closing stanzas in "The Sleeper," we discuss a shift in perspective, as the speaker finally admits that the lady sleeps in death. He hopes that her rest will be eternal; therefore, in "[s]oft may the worms about her creep!" he expresses an imperative (47), that worms should not disturb the lady's everlasting repose and that they respect her rest instead of desecrating the flesh. Thus, the line may not concern worms' predations. Although this reading runs counter to many others, it seems to be consistent with theme and form throughout the poem.

I also tell my classes to notice how the typical couplet form expands to a triplet in lines setting forth what amounts to a particularized hope in the speaker. This expansiveness emphasizes the repetition of "sleep," which, along with the rhyme words "deep" and "creep," emphasizes the lady's restfulness in death. Would a lover really incline toward visions of worms devouring his beloved? Students generally think not, preferring to read this passage as plausible thought, not revolting imagery. The strong sibilance in these lines compounds the stillness in motion and sound and suggests protection instead of decomposition. To students, the final lines bear out and make tenable such an explication because Poe contrasts sounds made when the lady, living, threw stones against the sepulcher door to the pervasive silence and restfulness effected once she is actually placed in the family mausoleum. Over all, drowsing and dreaming prevail.

The overarching structure in "The Sleeper" resembles customs connected with funeral preparations and services, thus making a fine coalescence of sound with sense that creates analogies between burial rites from the 1830s and those of today. Marshaled by the speaker, we move from the survivor's excited incoherence to restfulness to another high as the survivor enters denial and then admits the actuality of death, after which we finally move on to the graveyard and family mausoleum where the lady ultimately "sleeps." Another funeral tradition that makes Poe's poem comprehensible to contemporary readers is the indirect approach to viewing the corpse that precedes a funeral service. Just as the speaker in "The Sleeper" gradually leads us from the outdoors into the house, whether his direction invokes actual motion or his meditation-vision, persons today who pay respects to the dead do not enter a funeral home and immediately behold the corpse.

Such indirection unifies Poe's poem. The ordering effect in the typical couplet form—modulating into triplets when emotion heightens, as it does in the

speaker's linking forgetfulness and sleep—retards, if it does not altogether for-
bid, awakening, and is assisted by the *ake* rhymes in the opening stanza and in
the *ess* rhymes in the triplet that closes stanza 2. The result is a stately, dignified
rhythm wholly appropriate for funeral circumstances. Eventually arriving to
view the body, we then accompany it, through the speaker's thoughts, to the
family vault and repose, where the doors are closed, depicting the finality of actual death. Students frequently comment that, by now, they better comprehend
how Poe artistically combined theme and form in this poem.

I extend explicating and discussing "The Sleeper" because it is customary
to highlight its atrocities, supposed excrescences that may in fact have been
far more ordinary realities in Poe's day. The ambiguities in the poem are also
consistent with Poe's pronouncement, in the "Letter to Mr. —— ——," first
published in *Poems* (1831) and repeated with variations thereafter, where Poe
contends that poetry presents "perceptible images . . . with *in*definite sensations, to which end music is an *essential*" (17). The poetic music in "The
Sleeper" heightens the overall pleasant dream effect. In Claude Richard's
opinion, to which I direct students, the poem "rhythmically suggests general
drowsiness, a subduing of the prosodic beat; that sleepiness comes from a
muffled music which conveys, beyond words and cadences, the rise of the poetic spirit or sentiment" ("Heart" 203).[4] So much, then, for reading this poem
as a gallery of lurid horrors rather than for its realism. Students come away
better understanding why Poe's imaginative writings continue to appeal to
readers while those by many of his contemporaries have dwindled into obscurity or oblivion.

Other related poems receive less space here because they are usually more
familiar in college-university classrooms and have garnered more analysis.
"Lenore," "The Raven," "Ulalume," and "Annabel Lee" are often heralded as
premier Poe poems. "Lenore" is inspirited by deft alternations of emotional
calm and storm as other survivors of dead Lenore try to comfort her grief-
stricken lover, Guy de Vere, whose passionate retorts reveal that the other
mourners are really not grieved by Lenore's death. Counterpointing conven-
tionalities in the simulated grief expressed by the group, Guy's outbursts seem
to be far more sincere. As with those of the survivor-lover in the opening of
"The Sleeper," Guy's feeling—"tonight my heart is light" (25)—manifests erratic, but nonetheless plausible, emotions in a mourner. The strong feelings underlying the dialogue are enhanced by numerous internal rhymes and long
lines. The lyricism in the rhymes and the expansiveness in the line length are
excellent vehicles for conveying an aura of conflict that will not be silenced.
Asked about their reactions to sound effects in "Lenore," students reply that
they discern how Poe's poetic form enhances emotion.

A more decidedly hypnotic effect infuses "The Raven," "Ulalume," and
"Annabel Lee." I tell students that the "music" in the emphatic rhythms and
rhymes mimes the stately movement of funeral processions and that the lyrical

texture overall comports with emotional turbulence characteristic in mourners. For comparison, I refer to sound and sense in Tennyson's famous "Ode on the Death of the Duke of Wellington." "The Raven" is Poe's most renowned poem, students quickly respond, because excellent psychology underlies the hypnotic musical outreach. That Lenore is "lost" may be more figurative than literal (10). I tell students that her name devolves from the same root as Helen, who appeared in a much earlier poem, and whose name blends implications of dazzling light (stemming from the Greek for *lightning*—which also figures into the name Electra, that of another famous literary character) with overwhelming beauty, so there is no wonder that we, or the narrator, never behold this Lenore as a corporeal character. In "The Sleeper" and "The Raven," the survivor-speaker's imagination ignites with thoughts about a dead inamorata, but in "The Raven," Lenore's existence, predicated as it is on angelic "nam[ing]" (11), may symbolize an ideal—that of the light bringer–nurturer, a Psyche figure, without whose inspiration the male character becomes debilitated. Poe's pronouncement about undercurrents of meaning or indefinite rather than pleasurable poetry comes into play here, and I refer students to the "Letter to B——" and the preface to *Tales of the Grotesque and Arabesque* as good sources for his idea that to be plausible, it is essential for literature to convey psychological realities. Stress overwhelms the speaker in "The Raven" until it also physically limits him. Thus, he cannot leave his room, which is symbolic of his closing mind. He readily assumes that the raven is supernaturally endowed instead of merely seeking shelter on a cold night. That it has been taught to articulate one word, "Nevermore," unusual though it may be, does not require supernatural inspiration—a fact that initially surprises students, but that they quickly recognize as sensible.

I am frequently asked why Lenore is "rare and radiant," but "name[less]" (11–12), in other words, lost to the speaker, to which I respond that we may think of her as symbolizing a dynamic that once existed in the man's emotional-imaginative makeup but that has now departed. Students also want to know whether the speaker has "killed" Lenore, since several other Poe protagonists (in the tales) eliminate their female lovers. I reply that many readers think of these dead or debilitated women as symbolizing some major emotional part of what should be an integrated self that has been "murdered," that is, repressed by the male. As psychologists tell us, one cannot repress an important part of the self without a violent and destructive "return" eventuating.[5]

Such returns constitute mainsprings in "The Raven" and "Ulalume." In the latter poem, the protagonist will not heed the counsel of Psyche, who travels with him (on an emotional journey that concludes in dismay for him). Because he resists her urgings, both end at the tomb of Ulalume, the man's dead lover. That this symbolic journey takes place on Halloween night, as some students contend from reading the text, only reinforces implications of unpredictable, nonrational forces undoing the person who set them in motion. The tomb in

"Ulalume" may be considered both literal and figurative. "The Raven" concludes, fittingly, with man and bird "still"—silent and motionless. Once the raven is admitted to the narrator's "chamber," there can be no other outcome but death in life, stasis in body and mind.

In both "Ulalume" and "The Raven," students volunteer, sound coalesces with sense to produce maddening, deadening consequences in the heedless. Turning to "Annabel Lee," I propose to my classes that this poem does not demonstrate a fumbling Poe, the "jingle man" as the elderly Emerson jibed to the young William Dean Howells (qtd. in Howells 63), but is a product of Poe's genuine literary art. Naturally, the speaker expresses his shattered feelings, which persist after many years, in intensely lyrical fashion. That "song" indicates in its intense lyricalness a lasting, deranged grief, perhaps implying that the speaker has become senile, as revealed in his heated repetitions, representative of a mind obsessed. The speaker imagines that he can find rest only when he reposes by Annabel, but his lying down beside her is another ambiguity, which many readers have chosen to interpret as necrophilic desire when it might be nothing more than a fantasy in ideal planes. Students rapidly connect the situation here with that in "The Sleeper" and other works by Poe, allowing how in both poems—and in others—Poe's intent is not to repel but to create subtle psychology, not to be restrictively literal but richly figurative.

As outlined above, many of Poe's seemingly weirdest poems embody realism in theme and form. They bear out his dictum that terror emanates not from "Germany" (i.e., horrors created merely for cheap thrills' sake), but from the soul (Preface 129). By engaging with the types of readings recommended above, students may better grasp how Poe touches with knowledge and pressures the pulses of readers of all eras.

NOTES

[1] Most useful are Curl; Saum. For a more sentimentalized viewpoint on death from a contemporary of Poe, see Connors, as well as E. Davidson.

[2] Poe's other indication of his great esteem for "The Sleeper" appeared in his letter to James Russell Lowell, 2 July 1844 (*Letters* 1: 258), in which he lists what he deems his best poems. Kenneth Silverman notes that "The Sleeper" was one of three poems that Poe evidently considered his best when he submitted selections for Rufus W. Griswold's *The Poets and Poetry of America* (1842)—an impressively large and highly respected anthology (*Edgar* 213).

[3] See Quinn 185. His opinion resonates in many later academic critiques, e.g., Wagenknecht 154–55; Hoffman 20; and Kennedy, *Poe* 74–75. E. Davidson remarks that Quinn and George Edward Woodberry, an earlier biographer, gave only passing notice to *The Narrative of Arthur Gordon Pym* because they found it revolting (75). Similar revulsion probably accounts for Quinn's deploring the line about worms in "The Sleeper." I tell students about a similarly negative reading from a contemporary of Poe's, William Petrie, in the London *Literary Gazette* in 1846, where the closing of Poe's poem is said

to exemplify "bad taste and exaggeration" (qtd. in I. Walker 259). My (complementary) reading of the poem extends ideas expressed in my introduction to *Essential Tales and Poems of Edgar Allan Poe.*

[4] I point out in class that a contemporary of Poe's, Thomas Dunn English, had commented on the first fourteen lines as "one of the finest pictures of sleepy calm in the language" (qtd. in I. Walker 233).

[5] For example, see Wilbur; Gargano; and C. Jordan.

Rectangular Obscenities:
Poe, Taste, and Entertainment

Stephen Rachman

Literary opinion about Edgar Allan Poe has always been divided. Admired in his own century as an unalloyed genius by the French, especially Charles Baudelaire, Stéphane Mallarmé, and Paul Valéry, Poe was given mixed assessments in the United States. James Russell Lowell allowed three-fifths of Poe to be genius "and two-fifths sheer fudge" (315). Ralph Waldo Emerson witheringly referred to him as "the jingle man" (qtd. in Howells 62). While conceding Poe's originality, Henry James declared that Poe was a charlatan and that a passion for his work was "the mark of a decidedly primitive state of reflection." Truly, Poe had aspired to be a critical tastemaker in his own day, laying out the principal functions of fiction, poetry, and criticism. Because he attempted to define rigorously the purview of criticism and made occasional reference to "the heresy of *The Didactic*" ("Poetic Principle" 1435), he was claimed as a harbinger of the late-nineteenth-century aesthetic movement with its rallying cry of "art for art's sake." Ironically, Poe, of all nineteenth-century canonical authors, has been the most easily dismissed by critics of the last century, especially on aesthetic grounds. T. S. Eliot was puzzled but ultimately relegated Poe to juvenilia. Allen Tate ("Angelic Imagination") conceded to Eliot but then hedged. Yvor Winters fulminated over Poe's willful obscurantism and "the clumsiness and insensitivity" of his work (67). Harold Bloom called Poe's reputation as an aesthetic theorist a "French myth" and likened his writing style to the acting style of Vincent Price (Introduction 13). It may have been Poe's ideal that literature should "suit at once the popular and critical taste," as he explained in "The Philosophy of Composition," but, while his works have remained as popular as ever, the critics have been less consistently enamored (1375).

In contrast, students tend to like Poe even if they have never read him, or much of him. They are predisposed to approach him in the way we shiver with delight at the prospect of a scary or thrilling story even if the reading of the story itself actually terrifies us. They are attracted to the terrain of Poe, his dark Romanticism, psychopathology, violence, and preoccupation with death. The famous outlines of his life story, suffused with the aura of misunderstood genius, also have their appeal. Students continue to be fascinated by Poe's failings—real or mythical: his alcoholism, supposed drug use, and self-destructive tendencies. His orphanhood and struggles with his foster father, as well as his marriage to his thirteen-year-old first cousin reinforce a compelling impression of tribulation and turmoil. The language of the Poe tales most commonly taught present some obstacles to these initial impressions. The intricacies of Poe's grammar, the obscurity of his diction, and the abstractions of his philosophical disquisitions frequently challenge students to reconcile the textual surface of Poe with the terrors they narrate. Still, Poe seems to give historical and literary license to the popular, the sensational, and the fun of literature—and teachers know this. American literature specialists can reassure themselves that, in turning to Poe, they can expect renewed interest from students fatigued with the rigors of Emersonian rhetoric and the prolixity of Cooper. There may even be a whiff of pandering about this, a certain compromise in which high philosophical language is applied to the outre and the grotesque. We wonder if our students like Poe for the right reasons; his power seems undeniable, but questions of taste always abide as to how we value that power.

And so the question of the critical and the popular in Poe arises once again, like Madeline Usher from her tomb. Indeed, much of the debate over the value of Poe has been a battle of and over taste, but the aestheticization of Poe has obscured this conflict to a certain extent. This battle of and over taste has also been obscured by the choice of the particular Poe texts on which we choose to focus. Therefore, I shall reconsider Poe's concept of taste by way of the less frequently encountered angelic dialogue "The Colloquy of Monos and Una" (1841), from which this essay takes its title. While not as well known as other Poe texts, the angelic colloquies ("Monos and Una" and "Mellonta Tauta") present opportunities for students to ponder questions of taste on the broadest levels.

In "The Colloquy of Monos and Una," Monos looks back from a postapocalyptic or posthuman vantage on "man's general condition" in the nineteenth century and the "progress of our civilization," finding it the opposite of what it claimed to be (450). He describes a corrupt world that has embraced the routinized modernity of the industrial and its pollution, urban grids, and "rectangular obscenities," devoid of the serpentine line of beauty as it is found in nature:

> Meantime huge smoking cities arose, innumerable. Green leaves shrank before the hot breath of furnaces. The fair face of Nature was deformed as with the ravages of some loathsome disease. And methinks, sweet Una, even our slumbering sense of the forced and of the far-fetched might have arrested us here. But now it appears that we had worked out our own destruction in the perversion of our *taste*, or rather in the blind neglect of its culture in the schools. For, in truth, it was at this crisis that taste alone—that faculty which, holding a middle position between the pure intellect and the moral sense, could never safely have been disregarded— it was now that taste alone could have led us gently back to Beauty, to Nature, and to Life.   (451)

Poe here imagines a modern world that has sown the seeds of its own destruction in its doomed embrace of the notion of "progress," which entails a systematic perversion of its taste and "the blind neglect of its culture in the schools" (451). To be sure, Monos describes the mentality of a society as it seeks to define the beautiful—the province of aesthetics as well as taste. Observe, however, that the object of Monos's criticism is not art or even fine arts, narrowly defined, but rather a broad almost ecological sense of the beautiful that pertains to the ways that our environments and economies are structured. Poe expresses through Monos a powerful commitment to a culturally informed concept of taste. In what follows, I demonstrate the centrality of such taste to understanding Poe's relation to the critical and the popular, the artistic and the social, and the unstable and shifting value of his work in his own cultural moment and ours. Poe's expression of taste as a culturally integrated term in the conversation between Monos and Una offers a bridge between his own critical historical moment and ours as well as an opportunity for students to engage with critical problems of taste today.

But to understand the critical ambivalence that has always surrounded Poe's literary theory, one should bear in mind that the equation of aesthetic with taste stems in part from the overlapping emergence of theories of taste and aesthetics in the eighteenth and nineteenth centuries and the consequent interchangeable use of the two terms. Of course, to the extent that aesthetics is merely a systematic presentation of the properties that regulate taste, the two words may be construed as synonyms. As Raymond Williams writes, the word *aesthetic* is "a key formation in a group of meanings which at once emphasized and isolated subjective sense-activity as the basis of art and beauty as distinct, for example, from *social* or *cultural* interpretations" (32). The word *taste* is related to aesthetics because it too derives from a metaphorical abstraction of a physical sense and has been equated since the eighteenth century with discrimination, especially in regard to fine arts, decor, and food. But whereas *aesthetic* came to pertain to the formal properties of art or "the beautiful" in a way that was autonomous from cultural explanations, as Williams indicates, *taste* retains its application to a wider range of activities and remains embedded in the social, especially in consumer choice. While both words involve judgment, *aesthetic* is theoretical, formal, and elite whereas *taste* may or may not be formalized and pertains to both the connoisseur and the consumer. The concept of taste signifies an appreciation for the beautiful that is simultaneously critical and commercial. Poe's concept of taste was consonant with this polyvalent embrace of both the artistic and the social, the elite and the commercial, and the retroactive attempt by critics to place his works within aesthetic formations has distorted our grasp of his signal contributions to the understanding of literary value. Therefore, to understand the nexus between art and society in Poe—between the popular and the critical—a distinction between *taste* and *aesthetic* must be preserved.

Indeed, this distinction never wholly vanished from assessments of Poe, and it can be detected in the critical reproofs alluded to above. For Lowell, Emerson, and Winters, Poe, whatever his virtues, contained an inevitable degree of falsity, of the ersatz, of fudge. Eliot's and James's sense that Poe belongs properly to the immature or primitive and Bloom's dismissal of his style as hokey use aesthetic judgment to delimit Poe's cultural power. Poe's taste may have a curious childish power, but a taste for Poe cannot be part of a mature sensibility. These remarks all indicate that the commercial aspects of Poe's work are the most problematic, as if poetic compositions were mere "jingles," or advertisements. And yet it is precisely the line between the popular and the critical that Poe has always straddled, and arguments over the nature of Poe's taste and the value of his work invariably express the complex ideological relations of this divide. When praising Poe his critical faculties are exalted; when dismissing him his work is infantilized, seen as overblown. Of course, Poe recognized that he was courting these positions. By labeling his tales "grotesques" and "arabesques," he anticipated such criticism and offered a generic defense that was excessive by definition.

Poe's legacy similarly reproduces the tension between the popular and the critical. He is credited with the invention or modern development of popular literary genres, especially detective fiction, horror, and science fiction, and he is cited as a theorist of the short story, modern attention spans, and the literary effect. In Clement Greenberg's schema of culture, the critical reception of Poe has played out in such a way that he enjoys a simultaneously avant-garde (or retroactively avant-garde) and kitsch (ersatz) status—genius and fudge. Poe was the first theorist of the modern literary effect, but Eliot complained that the effect is "that all his ideas seem to be entertained rather than believed" (330). The high priest of modernism, Eliot searched for mature belief in Poe but found instead the shifting rhetorical sands of "entertainment." With Poe one finds what Terence Whalen has described as a fundamental tension between pleasure and truth that simultaneously offers and undercuts any stable notion of artistic or aesthetic value (*Edgar* 86). This tension produces a kind of ambient skepticism that lends many of Poe's pronouncements an overdetermined quality—the sense that Eliot perceived of Poe "entertaining" a position rather than holding it. The pervasive tension between pleasure and truth leads Poe, as Rachel Polonsky argues, "away from the possibility of theorizing about art" (44)—that is to say, away from formalized aesthetics and toward taste.

We repeatedly find in Poe's work a pattern of texts shuttling between truth and pleasure. Time and again the reader encounters a truth claim countered by the pleasures of a literary form: in the Dupin tales, ratiocinative analysis of analytic processes proceeds toward detective fiction; the credulity of the reading public leads to the hoax ("The Balloon-Hoax") and the pseudodocumentary (*The Narrative of Arthur Gordon Pym*); notions of human will and intentionality lead to the perverse ("The Imp of the Perverse"); plagiarism leads Poe to originality; and the ostensibly reliable narrator reveals his unreliability. "There are certain themes," begins the narration of "The Premature Burial,"

> of which the interest is all-absorbing, but which are too entirely horrible for the purposes of legitimate fiction. These the mere romanticist must eschew, if he do not wish to offend, or to disgust. They are with propriety

handled, only when the severity and majesty of Truth sanctify and sustain
them.   (666)

Poe argues that the actuality of a true but horrifying story gives the reader license to relish its "pleasurable pain" (666) in a way that the same story as a
mere fiction could never authorize. Truth turns out to be an enabling condition
of pleasure, and truth claims in the course of being entertained are transformed
into pleasure. We have tended to read the ideological play of Poe's entertainment as difference, as irony, as dichotomy, as a reproduction of a cultural impasse that is emblematic of modernity, or the emergent form of it found in the
antebellum American scene. As entertainment threatens belief, so entertainment culture threatens the concept of taste and the hierarchies of form and
genre. Thus, the idea that Poe is the purveyor of popular forms, of mere "en-
tertainments" (to use Graham Greene's term for sensational thrillers [qtd. in D.
Jones 62]), reproduces the question of taste that we have come to know so well.
The difficulty of knowing how seriously to take Poe's poetic principles or ratio-
nales lies in their slippage toward pleasure and entertainment.

It comes as no surprise that Poe's cultural status persists undiminished into
the twenty-first century, in part because Poe perceived how literature would be
increasingly bound up in "entertainment" culture. He understood that his
generic innovations (e.g., detective fiction) and his theories of the modern attention span and poetic repetition were directed at problems of modern taste in
an era of mass production and reproduction. Poe's well-known antipathy toward the mob, as Whalen has shown, expressed more than a fear of and con-
tempt for the masses; it also recognized the extent to which Poe was caught up
in the problems of writing for mass audiences. While Poe utilized the "aesthetic
distance" of the postapocalyptic afterworld of Monos and Una to call attention
to the general perversity of modern taste, he recognized that he too, as part of a
flourishing urban magazine culture, was caught up in that same perversion of
taste. Today, we are surrounded by a culture of entertainment that Poe, in part,
foresaw—one in which Poe's famous raven can sit happily as the logo of a National Football League franchise. Perhaps on this subject more than any other,
students can begin to interrogate their own taste, and, more important, the concept of taste itself. Is taste a product of something neglected or cultivated in our
schools? What does it mean to be "in good taste"? Our literary culture, whether
shocking or genteel, is embedded in a wider culture in which taste is subsumed
as part of entertainment. Undoubtedly, good taste and bad taste retain their
currency as terms of praise or criticism, but they are scarcely essential to the vi-
ability of any particular cultural artifact. Our consumerist democracy has grown
increasingly relativistic in matters of taste, challenging and blurring once distinct lines between elite and popular culture. This can be seen in the astronomical sale prices of pop art heroes like Andy Warhol and Roy Lichtenstein; the
junky outsize bric-a-brac Elvisiana of Jeff Koons; the canonization of postpunk,
postgrunge nihilism, such as the establishment of the Rock and Roll Hall of

Fame; the rise of NASCAR and professional wrestling; the mainstream popularity of cult films and *The Simpsons*. This process has been codified, to a greater or lesser degree, as it were, in Jane Stern and Michael Stern's *The Encyclopedia of Bad Taste*, and it signals a juncture in our cultural history in which "bad taste" might be celebrated with as much brio as good taste. Because we can no longer easily locate a traditional cultural ground on which to discuss taste, we grow increasingly sensitive in our own day and age to the quandaries of taste expressed by Poe and performed by his slippery positions. What does the question of taste pertain to in an era when bad taste has been canonized and when the designation of bad no longer signifies an absence of value? We live in an era that cheerfully accepts all manner of taste. Today, one can travel to Las Vegas to see major art exhibitions, and the memoirs of Internet pornographers are reviewed in national newspapers. What are we really to make of Eliot's diatribes about poor Poe's so-called stylistic foibles when Eliot's greatest impact on the culture has arguably been *Cats*?

Students can be extremely sensitive to these matters if an instructor is able to dispel the nonjudgmental posture that tends preliminarily to govern many discussions of taste. By encouraging students to generate lists of problematic examples of taste, a discussion can gravitate away from the merely scandalous toward the fundamental issue undergirding all questions of popular and critical literature. Students can then appreciate that part of Poe's abiding modernity and relevance consists of his ability to generate a conversation that continues to be at the heart of society. The problem of taste is the aftermath of a long popular revolution in our culture, as Michael Kammen has shown, involving a complex and shifting set of relations between popular and mass culture. Greenberg's sense of the tacky or ersatz quality of kitsch may well appear as hoary and elitist as Theodor Adorno and Max Horkheimer's complaints about Hollywood and the culture industry. As the high modernism of the mid–twentieth century recedes and globalized entertainment culture emerges, it may sensitize us anew—it may in fact bring us closer to Poe's era, in which, as Lawrence W. Levine has argued, the line between highbrow and lowbrow culture was much blurrier. Charges of mass production and commercialism have lost their sting. The power of commerce to convert and reproduce any kind of art has led not so much to a Benjaminian waning of aura in the individual work of art as to a sense that mass reproduction is no longer the acid test of value or taste or even a critical factor in a culture of "entertainment." Poe was aware of this phenomenon—was an innovator in it, but not a celebrant of it. In fact, as Poe anticipated, all works of art and literature, both high and low, critical and popular, must coexist and compete with the problems of mechanized reproduction and repetition. Poe wrote:

> The most exquisite pleasures grow dull in repetition. A strain of music enchants. Heard a second time it pleases. . . . We hear it a twentieth, and ask ourselves why we admired. At the fiftieth it [i]nduces ennui—at the hundredth disgust. ("Marginalia")

Poe rejected the notion that taste was relative or arbitrary. In 1841, around the time of his composition of "The Colloquy of Monos and Una," in a review of Henry Wadsworth Longfellow's *Ballads and Other Poems*, he openly disputed the Latin adage *De gustibus non est disputandum* ("there should be no disputing about taste" [679]). "So is it the part of taste alone to inform us of BEAUTY," Poe concluded, "And Poesy is the handmaiden but of Taste" (685). Indeed, Poe projected his theory of taste onto the world. In "The Poetic Principle," he explains:

> Dividing the world of mind into its three most immediately obvious distinctions, we have the Pure Intellect, Taste, and the Moral Sense. I place Taste in the middle, because it is just this position, which, in the mind, it occupies. It holds intimate relations with either extreme; but from the Moral Sense is separated by so faint a difference that Aristotle has not hesitated to place some of its operations among the virtues themselves. Nevertheless, we find the *offices* of the trio marked with a sufficient distinction. Just as the Intellect concerns itself with Truth, so Taste informs us of the Beautiful while the Moral Sense is regardful of Duty. Of this latter, while Conscience teaches the obligation, and Reason the expediency, Taste contents herself with displaying the charms:—waging war upon Vice solely on the ground of her deformity—her disproportion—her animosity to the fitting, to the appropriate, to the harmonious—in a word, to Beauty.   (1436)

Poe's choice of faculties derives from Immanuel Kant's tripartite paradigm of the mind described in *The Critique of Judgment*, but it is as if Poe had substituted taste for Samuel Taylor Coleridge's concept of imagination, replacing Coleridge's synthetic power with a selective one. Taste becomes a metaphor for sensory perception as experienced in consciousness. Taste becomes the site in the mind in which feeling, sensibility, and the perception of the beautiful are processed. Taste is a medial position between reason and conscience; to the extent that immorality is ugly, taste is moral, and feelings forever impinge on our powers of reason. Poe even likened taste to a phrenological organ. "Not the least important service which, hereafter, mankind will owe to *Phrenology*," Poe wrote, "may, perhaps, be recognized in an analysis of the real principles, and a digest of the resulting laws of taste" (Rev. of *Ballads* 679). Poe's theory of taste was a romantic processing of eighteenth-century ideas, and it offers an explanation of why Poe's writings continually slide between truth and pleasure—between intellect and taste as it were. In "The Colloquy of Monos and Una," as Poe charts the corruption of modern taste, however, his theory of taste acquires greater cultural resonance.

If taste is the faculty through which feelings are processed, then "Monos and Una" delineates a condition in which the consciousness of feeling is disorganized and dislocated—what Allen Tate referred to as Poe's synaesthetic sensibility ("Angelic Imagination" 406–07):

I breathed no longer. The pulses were still. The heart had ceased to beat. Volition had not departed, but was powerless. The senses were unusually active, although eccentrically so—assuming often each other's functions at random. The taste and the smell were inextricably confounded, and became one sentiment, abnormal and intense.   (453–54)

Sight is apprehended as sound, touch as sight, both evolving into an ecstasy of pure sensation. The disorganization of taste parallels that of feeling, creating a sensibility based on a confounding of the senses. Here, I suggest, Poe constructs an allegory of the problem of taste for modernity. A colossal disaster like the apocalypse that Monos describes might be attributable in some profound way to a perversion of taste experienced as a literal confusion of sensations and feelings. The "physical" confounding of the senses indicates that the perversion of taste is symptomatic of the described historical declination of the modern world. Turning away from nature, attacking it with "huge smoking cities," Poe seems to say, is what one feels when deprived of the ability to feel properly. Brilliantly, Poe has restored taste to physical sensation from its abstraction as Taste with a capital *T*, only to discover that in our social death it has been fundamentally altered. Synesthesia is therefore the physical condition that stands for the master trope of disorganized or "bad" taste. Unmoored from discrete senses taste physically enters into a realm of play in which feeling is "entertained."

Of all human perversities that Poe articulated, at the most apocalyptic core we find a perversion of taste. As Monos says, "our slumbering sense of the forced and of the far-fetched might have arrested us here." But no, "the harsh mathematical reason of the schools," and "the intemperance of knowledge" induced a premature old age in the world to the point that there appeared to be "no regeneration save in death." Faced with this predicament, Monos longs for catastrophic regeneration,

> when the Art-scarred surface of the Earth, having undergone that purification which alone could efface its rectangular obscenities, should clothe itself anew in the verdure and the mountain-slopes and the smiling waters of Paradise, and be rendered at length a fit dwelling-place for man.
> ("Colloquy" 452–53)

In "The Colloquy of Monos and Una," we find "taste on her deathbed," or, as Poe puts it in his derision of transcendentalist poetry, "Taste kicking *in articulo mortis*" ("Fifty Suggestions" 1303). One need not accept Poe's Kantian metaphysics of taste to recognize that he has reached a relevant social limit of imagining taste. If taste oscillates in our own time, it does so in part as a corrective process of old class distinctions. Poe's taste compels us to recognize that the ersatz of art is a relative burden shared not only by mass culture but by the whole mass of culture, critics, teachers, and students alike. We have been producing forms that are suited to this cultural predicament, tales of the grotesque and arabesque, limitless numbers of artifacts that straddle the line between art and entertainment. One might even see this predicament of taste as epiphenomena of global warming and urbanization and wait for the forces that will cleanse our own art-scarred earth of its rectangular obscenities. One can imagine an end to all this, Poe tells us, but one cannot escape its feeling.

A New-Historicist Approach to Teaching "The Black Cat"

Lesley Ginsberg

I have developed a unit on Poe, race, and gender that is part of a larger introductory undergraduate-level course on literary theory, titled Literary Criticism: Theory and Practice. After the students have been introduced to the
theory of new historicism through Ann B. Dobie's essay "Cultural Studies: New
Historicism," this assignment offers the tools for a direct experience of new-
historicist practice through engagement with a selection of both literary and
nonliterary primary sources. Using a lecture-discussion arrangement, I highlight some of the primary sources I have used to contextualize Poe with attention to the race and gender issues of his day. In so doing, I put students in
contact with materials used to historicize a literary work in terms of antebellum
attitudes toward race and gender while they gain the experience to critique
both the strengths and the weaknesses of new-historicist practice by direct engagement with the materials on which such readings are based. This method of
teaching Poe has consistently provoked lively discussions, both about the subjects (race, gender, and Poe) and about new historicism.

Whenever I ask undergraduates to name some of the authors who first ig-
nited their passion for literature, Poe's name is consistently mentioned. Yet it is
precisely their deep love for Poe's work that paradoxically breeds a resistance to
critical inquiry—the fear, perhaps, that the magic of Poe will evaporate under
the withering glare of academic scrutiny (and what term could be more drily
unappealing to certain English majors than the word *historicism*?). While I am
convinced that "The Black Cat" cries out for new-historicist analysis because of

its fundamental engagement with an alterity—troped through the human-animal divide—that speaks to a broad range of antebellum issues, this tale also works in the classroom as an introduction to new-historicist practice since it is familiar to students but not necessarily one of those works to which they are frequently attached (after the unit is completed, though, students are eager to reexplore their favorites). In addition, this course, by highlighting some of the extraliterary materials used to establish a new-historicist reading of Poe, gives students the tools to situate their interpretations of Poe in relation to some of the stronger currents of Poe criticism and allows them to leave the classroom with a demystified understanding of scholarly work more generally.

Alongside the tale featured in the assignment (I often include "The Raven" and "Hop-Frog"), students receive a representative sample of the first page of the paper in which "The Black Cat" was originally published; for many, this is one of the first times that they viscerally experience the fact that nineteenth-century American literature was printed in many venues, including magazines, giftbooks, newspapers, and story papers. From the beginning, then, students are taught that stories themselves appear in particular contexts, instead of being isolated in space and time from the world around them, as the aridity of the typical undergraduate literature anthology would suggest. Students are given a small packet of primary texts that includes selected excerpts from David Walker's *Appeal to the Coloured Citizens of the World*, Thomas R. Gray's *The Confessions of Nat Turner*, Joseph Holt Ingraham's *The South-West, by a Yankee* (along with a quotation from *The South-West* reprinted in James Kirke Paulding's 1836 *Slavery in the United States* [223]), Elizabeth Cady Stanton and Lucretia Mott's "Declaration of Sentiments," and George Fitzhugh's *Sociology for the South*; students also receive a brief biography of Poe. Poe's review of Ingraham's book in the *Southern Literary Messenger* ("South-West") is presented through the *Making of America* Web site, using "smart classroom" technology.

The teaching strategy I have developed is grounded in the work of such critics as Joan Dayan, John Carlos Rowe, Terrence Whalen, Teresa A. Goddu, and others.[1] However, though these critical sources are crucial, as a teacher I have found it far more powerful to introduce undergraduates to the primary sources used by scholars to link Poe to antebellum debates over slavery, race, and the status of women *before* they engage critical works that, in far more sophisticated and nuanced terms, essentially perform the work of the assignment. In other words, students proceed both deductively and inductively, and, by stressing the inductive portion of the assignment, the classroom becomes a creative space in which new historicism is both practiced and critiqued.

"Poe . . . rarely wrote about the contemporary scene. His fiction offers no glimpse of the whirlwind social changes wrought in nineteenth-century America by . . . hot debates over women's rights . . . and the abolition of slavery. . . . Poe's fictional world usually seems to mirror no particular place or time"

(Silverman 12, 24). This quotation from Kenneth Silverman's introduction to the 1993 collection *New Essays on Poe's Major Tales* serves as a useful corollary to our unit on Poe and the practice of new historicism. As students readily understand when I read Silverman's words aloud, his terms spell out what could be called the opposite of a new-historicist approach. I explain that many scholars of Poe have traditionally considered him a Romantic whose literary works for the most part deliberately avoided the political strife and the spirit of reform that both energized and divided his generation. I prompt students for some of those issues, usually writing at least three of them on the board: women's rights, abolitionism, and the temperance movement. Yet rather than risk oversimplification or monolithic thinking, this is the moment when I ask students to name the "place" and "time" in which "The Black Cat" is set. The stunned silence that this question usually elicits lets students acknowledge the validity of earlier positions about Poe's fiction, while I suggest that, by not limiting the setting to a specific place or time, the story invites itself to be read in the widest possible range of contexts—including Poe's own day and time. Further, I remind students that in his literary criticism Poe put literature on a pedestal that seemed to divorce it from the sordid materialism of everyday realities: "A poem, in my opinion, is opposed to a work of science by having, for its immediate object, pleasure, not truth" ("Letter to B——" 1371). Yet I also suggest that Poe used the literary essay to explore an abiding interest in the tension between the material and the ideal and to cultivate a persona. Instead of taking his dictum about poetry—and, by extension, literature as a whole—as "truth," we may take pleasure in the grandiose assurance of the narrator's pronouncements while recalling that the speaker's flamboyance needs also to be squared with the insecurities of an author who for most of his life was burdened with the ongoing struggle to establish himself financially as a writer. Finally, I argue that contained within the assumptions of other critical methodologies lie the questions that a new historicist would ask: how does Poe's fiction offer glimpses of the most important issues of his day? or, how does Poe's fiction mirror the particularities of his own day and age?

Having affirmed that new historicism would be deeply interested in the relation between Poe's fiction and the issues of his day, I then ask students to consider the American literature anthologies with which they are familiar from their larger survey classes (*The Norton Anthology* or *The Heath Anthology*). I point out that while anthologies may be cost-effective, such collections fail to reproduce the contexts in which a literary work actually appeared. Students recall that poetry and fiction published in the 1840s appeared in a wide variety of venues. Here I often highlight the *National Era*, the antislavery newspaper in which *Uncle Tom's Cabin* was first serialized. The *National Era* exemplifies a publication that looks to students like a contemporary newspaper, though it mixed news stories, fictional tales, and poetry to an extent that regularly startles undergraduates (even though they have heard such claims in lectures, the visceral charge of reviewing some photocopied pages from the *National Era* provides tangible emphasis. I circulate a page that shows how the last installment of Harriet Beecher Stowe's fictional novel is immediately followed by a reprinted editorial on Senator Salmon P. Chase and the Fugitive Slave Law; a fragment from the edition of 13 November 1851 shows poems by Phoebe Cary and James Russell Lowell placed next to state election results and reports from the Baltimore markets regarding prices for hogs and beef cattle).[2] These excerpts help concretize some of the theoretical claims of new historicists; or, as Dobie puts it in an essay that students read, under new historicism "a work of literature is no longer read as an autonomous entity" (167). Depending on what I have available to me, this is also a good moment to circulate an antebellum giftbook or a magazine—a gesture that not only reinforces the point that literary works are rarely "autonomous" but also tends to raise interest among students, most of whom have never handled older materials.

After establishing that antebellum short stories typically appeared in heterogeneous collections (often called miscellanies in Poe's day), I affirm that "The Black Cat" was first published in the *Saturday Evening Post* (then called the *United States Saturday Evening Post*). This story paper typically included serialized novel-length works, short fiction, poems, light news, and anecdotes reprinted from other papers, personal essays, and humorous editorials. As I remind students who peruse a representative copy of the masthead of this paper, like many other antebellum periodicals the *Saturday Evening Post* made a point of distancing itself from the political turmoil of the era, a gesture that seems calculated to sell more papers, despite antebellum political divides. I ask a student to read aloud the motto on the masthead of the *Post* in 1843: "A Family Newspaper: Neutral in Politics: Devoted to General News, Literature, Science, Morality, Agriculture and Amusement." Yet instead of assuming that this invites us to consider literature as separate from politics (a question often raised by students at this point), I suggest that the paper's professed detachment might also suggest the publisher's fear that overt politics will not sell well. A reference to Poe's poverty (mentioned in the brief biography students read) facilitates recognition of the material facts with which Poe struggled as he wrote the story at hand. This in turn helps build the argument that fiction too overtly partisan might not have been publishable in the venues Poe chose— and Poe had financial incentives to publish. Finally, I suggest that just as contemporary television watchers rarely limit themselves to one channel, antebellum readers typically read more than one paper, so that even those who subscribed to politically neutral story papers would have been well aware of contemporary obsessions and controversies.[3] And in his various editorial capacities for many magazines across the country, Poe was certainly aware of the breadth and depth of the print universe in his day and time; his book reviews for the January 1836 edition of the *Southern Literary Messenger* alone cover collections of poetry, a novel, travelogues, a memoir, and a conduct manual.

I remind students that thus far we have established some of the evidence that a new historicist would use to argue that Poe's stories could be considered alongside other print sources from his day and age, and I have also suggested that overtly partisan fiction potentially risked poor sales (a risk that meant a good deal to Poe given his financial precariousness). The class then turns to the packet of materials I have prepared to accompany Poe's stories. I remind students of Dobie's claim that new historicists analyze "the many discourses of a culture. . . . Literary interpretation involves acknowledging all the social concerns that surround a text" (167). If quoting Dobie is not enough to prompt a student to articulate a link between the various discourses represented in the packet, I briefly name some of the representative antebellum discourses students have at hand—proslavery discourse (Ingraham; Paulding; Fitzhugh), the discourse of women's rights (Stanton and Mott), and antislavery discourse (D. Walker). In broad terms, I sketch the plot of "The Black Cat" (convicted murderer confessing the murder of his wife) and read some key passages aloud—particularly highlighting the contrast between the narrator's cold-blooded account of the murder of his wife and the disposal of her body (603–04) with his hyperbolic account of the murder of his cat Pluto (599–600). I suggest that when the narrator calls the hanging of Pluto "a sin— a deadly sin" (599) while barely a moral quibble is articulated in recounting the murder of his wife, the narrator replicates the essential dilemma of slavery: its confusion between persons and things. By this stage, the class has moved to the question of pro- and antislavery discourses. I prompt students for the most common euphemisms for slavery in antebellum discourses: the domestic institution, the patriarchal institution, and the peculiar institution. Often a student will comment on the similarity between Ingraham's vision of slavery's patriarchal beneficence ("It is often the case that the children of the domestic servants become pets in the house, and the playmates of the white children of the family" [126]) and the narrator's aside, "Pluto—this was the cat's name—was my favorite pet and playmate" (598). I again remind students that Poe wrote a review of Ingraham's *The South-West* for the *Southern Literary Messenger*; even if he failed to read every word of the book, he had at least a passing familiarity with it (in a "smart classroom," I show the review to the class using the *Making of America* Web site). Poe's review of Ingraham also adds credence to the contention that Poe was conversant with nonliterary discourses, in this case proslavery discourse. I mention the common proslavery pseudoscientific belief that relegated people of African descent to the realm of the subhuman; at this point a student usually remarks on David Walker's attack on the *"insupportable insult"* that Africans are "not of the *human family*," but rather are "held . . . up as descending originally from the tribes of *Monkeys* or *Orang-Outangs*" (10). The proslavery argument that placed slaves in a less than human category is also attacked by Walker when he protests that "we (coloured people) and our children are *brutes!!* and of course are, and *ought to be* SLAVES to the American people and their children forever!!" (7). Students tend to link Walker's terms with the narrator's language in "The Black Cat":

> And now was I indeed wretched beyond the wretchedness of mere Humanity. And *a brute beast*—whose fellow I had contemptuously destroyed—*a brute beast* to work out for *me*—for me a man, fashioned in the image of the High God—so much of insufferable wo!   (603)

The narrator's obsession with the boundaries between human and animal—and his ultimate confusion of the two—is linked to discourses of slavery, including the tendency of proslavery discourses to equate slaves with animals.

I also raise the question of power dynamics in the tale. The narrator's almost absolute power over his dependents (wife, pets) is noted. I often read a quotation from Theodore Dwight Weld's *American Slavery As It Is*: "Arbitrary power is to the mind what alcohol is to the body; it intoxicates. . . . The possession of power, is such a fiery stimulant, that its lodgement in human hands is always perilous" (115–16). Weld's words help link the narrator's alcoholism to both the temperance movement and the question of slavery. Additionally, the antebellum interest in women's rights and its relation to abolition is highlighted through Stanton and Mott's "Declaration of Sentiments": "In the covenant of marriage, she is compelled to promise obedience to her husband, he becoming, to all intents and purposes, her master—the law giving him power to deprive her of her liberty, and to administer chastisement" (92). The dependent role of married women and its echo of the position of the slave is usually noted by students at this point in Fitzhugh's proslavery terms:

> Wives and apprentices are slaves; not in theory only, but often in fact. Children are slaves to their parents, guardians and teachers. Imprisoned culprits are slaves. Lunatics and idiots are slaves also. Three-fourths of free society are slaves.   (*Sociology* 86)

Students are encouraged to think broadly about the "domestic" and "patriarchal" language used to discuss slavery and its implications regarding gender. Students are critical of Fitzhugh's demonization of the North ("There, wife murder has become a mere holiday pastime" [84]) and are sensitive to the ironic juxtaposition of Fitzhugh's words to the wife murderer of "The Black Cat." The wife's namelessness is sometimes also raised, an omission that indicates the depersonalized manner in which the narrator portrays her; like a slave, the wife challenges the boundary between persons and things:

> The hideous murder accomplished, I set myself forthwith . . . to the task of concealing the body. . . . I deliberated . . . about packing it in a box, as if merchandize, with the usual arrangements, and so getting a porter to take it from the house.   (603–04)

Finally, I raise the issue of the narrator's motive; we seem to read the confession like that of Gray's introduction to *The Confessions of Nat Turner*, as a motiveless crime, or at least one whose motive (rage aimed at a cat) fails to satisfy. But just as Turner's motive for murdering whites is the institution of slavery, the masterlike power of the narrator over his wife and cat accorded to him by conventional antebellum patriarchal institutions suggests that Poe's story in some way reflects the major issues of his day, especially when read in the context of extraliterary antebellum discourses.

I conclude by inviting students to critique new historicism inductively, based on their in-class experience, and deductively, using their reading from Dobie. One of the first considerations raised by students is the problem of time—the time it takes to find and read extraliterary discourses, an author's letters and book reviews, and the sources in which literary works were originally printed (this exercise has the added benefit of making scholarly work visible to undergraduates). Student criticisms usually include the limitations of new-historicist focus in terms of what was left untreated—the mysterious cat, who returns after what seems to be his death, or the "spirit of PERVERSENESS" that serves as a plausible psychological motive for the narrator's misdeeds in "The Black Cat" (599). It is crucial for students to note the limitations of the method because doing so opens space for them to explore ideas (both in class and in their papers) that draw on what we have done in class while cultivating originality. And as part of a larger course on theory, I suggest to students that formulating a critique is central to acknowledging limitations of any theoretical framework, including new historicism. Students leave the class with a deeper appreciation of the extent to which Poe's stories reflect the central issues of his day, a richer understanding of antebellum print culture, and the satisfaction of having practiced new historicism. Finally, this unit leaves students better prepared to negotiate contemporary criticism of Poe and better able to situate their own papers on Poe in terms of multiple scholarly traditions.

NOTES

[1] For a nuanced reading of race in relation to Poe's Romanticism, see Lee.

[2] Barbara Hochman argues that the *National Era* was particularly promiscuous in its mixing of the literary and the nonliterary when compared with other antislavery papers.

[3] See Zboray 126–33. Though Zboray quotes Horace Greeley's memory of subscribing to just one weekly paper in his youth, Zboray comments that "[t]he great number of newspapers, their easy availability, and their low cost assured most Americans of an ample supply of ephemeral prints" (126).

Reader Response and the Interpretation of "Hop-Frog," "How to Write a Blackwood Article," and "The Tell-Tale Heart"

Brian Yothers

Pedagogy, criticism, and theory rarely interact as richly as they do in a class on the works of Edgar Allan Poe. Poe's stated intention of creating a powerful "effect" with each of his stories ("Poetic Principle" 1431), when combined with his pervasive use of irony and misdirection, allows the classroom to become a critical laboratory in which the effects of Poe's tales on a rapidly evolving interpretive community can be observed and analyzed. Both students and instructors can profit immensely from analyzing the creation of effect in Poe's tales. Students who might normally consider critical theory baffling find themselves speaking authoritatively about complex critical issues, and instructors are able to evaluate critical claims about the effects that Poe achieves in his tales by observing student responses, some naive but many increasingly complex as the semester progresses, to these effects.

In my senior-level undergraduate seminar on Poe, students are asked to write one-hundred-word responses to each of the stories, poems, and essays that they read throughout the semester. Assignments of this length allow students to construct focused readings of a particular aspect of the text and to share these readings with one another. Students are able to learn from one another's responses to the texts, both those that are naive and those that, as the semester goes on, become increasingly sophisticated. Moreover, students are able to evaluate the persuasiveness of their critical efforts and those of their peers based on both textual and contextual concerns. As a result, they are also in a better position to evaluate and synthesize the readings presented by professional literary critics and scholars.

In the following pages, I examine the ways in which the student responses that I gathered during the fall 2004 semester can help illuminate critical controversies about the affective qualities of Poe's works. I also suggest that using student responses as a way to understand the affective elements (verbal strategies that are applied to elicit specific emotional responses) in Poe's texts can be a means of developing both critical acuity and confidence in undergraduates who are on the verge of graduate school or secondary teaching. I proceed by examining student responses to two of Poe's lesser-known tales, "Hop-Frog; or, The Eight Chained Ourang-Outangs" and "How to Write a Blackwood Article," and suggesting how those responses can enhance their comprehension of the texts and enter them into the critical debates about Poe. I conclude by discussing how this method can be applied to one of Poe's most famous and frequently assigned works, "The Tell-Tale Heart."

Poe's often overlooked story "Hop-Frog" exemplifies how the classroom can contribute to critical praxis. Articles regarding the relation between "Hop-Frog" and antebellum slavery have made the affective response elicited from readers by this story a keystone of their argument that Poe should be viewed as a typical proslavery Southerner.[1] In this reading, developed, for example, by Paul Christian Jones, Poe uses readers' initial sympathy with the title character and the revulsion that readers feel after Hop-Frog has taken his revenge to construct a critique of abolitionist rhetoric that ultimately justifies the antebellum status quo. Student responses, which often include visceral reactions to the sensational aspects of Poe's tales, can provide a means of evaluating the persuasiveness of this argument. If indeed the most common reaction is revulsion, then Jones's argument appears very strong. If, however, the interpretive community in the classroom reacts by finding that Hop-Frog's revenge is emotionally satisfying, then this conclusion raises questions about whether Poe's story indeed does work as an antiabolitionist cautionary tale.

When I last taught "Hop-Frog," during the fall 2004 semester, I made Jones's thesis a major part of our class discussion. Before the students read the story, I asked them to think carefully about the matter of sympathy and to consider with whom they sympathized most in the story. As a result, when the students came to class on the day of our discussion, many of them had written detailed analyses of their own affective response to the story. To keep students from having their response shaped by their agreement or disagreement with Jones's thesis, I did not supply them with the article in advance. Rather, I read relevant portions of the article to them after they had already gone on record regarding their initial response to the text. When I introduced Jones's reading of the story, many of them objected on the grounds that they had not, in fact, experienced a feeling of revulsion at Hop-Frog's gruesome revenge but had concluded that, as one of the students wrote in her response: "I absolutely loved the ending of this tale; the king and his ministers deserved to be burnt to a crisp." One student went so far in her response as to see the story as a refutation of the common charge of racism against Poe precisely because of what she saw as his evident sympathy for the enslaved Hop-Frog.[2] Others, having experienced revulsion at the excessiveness of Hop-Frog's revenge, found Jones's argument more persuasive.

This interpretative impasse led the class into some interesting questions: What is the relation between our diverse affective responses to the story and Poe's intended "effect"? What is the relation between our responses to the story and those of nineteenth-century United States readers? Would they be as divided as we are? How can we find out about their responses? This series of questions led us into a discussion of the sort of historical reader-response criticism that Cathy Davidson has applied effectively to early-nineteenth-century American literature.[3] Furthermore, students were able to historicize their own affective responses to the story in relation to their own twenty-first-century cultural context.

The result of the discussion was not that the class reached a final judgment on Jones's article. Instead, students saw how a work of criticism can raise important and engaging questions about the text and the world beyond it and how their responses can provide evidence used in assessing critical claims. Moreover, the students were beginning to see how close reading, historical research, literary theory, and a personal appreciation of a text can be complementary rather than antagonistic.

If students' responses to Poe's revenge tale "Hop-Frog" proved illuminating in surprising ways, their responses to "How to Write a Blackwood Article" showed both analytic zeal and genuine zest for the writing of parody. Although our discussion of this text also included a discussion of the role of race, the class found that formal concerns were of considerable interest as well. One of my goals in teaching Poe is to help my students develop an eye for irony and parody in Poe's work.[4] Although at first they are surprised that this element is a part of Poe's oeuvre, as members of a generation that grew up watching *The Simpsons*, they quickly find that these elements in his work are both interesting and familiar. When I taught "How to Write a Blackwood Article" in the fall 2004 semester, I assigned students the sample articles from *Blackwood's* that are included in the Norton Critical Edition *Selected Writings*, edited by G. R. Thompson. I then gave the students the chance to write their own parodies of the Blackwood articles in place of their daily response to the assigned stories. As a result, about half the class wrote their regularly scheduled response to "How to Write a Blackwood Article," and half the class wrote their own parodies of Blackwood articles. In our discussion, we were able to see the elements in *Blackwood's* sensation fiction that Poe mocks and appropriates in many of his own stories. Several of my students took the opportunity provided by the assignment to parody Poe's own agonistic relation with his contemporaries.

As we discussed in my class, Poe's parody of the Blackwood genre of sensation fiction is surprisingly complex because Poe is able to mock a genre that also figures as an influence on his own more serious works. One of the "effects" of "How to Write a Blackwood Article" is the display of Poe's virtuosity as an artist. He successfully parodies work that in many ways resembles his own, and, by doing so, he demonstrates his mastery of the sensation-tale genre and his ability to comment ironically on his own style of writing. The students who chose to write parodies found themselves drawn into Poe's competition with the Blackwood writers. One of the most accomplished parodies, a favorite of the class, combined Poe's fascination with phrenology with the style that Signora Psyche Zenobia adopts in "How to Write a Blackwood Article." In a scene in which a mad scientist is stimulating the speaker's brain with electrodes, the student wrote:

> He pressed the button for Firmness—I resolved to escape. He pressed Beauty—I saw my jar as the most delightful habitation. He pressed Grandeur—the jar seemed endless. He pressed Observation—my eyes moved about everywhere. . . . He pressed Destruction—I swore to kill him. He pressed Kindness—I forgave him at once. (Stolar)

This parody, of course, echoes Signora Psyche Zenobia's narration of her own predicament: "The dogs danced! *I*—I could not. They frisked—I wept. They capered—I sobbed aloud" (288). As the students shared their parodies and noted the ways in which the parodies' success depended on careful imitation of sentence structure and tone, they learned to attend more carefully to the formal aspects of Poe's work as well as the thematic issues that we discussed throughout the semester.

My first two examples show methods for introducing some of Poe's lesser-known short fiction in the undergraduate classroom. This raises the obvious question of how a response-oriented approach can address a text that is familiar and frequently assigned. "The Tell-Tale Heart" illustrates the challenge a text that many students have read in middle school, and almost certainly in high school, can pose for the instructor who uses student responses as a means of analyzing Poe's effects. Initial student responses to this tale are shaped not by naive first encounters but by previous—in many cases multiple—encounters. Their readings are further shaped by readings that have been proposed to them by previous instructors, ranging from the middle-school to the university level. Moreover, the availability of Internet sites that offer to "decode" popular stories like this one results in students bringing to class a complicated array of responses that resemble palimpsests, in which their own responses are intermingled with those of prior instructors and easily available outside resources in addition to those assigned for the class.

My solution to this situation, both in Poe and survey courses, is to ask students to engage directly with the big questions of interpretation. I ask them to come up with criteria for evaluating readings of the text that they have previously encountered. Which readings do they find persuasive? Which readings seem untenable? What makes the difference? In this case the role that written responses can play is different from the role that they play in relation to Poe's lesser-known stories.

Another strategy for discussing "The Tell-Tale Heart" is to ask students to "bracket out" their earlier experiences with the story and attempt to approach the story as if they had not seen it before. This strategy accomplishes two things: First, it allows students to realize just how difficult it is to see a story afresh after becoming accustomed to seeing it through a particular set of lenses. This realization leads to an opportunity to discuss Poe's own concern with epistemological issues alongside more general epistemological questions about the nature of reading. Second, when students succeed in approaching the story as if for the first time, they sometimes uncover provocative possibilities in their readings of the story. For example, one of my students in the fall 2004 term produced a thoughtful reading of the relation of military metaphors in "The Tell-Tale Heart" to the narrator's justification for his attack on the old man.

The three stories discussed above illustrate three discrete approaches to using students' responses to Poe's work in the classroom. My approach in the case of "Hop-Frog" draws on the students' naive affective responses as grounds for both critical speculation and classroom discussion. In the case of "How to Write a Blackwood Article," my approach depends on the students' ability to engage in the kind of agonistic relationship with Poe implied by the genre of parody and thus come to a richer understanding of Poe's formal strategies. Finally, in the case of "The Tell-Tale Heart," my approach encourages students to engage directly with the wider world of critical discourse. There are two major benefits of making use of these sorts of written student responses: the contribution that studying naive responses to the text can make to critical discourse and thus to future generations of teachers and the pedagogical contribution that these responses make to student comprehension and intellectual growth.

I suggest that when an instructor makes student responses part of the larger critical discussion and explains theoretical and critical issues in relation to these responses, he or she gives students a stake in the current critical debate surrounding Poe. Once students have this stake, they are more prepared to understand knotty theoretical and critical issues and to evaluate critical positions in a nuanced manner, avoiding the common false dilemma that portrays the critic as either an omniscient superinterpreter or an addled egghead who "always reads too much into the story."

As I learned teaching Poe, pedagogy, critical praxis, and theory can coincide fruitfully in the use of student responses. Most significantly, the use of written student responses to Poe's fiction can produce the "double effect" of contributing to the existing critical discourse and of helping our students develop their own emerging critical voices.

NOTES

[1] For a useful series of discussions of Poe's views on race, see Kennedy and Weissberg.

[2] Most students who gave permission for their work to be cited in this essay wished to remain anonymous, so I only include the name of one who wished his name to be used.

[3] Davidson's *Revolution and the Word: The Rise of the Novel in America* investigates the recorded responses of late-eighteenth-century and early-nineteenth-century American readers to the novels of the period. It is a particularly fine example of the combination of reader-response theory with careful historical research that I suggest can both give our criticism firm epistemological grounding and provide us with clearer answers to students' questions about what it is that literary critics do.

[4] In my emphasis on the importance of parody and humor in Poe's work, I follow the work of G. R. Thompson in his introduction to *Great Short Works of Edgar Allan Poe: Poems, Tales, Criticism*.

Teaching "The Purloined Letter"and Lacan's *Seminar*: Introducing Students to Psychoanalysis through Poe

Diane Long Hoeveler

In April 1955, Jacques Lacan presented a seminar on Poe's "The Purloined Letter" as part of his year-long seminar on the meaning of repetition and memory in Sigmund Freud's *Beyond the Pleasure Principle*. The essay was apparently so significant to Lacan that he chose to publish it in his collection *The Seminar of Jacques Lacan. Book II: The Ego in Freud's Theory and in the Technique of Psychoanalysis, 1954–1955*. Freud had also famously based a number of his central psychoanalytic theories on literary texts (e.g., Oedipus, Hoffman's *Sandman*, Jensen's *Gradiva*, fairy tales, *King Lear*), and in his *Interpretation of Dreams* he identified condensation and displacement as the key indications of unconscious material in texts as well as dreams. Lacan was to some extent following in Freud's footsteps by analyzing Poe's short story, and certainly literary critics with a psychoanalytic bent were attracted to Poe long before Marie Bonaparte's famous biography put his so-called mother fixation on public display. They have also, however, acknowledged that following the siren's song of psychoanalysis and sailing into Poe biographical-psychological territory can leave one on the rocks of confusion, not to mention potential pedagogical disaster.[1]

This essay charts one approach I have taken to teaching Poe through the psychoanalytic theories of Freud as filtered through Lacan. I teach "The Purloined Letter" and Lacan's "Seminar on 'The Purloined Letter' " in a course titled Literature and Psychology, and the students enrolled in the course are about evenly split between upper-level English and psychology majors. Even so, their knowledge of psychoanalysis is minimal when the course begins. I mention this at the outset because I have learned that undergraduates often find reading Freud's essays, not to mention Lacan's works, difficult. I will make a case here for claiming that teaching Poe's short story in relation to Lacan's essay allows an instructor to interrogate not only Poe's literary techniques but also the method and intentions of psychoanalysis as an interpretive tool. Earlier in the course, students read E. T. A. Hoffman's "The Sandman" in conjunction with Freud's analysis of the story, "The Uncanny," so they understand that psychoanalysts have often used literary texts as psychological case studies, reading the symptoms of literary characters as if they were real clients with psychological histories and problems who had found their ways to Freud's couch. Other pairings that have been successful in demonstrating this method are Poe's "William Wilson" alongside Otto Rank's "The Double" or Poe's "The Tell-Tale Heart" and "The Black Cat" alongside Freud's essay "A Child Is Being Beaten."

To introduce Lacan, I inform students that Lacan is generally regarded as a modernizer of Freud. Instead of relying on Freud's tendency to ferret out hidden meanings from the unconscious mind, Lacan focuses on how the mind's processes can be read through the use of language. Using the theories of the linguist Ferdinand de Saussure, Lacan's approach centers on those moments of slippage or the gaps that occur between our understanding of the sign (the physical object) and the signifier (the word or the abstract representation of an object). In the class, I begin with the premise that all literary texts convey more on the implicit level than they do on the explicit, and yet it is necessary to place these two levels of meaning into a dialogue with each other in order to demonstrate how the textual unconscious reveals itself. By putting literary texts to the psychoanalytic question, so to speak, we are teasing out symptoms and traces of the author, the characters, and finally the reader.

To begin, I state that Poe's "Purloined Letter" presents us with three primary formalistic literary devices that I will emphasize in my teaching of the tale: repetitive actions involving substitutions, interconnecting subjects, and symbolism. Lacan's post-Freudian approach to the story builds on these literary devices but transforms each of them into a psychoanalytic approach: repetition becomes understood through metonymy and metaphor; interconnected subjects become condensed and displaced as the oedipal triangle; and the symbolism of the letter, the queen, and the curse at the conclusion of the story become the moments at which signification and desire erupt in the text. I routinely use the blackboard in all my classes to outline how interpretive strategies can be applied to the literary text under study. With these two texts I list "Poe: Literary Formalist Devices" on the left side of the board and then, parallel to that column, I list "Lacan/Freud: Psychoanalytic Approaches." By keeping the two lists running parallel to each other throughout the class discussion, I have seen students anticipate connections and participate actively.

Repetition: Metonymy and Metaphor

Poe's "Purloined Letter" begins when an unnamed narrator and C. Auguste Dupin, Poe's recurring French detective, are sitting around one evening reminiscing about the earlier cases of the murder in the Rue Morgue and the murder of Marie Rogêt (680). The body of this dead woman functions as a metonymy (a substitution of the murdered woman for the queen, the object of the son's rage), hovering over this later story in an ominous way, reminding Poe's readers that violence against women lurks in the most civilized of cities. But "The Purloined Letter" is a curiously cerebral story on the surface, with all its threatened violence contained on a letter that passes—and becomes increasingly "soiled"—between the hands of men and over, so to speak, the elided body of the woman. It is necessary to point out to students that the dominant metaphor in the story is the narrative that Dupin tells of the odd and even game that is played by a cunning child to outwit his slower peers of their money (689). This game and gaming itself stand as a metaphor for the detective game that Dupin plays with Minister D——, for, just as the child is able to place himself in the position of his opponents, so is Dupin able to assume the face of his antagonist ("I fashion the expression of my face, as accurately as possible, in accordance with the expression of his, and then wait to see what thoughts or sentiments arise in my mind or heart, as if to match or correspond with the expression" [690]). By donning green glasses to conceal his scrutiny of Minister D——'s room, Dupin reveals to his audience of one (the narrator) how his system of displaced physiognomy works. By mimicking Minister D——, who was the third party between the king and queen, Dupin has also placed himself in the position of the blinded Oedipus seeking the truth about the mother in another man's bedroom (locating her defaced "body" in the letter and rescuing her for the rightful and phallic father figure, the king).

The story is also structured around two repeated scenes of theft, the first one related by Monsieur G——, the prefect of the Parisian police (681–82), and the second one by Dupin (696–97). In the first scene, which Lacan refers to as "the primal scene" (34), three people are in the boudoir of the queen, and, although this is only implied, we can infer that these three people are the cuckolded king, the adulterous queen, and the wily thief of the incriminating letter (Minister D——) who steals the letter in plain view of the queen in order to hold political power over her, in effect, to blackmail her.[2] This theft of the letter occurred when the minister quickly substituted one of his own letters, with a similar heading and lettering, in place of the queen's, which she had hurriedly placed on the top of her table. Although she was able to see exactly what he was doing, she was powerless to draw attention to his act without alerting the king to the contents of the original letter. Later this scene is repeated when Dupin insinuates himself into the minister's room, locates the soiled and disguised letter in plain view above the fireplace of the minister, and substitutes his own letter, signed with an ominous curse (more on that anon).

While Poe uses these two scenes of theft to structure his story like two sides of a folding panel, with much theoretical discussion of gaming and psychological identification between the two scenes, Lacan does something else with the two thefts. For him, as for Freud, all repetition is a recourse to and reenactment of the death drive (Thanatos), an earlier and ultimately much more powerful impulse than the pleasure principle (Eros) that supposedly motivates human behavior. In their pursuit of the purloined letter, both the police (the patriarchy) and Dupin appear to be caught up in the family romance, with the letter functioning as a displaced substitute for the mother's body. As Lacan notes, the letter can only be understood as "a pure signifier" (32), although the two theft scenes, in their sheer repetitiveness, have to be understood as part of a sign of "the signifying chain," which itself is controlled by the "specific laws of . . . foreclosure (*Verwerfung*), repression (*Verdrängung*), denial (*Verneinung*), and displacement (*Entstellung*)" (29). In placing these two, signifier (letter) and sign (the thefts), against each other, students can see in much more concrete terms how Lacan defines his own slippery concepts, how they differ, and how psychoanalytic properties like repression enter into Poe's text. But what exactly is being repressed and displaced in this text?

Interconnected Subjects: The Oedipal Triangle

Poe's story places the central personages of childhood fantasy, the king and queen, at the center of the action, albeit in a fairly displaced fashion; in fact, protecting the queen's honor and status becomes for Dupin and the police force the focus of all their actions. Although Lacan does not refer to Freud's essay "A Special Type of Choice of Object Made by Men," he clearly seems to suggest that the impetus for locating the letter can be found in what Freud labeled the "rescue fantasy," wherein a man seeks out as a love object a prostitute or sexually compromised woman in order to "rescue" her (recall Somerset Maugham's *Of Human Bondage*). Such a fantasy has its origins in repressed oedipal fixations on the mother that occur when the male child first begins to understand the nature of sexuality and his own conception. Such a complex, of course, gives rise to what Freud defined as the "primal-scene phantasy" ("Paths" 459), a situation in which a child or childlike subject position stands as voyeur to the act of parental intercourse, itself a symbol to the viewer of the sexual power of the parents and the viewer's own desire to witness his or her own conception.

When Lacan identifies the first purloining of the letter in the queen's *boudoir* as something like a primal scene (195), he is situating his own reading of the power of language to circulate and mutate (like the letter) within traditional oedipal Freudian theory. Such a reading makes Minister D—— the child in a nursery drama, caught in a displaced and elided power struggle between two powerful parental figures (the "king" and "queen"). That Minister D—— chooses to threaten to expose the sexually compromised queen recalls Hamlet, or, as Freud would observe, the male child's rage and jealousy that he is forced to share his mother with another, and more powerful, male.

Symbolism and the Moments of Desire in a Text

Clearly, by this point in our discussion students see that the purloined letter is the central symbol in the story, but they also see that there is no easy equation in what that letter signifies, for its meaning has shifted throughout the course of the story. In Dupin's recovery of the letter, we begin to see how complex and complicated that letter really is. When Dupin enters the sitting room of Minister D——, he quickly scans the surroundings and realizes that his opponent would have counted on the police to ferret out every secret nook and cranny of his rooms, and so he has outwitted them by hiding the letter in plain sight. The letter is now hanging on a pasteboard rack on the mantelpiece, "soiled and crumpled. . . . nearly torn in two, across the middle" (695). A more symbolic description of the sexually compromised mother could hardly be imagined, but the author actually goes further in his defacement of the female body: it now appears "entirely worthless, had been altered, . . . [with] a large black seal, bearing the D—— cipher very conspicuously, and was addressed, in a diminutive female hand, to D——, the minister himself" (695). So whereas earlier in the story we were led to believe that the motive for stealing the letter was political, now it appears clearly oedipal. The letter has been seized by the son so that he can, through his own fantasy work and calligraphic flourishes, become the queen's lover himself. He has even gone so far as to imitate her handwriting and conduct an imaginary affair, with himself playing both parts (recall Narcissus). This scene is, I advise the students, the first scene of displaced and substituted desire, with the body of the letter serving as a displacement for the queen's body.

But a second and perhaps even more bizarre (or "odd" in the rhetoric of the story) moment of desire occurs. Dupin goes home, prepares a substitute letter, and stages an interruption and theft that mimics the minister's purloining of the original letter. Dupin's letter is not blank inside, because he claims that the minister at one time "did me an evil turn," and therefore Dupin is determined to leave him "a clue" as to who had outwitted him. To do this he copies the passage: "—Un dessein si funeste, / S'il n'est digne d'Atrée, est digne de Thyeste. . . . in Crébillon's 'Atrée' " (698), translated by Mabbott as "so baleful a plan, if unworthy of Atreus, is worthy of Thyestes" (3: 997n27). This intertextual passage, of course, stands as the ultimate moment of desire in the text, revealing that the letter has been passed between the men (the "brothers" Dupin and the minister) just as the bodies of women have been throughout history. In its allusion to the curse of the house of Atreus, the passage fingers the ancient wounds of murder, adultery, fratricide, incest, cannibalism, power, and revenge. Few allusions carry so much freight in such a compact space. Twin sons, Atreus and Thyeste, killed their half-brother Crysippos at the instigation of their mother, Hippodamie, and then began their manic struggle to gain the throne of Mycene. Thyeste seduced his brother's wife Aerope, and Atreus retaliated by cooking the sons of Thyeste and serving them, as well as their decapitated heads, to their father at a feast. The curse that Thyeste placed on his brother was soon fulfilled when the only one of Thyeste's surviving sons, Egisthe, the product of incest himself, killed Atreus and thereby restored his father Thyeste to the throne. By placing this passage with its horrific allusions to familial perversions in his own letter, Dupin reveals more about himself than he perhaps realizes. Full of self-righteous anger toward Minister D—— for the theft and dishonor of a "lady," he repeats in substituted form the same theft of the same letter, thereby placing himself in a chain of signification that allies him to his dark brother, the minister, in an act of displaced incestuous longing. Like the doubles in "William Wilson," Dupin and the minister shadow each other in their actions and pursuit of what Lacan calls "the oddest *odor di femina*" (48), "the immense female body stretch[ed] out across the Minister's office" (48), until the reader knows that these two characters are meant to be understood as the split-off manifestations of a single yet bifurcated psyche.

But beyond the pursuit and recovery of the letter as a substituted and displaced quest to regain the unsullied mother, the chain of signification in this story leads, according to Lacan, to an awareness of the inescapability of death: "What are you, figure of the die I turn over in your encounter (*tyche*) with my fortune? Nothing, if not that presence of death which makes of human life a reprieve obtained from morning to morning in the name of meanings whose sign is your crook" (51). What I finally try to enable students to understand is that in the act of reading about the circulation of a letter of desire written to a desirable woman, we are inserting ourselves into those moments of desire in the text when it speaks the author's, the characters', and finally our own desires. Like literary voyeurs, we place ourselves in the boudoir, between figures on a page who are ultimately acting out the fantasies that we read in them.

NOTE

[1] The bibliography of secondary sources on the Poe-Lacan connection or on Poe and the vexed question of psychoanalysis as an interpretive tool for reading his fiction is fairly extensive. I prepare a bibliography for students and encourage them to read for their research papers from the following: C. Bloom; Bonaparte; Feldstein, Fink, and Jaanus; Muller and Richardson; Parkin-Gounelas; Rosenheim; L. Williams.

[2] All citations to Lacan are from Mehlman's transation in *Purloined Poe*.

The Linguistic Turn, First-Person Experience, and the Terror of Relativism: "The Purloined Letter" and the Affective Limits of Ratiocination

A. Samuel Kimball

> Dupin: "[Y]et we forget ourselves continuously. . . ."
> —Poe, "The Purloined Letter"

As anyone will recognize who has tackled Jacques Lacan's "Seminar on 'The Purloined Letter,'" Jacques Derrida's extended critique of Lacan's exposition, and Barbara Johnson's ironic reading of Derrida and Lacan or who has made his or her way through the many other articles on Poe's story, the poststructuralist and postmodern criticism of Poe's most famous tale of ratiocination is forbidding, often vertiginously so.[1] This criticism is provocative and intellectually exciting, and yet its difficulties of language and style, its engagement with a vast philosophical and psychoanalytic literature, and its often extraordinary abstractness can also be terribly alienating.

In the pages that follow, I suggest a way of introducing students not to the particular arguments of such criticism but to one of the more general interpretive issues this criticism addresses by way of these arguments, an issue that I believe is at the heart of literature and literary study. I raise this issue to broach a central pedagogical challenge, which is how to negotiate the enormous distance between the intellectual sophistication and demandingness of much literary criticism, on the one hand, and, on the other, the limited practice many students have at recognizing and articulating what might be at stake for them, not abstractly but in an affectively charged way, in reading literature. In this regard I believe that "The Purloined Letter" offers a fascinating opportunity, for the intellectual gamesmanship of the story conceals a deeply problematic emotionality. If students can get a grip on the story's hidden affect, they will come a long way in preparing themselves for what many contemporary critics are trying to theorize about a paradoxical limit to certain experiences of oneself, a limit to experience that cannot itself be experienced.

The hermeneutical issue I focus on, then, concerns a blind spot within "first-person" access to oneself, to one's own mind, that does not exist in "second-" or "third-person" access to someone else's mind. The insight, deceptively easy to state, is that self-consciousness is problematic in ways that are exceedingly difficult to experience, let alone admit. There is something about the privileged sense of being present to oneself, of knowing what one knows, of being able to say "I" that blocks apprehension of how rational knowledge is embedded in nonrational—specifically affective, desire-based—mental processes of which one does not have an immediate, first-person awareness. And yet, unless and until one begins to apprehend not what is untrustworthy about *other* people's consciousness of themselves but what is questionable about self-consciousness, one will miss a signal value of the literary theories that examine what it means to think about one's being in the world and to integrate such self-reflection into individual emotional life.

To bridge the gap between the headiness of the professional discourse (for example, psychoanalytic, deconstructive, new historical) on the meaning of Poe's story and the affective energy and forces that are involved in this meaning, I briefly explain below what is meant by the linguistic turn, an intellectual development that calls into question the self-certainty associated with first-person experience, and then outline the paradoxical blindness that inheres in this characteristic experience, by which it is impossible for an individual to know he or she is wrong at the moment of knowing that he or she is right. I then turn to "The Purloined Letter" to show how it dramatizes, by hiding in the open, the potentially destructive emotional consequences of seeking to capitalize on another's self-blindness while refusing to admit or while defending against one's own. I conclude by identifying the general existential—that is, both personal and social or political—challenge that this line of reflection might help clarify for students.

In teaching the following material, I am interested in the pedagogical challenge, for students and teachers alike, in recognizing the extent to which self-interests, especially unavowed emotional investments, might drive one's intellectual positions and the interpretations that derive from them. Aristotle understood these investments as the focus of tragic anagnorisis, wherein the emotional force of tragedy emerges in the frightful and yet compassion-evoking process by which an audience comes to a significant new awareness, one that takes audience members to the limit of their knowledge *and* their emotional resources. Here, tragedy models a kind of learning that can transpire only when one confronts the impertinence of what one knows or thinks one knows and the irrelevance if not danger of feeling grounded, at home, self-confident, or otherwise emotionally well adapted. In endeavoring to produce this confrontation, I ask my students to try to specify what is at stake for them in believing what they believe and what they fear would happen to their vision of life if they were to discover that their intellectual positions were ill founded.

To make this demand of students is emotionally tricky, since it requires that students feel secure enough to enter into the potentially frightening process of self-questioning by which they put that very sense of security at risk. How one gets students to work through this paradox is part of what makes teaching an art.

The Linguistic Turn and the Phenomenological Limits of First-Person Experience

Contemporary literary scholars write in the wake of the so-called linguistic turn, which refers to the recognition that human thought and perception provide not

immediate, direct, intuitive access to the world but indirect, linguistically mediated access.[2] The linguistic turn does not stipulate that there is no objective reality; rather, it indicates that every attempt to define reality necessarily occurs in
cultural contexts that depend on systems of signs—on language, discourses of all
sorts, communicative conventions, different forms of symbolic representation,
countless strategies of persuasion, historically conditioned categories of thought,
and so on. Not surprisingly, the linguistic turn emphasizes that human beings do
not, indeed cannot, perceive themselves and others independently of the many
ways they are "inscribed" or "situated" within an existential horizon, which is
constituted by many cultural formations—structures, institutions, historical processes, economic conditions, geopolitical developments, and so on—and which
exerts a consciousness-shaping influence of which human beings are often or
mostly unconscious. The linguistic turn says that people do not simply respond
to what is "out there" but encounter what is "given" to them in the discursive
practices into which they are born and acculturated. For this reason the linguistic turn cautions that there is no metalevel or "transcendental" position from
which human beings can survey the world and their place in it.

The belief that one occupies such a position of mastery constitutes one kind
of first-person illusion.[3] The transition figure between medieval and modern
philosophy René Descartes sought to overcome this illusion by determining
that something about an individual's own mental states puts him or her beyond
doubt. He concluded that an individual might be deluded in any number of
ways but could not be deluded into thinking he or she exists if he or she does
not. Therefore, if the individual thinks, then this person must exist: *Cogito ergo
sum* ("I think, therefore I am"). For this reason Descartes assigns to first-person
knowledge an immunity to error—an apodictic certitude—and hence a privileged status.

Many twentieth-century thinkers—from Wittgenstein to Lacan to Derrida—
have analyzed the difficulties with Descartes's efforts to find in self-consciousness
a foundation for knowledge. Nevertheless, Descartes's "move" is readily understandable from the way people experience their own minds.

The temptation to assign a special significance to first-person knowledge is a
consequence of the way human beings experience themselves. Any person, any
I, seems able to inspect his or her own mind in a way that is denied to others.
Each person's mind appears to be transparent to itself but not to someone else's
mind. I know what I am thinking by virtue of my reflection on my act of thinking, by virtue of turning my attention on myself. My introspection of myself,
however, will not disclose to me what someone else is thinking, only what I
think they might be thinking. My self-introspection will make explicit only that
I am engaged in the process of trying to infer the other person's mental states;
it will not present me with this person's mental states. Thus, while my thoughts
present themselves to me seemingly without the mediation of signs, I do not
have such a direct intuition of another person's thoughts. To know what someone else is thinking, I must rely on the signs of this person's consciousness (his

or her words as well as his or her nonverbal cues, such as facial expressions and bodily gestures), by which this person signifies what he or she is thinking. In sum, I cannot enter into the other's self-consciousness in the same way that it appears I can and do enter into my own.

This gap between my first-person experience of myself and my second- or third-person experience of another constitutes an irreducible *epistemological asymmetry*, or barrier, between any I and any you (any other), and it raises a profound cognitive challenge. The challenge arises because human beings tend to experience their self-consciousness narcissistically—that is, as superior to the consciousness someone else has of them. The test of this narcissism is simple: Whose consciousness of yourself do you value more, the other's or your own? On this count one criterion of emotional development is whether one has the equanimity necessary to hear someone's different view of oneself, especially if it is highly critical.

Such suspension of self-belief is difficult in part because it involves accepting something that is counterintuitive about the sense of certainty that accompanies the experience of knowing, and especially of knowing that one knows, something. If I think I know something, I cannot at the same time also know that I am wrong, if I am. I might later come to know that what I thought I knew has turned out not to be so, but it is self-evident that I cannot both think I know something and know that I am wrong. However, others might know that I am mistaken in thinking that I am right.[4]

The situation of knowing or not knowing quickly gets very complicated, of course, because those who are convinced they know that I do not know that I am wrong might themselves be caught up in the same conundrum, the same situation of experiencing themselves to be certain of what they know. The point is that if one is mistaken about what one thinks one knows, the experience of having direct access to one's own mind can be catastrophic. Indeed, the experience of thinking one knows the truth is particularly dangerous when it excites one to protect oneself against what one knows or thinks one knows are the false beliefs of others.

In my experience students are both troubled and fascinated by and thus eager to explore the ramifications of the idea that first-person experience might be a false guide to reality. For advanced students, the concept in question provides an accessible entry point into Lacan's critique of ego psychology. For example, in Lacanian terms, the first-person illusion constitutes an imaginary escape from the symbolic order, an escape that deludes one into believing that the I is the source of itself, its being in the world, and its values. Students without training in literary theory can readily understand the power of the first-person illusion by considering the acts of violence that some people justify in terms of their first-person declarations of faith: I believe in my God, who has called me to protect myself from your evil, and to do so by engaging in behavior you call violent or terrorist but I call justice. Students understand the danger of such a first-person insistence coming from someone else; they are often deeply disturbed when they begin to reflect on how much they themselves rely on a first-person perspective to ground their beliefs, attitudes, and actions. In any event, they grasp the problem of how warring parties alike appeal to first-person experience to justify the most violent of actions each takes against the other. The pedagogical issue is straightforward and yet intractable: the sense of certainty that attaches to first-person experience is not a solution to the deepest existential problems but a response that worsens them.

I have found students to be eager to try to explain their understanding of the problems associated with first-person experience and to put into words the emotional urgency of these problems. They can be very alert to how discourse—especially public and quasi-public discourse—can be a site of conflicting first-person claims. In my experience students often, at least initially, want to take up positions with regard to such claims. However, they are also capable of identifying their emotional investments in whatever position they feel impelled to take and then of beginning to analyze how their self-interest might be affecting their first-person perceptions, attitudes, and actions with respect to the issue in question.

To identify the possible self-interest behind or within someone's first-person point of view immediately raises the specter that knowledge is perspectival and therefore that values are relative. Students tend to take the value of the concept of value for granted. For this reason one of the most challenging questions to ask is not, what do you value? or why do you value it? but what is the value of some particular value that you hold? Responses to this question invariably reveal that the value of the particular value (of love, for example, or faith, or first-person experience) is its false promise of a solution to the problem of relativism. The solution is false because affirming in the first person one's adherence to a set of values invariably leads to conflict when confronted with someone who affirms, also in the first person, their adherence to an incompatible value.

On this matter much literary criticism, especially of a poststructuralist and postmodernist cast, can be understood as a study of the strategies by which literary texts address the problems that arise, and especially the violence and destruction that is unleashed, when human beings fall victim to the illusion that their first-person knowledge provides a secure foundation and frame of reference for the value of their presence, their being, in the world. It is no accident that this criticism would be fascinated by "The Purloined Letter," for the story is a case study not only in the erroneousness of the first-person perspective but in the relativism, cynically triumphant self-interest, and primitive desire for revenge that this perspective excites. The story is an object lesson concerning the self-interest and emotionality that power the first-person discourse of a character, in this case Dupin, and that give this discourse the misleading appearance of a rationality able to overcome the nefariousness of this character's enemy.

Desire, Self-Interest, Power: The Emotional
Context of Cognition in "The Purloined Letter"

The symbolic action of Poe's story is organized around situations of knowing and not knowing—above all around knowing that others do not know that they do not know something that they think they do. At the political center of the story is a "personage of most exalted station," presumably the king, who does not know that his wife, the story's other "illustrious personage," has received a compromising letter, perhaps a missive from a lover ("Purloined Letter" 682). When Minister D—— discovers that the king is unaware that the woman in question has a secret, he steals the letter from under her nose so he can thereafter blackmail her with impunity. The woman knows she is vulnerable and is desperate to keep her secret. Her husband, however, is unaware that his political authority is in jeopardy and is thus vulnerable to the kind of (insurgent) surprise attack that could bring down his reign.

The narrative trajectory of the story involves a complex doubling and reversal of the queen's defenselessness. Dupin steals the letter from Minister D—— when this man's back is turned and substitutes for it a "facsimile." Dupin thus puts the minister in the position not of the queen but of the king—that is, of the person who thinks he has all the power but in fact does not know (and perforce does not know that he does not know) that he does not. The result for the minister is that he is in a politically precarious position, of which he is unaware:

> For eighteen months the Minister has had [the queen] in his power. She now has him in hers; since, being unaware that the letter is not in his possession, he will proceed with his exactions as if it was. Thus will he inevitably commit himself, at once, to his political destruction.   (697)

Knowledge in this story does not provide access to truth but to power—specifically, to a power that enables one to discharge the potential aggressivity, the violence, the destructiveness, even the terrorism of one's desire. The value of knowledge is not in the knowledge as knowledge but in this knowledge as power (here to terrorize). In relation to a post–9/11 world, *terror* is not too strong a word, for Dupin is willing to risk a riot to regain the letter and reduce the minister to a position of not knowing, a position that will lead to his downfall. Thus, at the end of the story, Dupin hires an associate to fire a pistol in the crowded street below the minister's window. Those who hear the report do not know that the gun is not loaded. Frightened, they erupt into the "fearful screams" and "shoutings" of a mob (697).

Why does Dupin emphasize the terrified reaction of the mob? What does he want the minister to see when this man looks out the window to determine what is causing the noise? What does he want the minister to remember about how Dupin has tricked him? Such questions, of course, bring to the fore

Dupin's undeclared motivation, the passion that drives him: to get even. Thus, Dupin wants to evoke the most appalling spectacle of violence as a way of communicating to the minister—a *"monstrum horrendum,* an unprincipled man of genius," who once "did me an evil turn," Dupin says—the meaning of the downfall that will descend on him (697). Thus, too, Dupin tips his hand about the savagery of his desire when he explains how he has copied into the facsimile letter the words from a French tragedy that retells the story of how Atreus takes revenge against his brother Thyestes by killing his children and serving them to their father. Finally, Dupin does and does not want to admit the profoundly primitive—indeed, Darwinian—urge to destroy that underwrites his behavior.

From the beginning of the story to the end, the value of knowing is not in the access to the truth that knowledge provides but in the way it enables the different characters to act out their desire, self-interest, and power, especially the power to take revenge and to exult in one's triumph over another, defeat of another, ability to make another pay, and success at destroying another's life.

Once students know how to frame the problem of the limits of first-person self-reporting, they have a means and a reason to identify the ways, subtle and not so subtle, in which literary characters conceal their self-interest from others as well as from themselves. Part of what makes Dupin fascinating is that he both hides and reveals his cynicism about knowledge as a vehicle of power. He does so, for example, when he recalls the childhood game of "even and odd" and the strategy by which a boy, who has a highly developed ability to use his "reasoner's intellect" to "identif[y]" with the intellect "of his opponent," is thereby able to win whatever is at stake in the game—marbles in the case at hand (689). The stakes for Dupin in his version of the game are much greater— nothing less than the political head of his nemesis. Students are quick to point out that those stakes underscore the uses to which Dupin puts his intellect. In explaining the strategy of "thorough identification" by which he will defeat the minister, Dupin describes the process of discovering what others do not know they do not know as a strategy for gaining a material advantage over them. Dupin thereby elucidates how second- and third-person points of view expose the false sense of security, the false sense of mastery, the false sense of self-presence and self-possession that accompany the first-person point of view. The one who thinks he or she knows but does not is the one who is the most helpless, the most vulnerable to unimagined threats. Not surprisingly, Dupin declares that second- and third-person knowledge of the limits of first-person knowledge constitute the cynical wisdom of "Rochefoucault," "La Bougive," "Machiavelli," and "Campanella," who evidently believed that human behavior is ultimately if not immediately self-serving (690). Invoking their names, Dupin identifies the nihilistic relativism that underwrites his attitude toward (the knowledge of) self and other.

Dupin's relativism is evident in his effort to "make a killing" on the market by waiting until the reward for the letter doubles.[5] Only then does he turn the letter over to the police, who for their part return the letter for a huge reward to the queen, who presumably either destroys the letter or keeps it away from the person in whom the very law of the land is vested—the ignorant king. In this way the letter, with its unknown contents, comes to symbolize the affective context of knowing, the way knowledge arises from desire for power over the other by way of the other's self-ignorance at the very moment the other harbors the illusion of self-mastery.

The story translates its relativistic and nihilistic view of knowing in one of its most conspicuous stylistic features—its use of negation. In an article on negation in "The Purloined Letter," John Muller points out that 118 of the story's 332 sentences (36%) contain various kinds of negation. The first word of the story is the Latin *nil* ("nothing") in the epigraph from Seneca; the penultimate line of the story, the citation from Crébillon, turns on a syntax of negation. The very scene of narration is marked by negation since Dupin and the narrator are in an apartment at "*No*. 33, Rue Du*not*" (emphasis mine). The engine of the plot is the action of negating the king's authority and power on the one hand and the action of taking revenge against the minister on the other. The letter itself undergoes various negations in the way it is turned upside down and then inside out and is later replaced with a copy on which is written a statement that alludes to the negation of the future through the destruction of the children of one's enemy.

Not only in "The Purloined Letter" but also in all his works Poe relies on an astonishing range of techniques of negation. These techniques include the use of privatives (*in-*, *un-*, and *-less*), negative adverbs, adjectives, conjunctions, and prepositions (for example, *no, nor, not, beyond*) that negate by denying an otherwise affirmative predication; negative intensifiers; foreboding descriptions; alliterations that reinforce a sense of disaster and deathliness; sequences with a falling rhythm; images of downward movement; contaminations of characters by the physical environment; contaminations of a place by the person in it; typographic interruptions; the passive voice in conjunction with suggestions of helplessness and vulnerability; and numerous means (repetitions, personifications, prosopopoeia) of evoking not only a nonrational world but a chaotic, entropic, self-dissipating, or self-destructive world that is beyond empirical measure, beyond intellection, beyond ratiocination. All these techniques point to the problematic nature of the sacred in Poe's work, to how his characters and narrators invariably negate, deny, nullify, or disaffirm the sacred in the very act of trying to gain access to it.

Once students understand how technical aspects of grammar, such as Poe's technique of negation, reflect the uncertain location and character of the sacred in Poe, they are in a strong position to explore the relation between a text's style and the moral, theological, and other value-laden implications of its storyline. In my experience students are not only open to examining but enthusiastic about exploring the conflicts, aggression, and destruction that follow from attempting to ground one's values in any belief that depends on first-person attestation.

The Existential Challenge

Over and over, the negativity of "The Purloined Letter" story foregrounds the (potential) destructiveness of the desire that motivates the impulse to know. The result is an extraordinarily bleak vision of ratiocination, Dupin's triumph notwithstanding. Indeed, the story's depiction of Dupin's perspicuity is all the bleaker for the glibness with which he pretends that his revenge is but a "good natured" move in a boyhood game of "even and odd" and not a deadly serious game of political vengeance. The story's linkage of Dupin's intellectual lucidity to his astonishingly violent fantasy of an infanticidal and cannibalistic revenge, for example, gives the lie to the cool detachment with which Dupin recounts the manner in which he deceived Minister D——. In the end, then, the story dramatizes the destructiveness that is unleashed when the likes of a Dupin gives himself over to rather than examines critically the affective basis of his hyperintellection.

The emotional virulence that powers the story raises the difficult question of how to affirm one's own being in the world and the being of the other in view of the fact that first-person knowledge is inherently self-limiting. This question has new force and urgency in the age of political terrorism, especially when anonymous others justify their violence in the name of a first-person experience—of faith, for example, in some transcendental agency or principle—that they claim calls them to their destructiveness. Such an experience of knowing, or claiming to know, eliminates one's accountability to others; it makes one accountable only to what one knows or thinks one knows.

Students are simultaneously afraid of being held accountable and concerned with living responsibly. Why the fear? Because they intuit that their first-person sense of themselves is unreliable even as it offers an immediate narcissistic satisfaction, a satisfaction catered to by the massive forces of the modern market. For this reason, then, students tend to be, at least in my experience, first shocked and then mobilized into excited self-scrutiny when confronted with the kind of questions that are at the heart of poststructuralist and postmodern criticism. These are the questions that demystify the forms of false belief that arise from a blind spot within the very experience of knowing oneself. These are the questions that bring students to the point of being able to articulate not what they believe and not why they believe whatever they might believe but what is emotionally, psychologically, and spiritually at stake for them in so believing, and thus what they would have to give up emotionally, psychologically, and spiritually if their beliefs turned out to be mistaken. In other words, these are the kinds of questions that lead students to internalize the desire to ask critical questions. And that is a particularly rich pedagogical payoff for confronting the costs, the damages, in a word the violence—one of the more heinous forms of which "The Purloined Letter" hides in the open—of actually believing one's first-person illusions.

NOTES

[1] In *The Purloined Poe*, Muller and Richardson reprint the articles by Lacan, Derrida, and Johnson along with articles on "The Purloined Letter" by nine others. Among the many additional commentaries pertinent to the present discussion are those by Bretzius; Charney; Hull; Irwin, *Mystery;* Kimball; Mehlman; Pease ("Marginal Politics"); Porter; Richard, "Destin"; Riddell; and Woodward.

[2] Richard Rorty's 1967 work, *The Linguistic Turn*, provides an excellent introduction to the philosophical consequences of this development in the history of ideas. A recent collection of essays edited by Elizabeth Clark, *History, Theory, Text*, provides valuable perspectives on the implications of the linguistic turn for the so-called new historicisim.

[3] This discussion of the first-person illusion is adapted from a similar exposition in my analysis of the infanticidal implications in Dupin's desire for revenge against Minister D——. See also the discussion of "epistemological asymmetry" in Donovan, Kimball, and Smith.

[4] In a notorious Department of Defense briefing, Secretary of Defense Donald Rumsfeld acknowledged just this problem: "as we know, there are known knowns; there are things we know we know. We also know there are known unknowns; that is to say, we know there are some things we do not know. But there are also unknown unknowns, the ones we don't know we don't know" (United States). Ralph Waldo Emerson restates the problem of first-person point of view in terms of his famous metaphor of the eye: "The eye is the first circle; the horizon which it forms is the second. . . . Our life is an apprenticeship to the truth that around every circle another can be drawn . . ." ("Circles" 225). In their Johari Window, Joseph Luft and Harry Ingham provide a well-known schematization of the general epistemological asymmetry between self and other. Thus, one might know about oneself what others know; one might know what others do not; and one might be ignorant of or blind to what others know. The most interesting situation arises when both self and others alike do not know that they do not know something, a circumstance of unknowing that is often the effect of ideology. Much contemporary literary theory is devoted to analyzing how people unknowingly internalize the ideological conditions of self-consciousness.

[5] Students who work while attending college are particularly attuned to the necessity of weighing benefits against costs in the allocation of their scarcest resource—time. For this reason their first-person experience can be especially valuable in discussions of the economic motifs in works of literature, including "The Purloined Letter."

The "Visionary" Project:
Poe and the Textual Condition

Derek Furr

Elusiveness is an essential trope of Poe's early short story "The Visionary," as it is in much of Poe's work.[1] The elusive qualities of the unnamed "ill-fated and mysterious man" (200) who is (ostensibly) the narrative's subject are replicated in the narrator's arabesque discourse, as well as in the story's veiled allusions and changing epigraphs. Furthermore, when we take the lead of these allusions and move outside the story proper, what constitutes the text of "The Visionary" and of "To One in Paradise," the poem embedded in it, proves as difficult to pinpoint as the narrator's perspective on his bizarre tale. The meanings of story and poem, that is to say, are carried forward and complicated by the histories of the texts and the play of intertexts. Readers of "The Visionary" and, I would argue, of Poe in general are confronted by what Jerome McGann has called "the textual condition." As Poe's first publication in a national magazine, "The Visionary" forecasts patterns of textual change that will hold true in much of the writer's later, more familiar, work. For that reason, it is worth careful analysis, particularly in classes that seek to represent Poe's development as a writer. So in my classes on Poe, students and I engage in bibliographic and historical research on "The Visionary" as an entry point into considerations of the complex nature of textuality in much of Poe's writing, including commonly taught texts such as "The Raven" and "The Fall of the House of Usher."

The changeable nature of Poe's stories and poems calls for teaching that takes into account issues raised by advanced textual study of the kind implicit in McGann's concept of the textual condition. McGann argues that all literary texts change and accrue meaning over time, and not simply because authors make revisions to the lexical elements. How texts are read (their "reception histories"), how they converse with other texts (what Julia Kristeva called their intertextuality), and how they are published (the material conditions of format, for example) are integral to a text's meanings. "To study texts and textualities, then," McGann writes, "we have to study these complex (and open-ended) histories of textual change and variance" (*Textual Condition* 9). Bibliography, histories of the book, and histories of reading have proved increasingly important as technological advances make various editions of texts easily accessible and arcane bibliographic coding obsolete. As the textual scholar Kathryn Sutherland has written, "Textuality . . . requires that we consider the unfixity of text, the promiscuity as opposed to integrity of its identity in an age when text has a diverse, non-book existence" (Introduction 5). Poe's work requires the same considerations. Thomas Ollive Mabbott's important critical edition of Poe makes it apparent that "change" or "unfixity" is essential to Poe's writings. Not only did much of Poe's work undergo frequent revision, but many of the stories and poems also changed significantly with each publication. In addition, the publication venues themselves varied considerably, from lady's magazines to story collections.

My classes on Poe involve students in the research and construction of an edition of a Poe text, most recently "The Visionary"—initially as paper and imagined prototype, then as a hypermedia archive. The "Visionary" project began midway through a course on Romanticism and historicism, in which we considered historicist approaches to reading and teaching British and American Romantic texts. Drawing on principles from Grant Wiggins and Jay McTighe's *Understanding by Design*, the project was grounded in two essential questions: what is the vision of "The Visionary"? And, whose vision is it? Before we began the research, everyone read the story in its original version, and, through a series of writing and thinking activities, we derived preliminary answers to the essential questions.[2] The initial writing prompt focused attention on the peculiar tone of the first three paragraphs of the story: why does the narrator dwell on the name of the character whose name he will conceal?

From the conversation that followed, we moved into the apartment of the mysterious stranger, "an apartment whose unparalleled splendor burst through the opening door with an actual glare, making [the narrator] blind and dizzy with luxuriousness" (204). We reread this section of the story, noting the stranger's pyrotechnic display of material wealth and erudition and the narrator's comments on "the manner of the true gentleman" as distinguished from "the vulgar" (207). We then wrote to a second set of prompts, this time considering the poem: how do sighs function in this lyric? And, why does the narrator want us to question that the poem was written by the stranger? This second question brought up the issue of indeterminacy. On one level, the narrator is drawing our attention to the instability of text and authorship; on another, these lines are part of an intertextual game that Poe is playing, which research would bring forward.

After considering the outcome of the story, we returned to the beginning for a final writing exercise designed to open up an avenue of our research: Poe later changed the title of this story to "The Assignation." How does the change frame the story differently? While "assignation" most clearly refers to the tryst between the stranger and the marchesa, the word's roots in *assign* and the variety of meanings that derive from that are significant in this story about the ambiguities of identity, attribution, and influence.

Having noted one of Poe's many alterations, students next formed research groups that looked into textual history, reception history, and the story's allusions and intertexts. Overlap in the concerns of the three groups was inevitable and desirable; for these projects, the groups are a tidy organizational structure laid across the necessarily untidy scene of bibliographic and historical research. Our goal, I pointed out, would be to lay the groundwork for a hypertext of "The Visionary"—a hypertext that would be useful to students of Poe and that would help us answer our essential questions about the story. I provided each group with the following guidelines, understanding that unanticipated questions or directions may arise from the work:

> Reception-history group: Construct a focused reception history of Poe, with an emphasis on "The Visionary" and its poem, using I. M. Walker's *Poe: The Critical Heritage* and other sources. Include an account of nineteenth-century Poe reception and recent work on the story itself. You may choose how to focus your account of the nineteenth-century reception.
>
> Textual history group: Using Mabbott and other sources, construct a textual history of "The Visionary" and the poem embedded in it, "To One in Paradise." While you will not have time to be exhaustive in your research, your textual history should review the nineteenth-century contexts of the story or poem's publication, significant variants in the text(s) over time, and important paratextual elements.
>
> Intertext group: Research Poe's biography and letters, as well as Poe criticism, to trace important allusions in the texts and to locate significant intertexts.

I provided these guidelines as well as a list of resources that would be helpful to the groups and required students to read essays on hypertext and literary study (specifically, articles from the Sutherland text and chapters from McGann's *Radiant Textuality*). Groups were given several weeks to carry out the research. During that time, we devoted a small portion of our class meetings to discussion of the status of the research, and I required each group to meet with me at least once in a more formal manner outside class.

Presentations of the research and preliminary designs for the archive were the agenda for the penultimate meeting of the historicism and Romanticism course. Students in the textual-history group led a review of the variants of "The Visionary." Seven variants were published during Poe's lifetime. The first appeared in the *Lady's Book*, January 1834, and underwent substantial revisions before being published again in *Southern Literary Messenger* for July 1835. In his 1842 *Phantasy-Pieces*, Poe renamed the story "The Assignation," the title it has been known by ever since. Changes in these variants repay close scrutiny—particularly the ways that Poe changed the epigraphs and initial paragraphs between 1834 and 1835—as does the far more complicated textual history of "To One in Paradise." The poem was published in several different versions over nearly two decades. Tracing the changes in the poem provides insight not only into Poe's craftsmanship but also into his efforts to make the poem stand independent of the story and its Byronic main character, who claims to have composed it.

The textual-history group offered this overview and an interesting analysis of the story's epigraphs and poem. In the *Lady's Book* version, the epigraphs are drawn from Johann Wolfgang von Goethe's "Das Veilchen" and Friedrich

Schiller's "Wallenstein"; later versions quote from Henry King's "Exequy." As the students pointed out, the first epigraphs turn attention to the speaker himself, whereas the King gestures toward an assignation. We talked about what "Goethe" and "Schiller" signified in the periodical writings of the time, given the many epigraphs from these two German Romantics we had encountered in other poems and stories from the 1820s and 1830s. The textual-history group also brought collations of three versions of the stranger's poem: the untitled *Lady's Book* version, "To Ianthe in Heaven" from the July 1839 *Burton's Gentleman's Magazine*, and the 1849 "To One in Paradise." Of the many changes in the language and prosody of the poem, the group found most telling the differences in line 15—from "Ambition—all—is o'er" to "The light of Life is o'er" (Mabbot). As in the epigraphs, the change shifts attention from the Byronic stranger to his idealized love.

Poe's use of "Ianthe"—Byron's name for Charlotte Harley in the dedication of *Childe Harold's Pilgrimage*—provided a segue from our discussion of text to intertext and reception history. Students in those two groups found significant overlap in their research because of the importance of Byron, both to Poe and to Poe's readers. As the reception group noted, critics have generally agreed that on many levels, "The Visionary" dramatizes Poe's vexed relation with his literary father, Byron. Mabbott considered it "obvious" that the protagonist is modeled on Byron, and his notes to the story point out parallels between the protagonist's life and loves and those of Byron, as set forth in Thomas Moore's *Letters and Journals of Lord Byron* (Mabbott 2: 148–49). Dennis Pahl's "Recovering Byron" argues that Byron stands as "Poe's other, an other from which Poe's 'identity' cannot extricate itself," but that in the story, Poe "ironizes . . . the romantic quest for origins" and thus the very critical act that would name him or his story "Byronic" (Pahl 224–25). Susan Amper has tied the story more directly to Moore's *Life*. While the extent to which "The Visionary" is about Byron or about Poe's relation to him is debatable, Byron haunts the tale, and his life and works are some of its principal intertexts.

To this contemporary reception of Byron and Poe, the intertext group added extensive research on Poe's use of Moore's Byron biography. The scene in the stranger's splendid apartment draws directly on Moore's *Letters and Journals of Lord Byron*, a text that Poe knew well. In the stranger's manic behavior and pretentiousness, Poe echoes Moore's tongue-in-cheek presentation of Byron, a fact pointed out by Richard P. Benton in "Is Poe's 'The Assignation' a Hoax?" Byron's affair with Contessa Guiccioli, as reported by Moore, factors into the stranger and the marchesa's illicit relationship, and Byron's poetry to his first love, Mary Chaworth, is an intertextual field for "To One in Paradise." In the first edition of his Byron biography, Moore mistakenly attributed a poem to Byron that the poet had written in a book belonging to Chaworth; in the second edition, Moore admits his error, though the lyric can certainly be called Byronic.[3] As the intertext group noted, Poe may have had these editorial blunders in mind, for he has his narrator question whether the stranger actually composed the poem "written in a hand so very different from the peculiar character of my acquaintance, that I had some difficulty in recognizing it as his own" (208).

The most provocative contributions from the reception-history group were handlists of excerpts from a range of nineteenth-century Poe commentary coupled with Poe's own troubled reflections on his ambitions and his work as a magazinist. The lists were compiled from Poe's letters and I. M. Walker's useful text in the Critical Heritage series. The lists generated discussion about literature as commodity and about the received assumptions about Poe we bring to our readings of (formerly) unfamiliar texts like "The Visionary."

Collating all this information in a meaningful and useful way was the next step in the project and became the master's thesis work of one student, Kathy Dudley. At the time of this writing, a hypertext archive based on the students' research is under revision. The particular technical issues that have arisen as Dudley and I have worked on the archive have important theoretical implications for literary scholars, and, while a detailed account of the issues is outside the scope of the essay, sample questions include the following:

What shall we include in the archive, what shall we exclude, and how are our inclusions/exclusions interpretative?

Can we adequately re-present the "materiality" of Poe's story in its nineteenth-century versions—elements such as the magazine covers and book bindings? The ornate cover of the January 1834 *Lady's Book: A Monthly Magazine of Belles-Lettres and Arts*, for example, promises "Literary Compositions Embellished with several Hundred different Engravings," capitalizing thereby on the popular giftbook trade; the magazine also includes "beautiful illustrations of the prevailing Fashions" and music for pianoforte. Surely reading "The Visionary" in such a context would be suggestive.

How much should we gloss or interpret the texts? How "present," if at all, should our glosses be in the primary texts?

Who is the intended audience for this archive: public school students, college students, or advanced scholars?

What virtue might there be in constructing the archive in SGML, rather than using commercial software? We want the hypertext to be open to revision, allowing future classes to extend it or rework it based on their own research findings and interpretations.

Because my students are future English teachers in middle and high schools, the desire to make the archive accessible to adolescents and useful to public school teachers was strong. Having access to some of the materials that college literature teachers rely on—scholarly editions of Poe's works, period magazines, literary criticism—and support for using the materials (hence our question about glosses) could make classroom research projects like our "Visionary" project realizable in the middle school or high school classroom. More to the point, such projects involve secondary school teachers and their students in authentic questions of textuality, literary history, and interpretation that can culminate in the production of an edition—even if a paper edition—that has utility for future classes.

As I have suggested, the interpretive issues presented by "The Visionary" recur throughout Poe's oeuvre—not only in the lesser-known texts but also in poems and stories that are commonly taught in secondary and college classrooms. Consider, for example, the first version of "The Raven" from *American Review: A Whig Journal of Politics, Literature, Art and Science* for February 1845. It is prefaced by editorial commentary—probably cowritten by Poe—in which the poem's "ludicrous touches" are defended and its "unique rhyming" is praised. The second version, from the *Evening Mirror*, of the poem is also preceded by editorial commentary, which describes it as the "single most effective example of 'fugitive poetry' ever published in this country"[4] How do these prefaces— left out of most anthologized versions of "The Raven" or, at best, relegated to the endnotes—frame an understanding of the poem? Moreover, the first version was published pseudonymously, "by — Quarles." What might students of Poe learn by seriously considering this allusion to the seventheenth-century metaphysical poet Geoffrey Quarles and reading his *Emblems* as intertexts with "The Raven"? Attention to details of textual history is also rewarded in studying "The Fall of the House of Usher." This famous story contains the poem "The Haunted Palace." Like "The Visionary," both story and poem went through several significant changes, though "The Haunted Palace" was composed and published before it came to be a part of "The Fall of the House of Usher." What can we learn about both texts by researching the poem's complex life outside the story? When we bring back into our line of vision the histories of well-known texts like "Usher" and "Raven," the familiar quickly becomes unfamiliar, inviting new interpretations.

Poe's "The Visionary"—like most of the work that followed it—asks us to construct teaching environments in which the multivalenced nature of text is foregrounded. As collaborative researchers in the development of a hypertext, students not only interpret a tale's meaning but also recognize the textual and contextual contingencies of meaning construction. At the linguistic, semantic, and textual levels of his story and poem, Poe confronts these very contingencies.

NOTES

[1] In 1842, Poe gave the "The Visionary" a new name, "The Assignation," which is the title used in the edition cited in this volume. All citations to "The Visionary" can thus be found in the works-cited list under "The Assignation."

[2] Based on Mabbott's collations, three variants of the story—1834 *Lady's Book*, 1840 *Tales of Grotesque and Arabesque*, and 1850 *Collected Works*—are available on the Poe

Society Web site (www.eapoe.org/works/taless/assiga.htm). A digital reproduction of the original magazine pages can be found in the database *American Periodicals Series On-line, 1740–1900*.

[3] Mabbott glosses this in his notes to "To One in Paradise" and quotes the poem falsely attributed to Byron. Poe probably read the account in Murray's edition of Byron's works, which includes the second edition of Moore's *Life*.

[4] For variant texts of "The Raven," see *Edgar Allan Poe: "The Raven."*

Teaching Poe's Ironic Approach to German Learners of English: The Didactic Complexities of "The Cask of Amontillado"

Erik Redling

Edgar Allan Poe's fame in Germany rests not only on the well-known poem "The Raven" (1845) but also on his tales of the grotesque that established him as an important and influential writer in the United States and abroad. These stories derive their impact from a link between darkly Romantic themes and an ironic method of foreshadowing that causes fear and horror. This essay focuses on my attempts to teach this mixture of theme and method to German EFL (English as a foreign language) students. I illustrate specifically the challenges that arose from Poe's ironic method when I taught his tale "The Cask of Amontillado," both because of the students' background in German Romantic literature and because of the typical inclination of EFL students to interpret literally.

Preparing the Course

First of all, it appealed to me that Fortunato, the murdered jester in "The Cask of Amontillado," almost prototypically represents one of those distorted whimsical dark figures found in subterranean grottos during the fifteenth and sixteenth centuries that gave rise to the term *grotesque* (from Italian *grotteschi* ["grottoes"]). It was likely that my students would have read about such strange and capricious figures in stories by German Romantic writers, such as Karl Grosse, Ludwig Tieck, and E. T. A. Hoffmann. The themes of carnivalistic costume and drinking, the walk through the catacombs, the walling up, and the planned revenge would remind them of nineteenth-century tales. The story is also embellished by the idea of carnivalistic reversal in which the king becomes a fool and the fool becomes a king. One day, Fortunato is the King of Carnival; the next day, he is walled up in a grotto.

A colleague of mine who had taught Poe confirmed my expectations but warned me about paying too much attention to the Romantic similarities, since the students' main problem would be to discover Poe's ironic method of foreshadowing. They would recognize all the Romantic themes presented literally in the text but would also take the narrator's (that is, the killer's) pleasantries with which he beguiles Fortunato literally. I realized that the Romantic themes thus could become an impediment to understanding and that the real problem would be how to guide the students toward recognizing Montresor's gloating, which Montresor aims at his confidante, the reader, while flattering Fortunato. I asked myself how my students would understand, for instance, Montresor's greeting of Fortunato: "My dear Fortunato, you are luckily met" (848). Would they think of the greeting as being one of Montresor's attempts to befriend and

deceive Fortunato by topping his show of extreme joviality with a pun on Fortunato's name? Or would they, unaided, understand it as an aside to the reader,
which, as a sardonic irony, already foreshadows the murder? Would nonnative
readers who are grappling with the progressive acquisition of Poe's strangely
old-fashioned and Latinized vocabulary (e.g., "hearken," "pipe," "motley," "immolation," and "rheum") be able to uncover the destructive irony? Because if
they did not—if they were only concerned with language acquisition and were
reading the pleasantries only in terms of a deceptive friendliness—then the
murder itself would appear to them to be unmotivated and without a progressive emotional foreshadowing. At the end of the story, they would probably
question the story's point, since it would appear that the author does not give
Fortunato a chance to find out why he is going to be killed. And what purpose is
there in killing someone who is presented as drunk and stupid? Even when, toward the end of the story, he is sober and sees himself being walled up, Fortunato
calls the act "a very good joke indeed—an excellent jest" (854). My conclusion
was that EFL students would be baffled by a senseless murder and miss the experience of rising horror unless they were enabled to see through Montresor's
sinister gloating.[1]

The first EFL reference book that I consulted on teaching irony was Christine Nuttal's *Teaching Reading Skills in a Foreign Language*. It simply advises
against using irony with foreign students since it is "the most difficult of all uses
of language for the student to interpret; even though it is not very common in
nonliterary writing, advanced students should be helped to deal with it" (78).
But I needed much more teaching advice than a suggestion on how to cope
with ironically stated words or phrases because Montresor, the murderer, talks
on different levels and to different addressees simultaneously. On the one hand,
he desires to adapt to the Romantic level of the "Italian" braggart, Fortunato,
and to flatteringly describe him as the greatest connoisseur in order to lure him
to his own burial place. On the other hand, Montresor has to impart to the
reader his repugnance toward Fortunato's villainous stupidity, which forewarns
the reader of the upcoming murder. Thus, I needed to unravel the dual layers
of addressees and find a way to reveal this to the students.

For my purpose, Ralf Weskamp's suggestions on teaching literature turned
out to be useful for me. Weskamp favors two general approaches, which a literary critic will recognize as didactic adaptations of Hans-Georg Gadamer's and
Wolfgang Iser's literary theories: first, a hermeneutical-aesthetic approach that
aims at generally acceptable methods and interpretations; second, a construc-
tivist approach that ties literary interpretation to the subjective mental processes of EFL learners. Weskamp himself favors Lothar Bredella's aesthetic
approach (Weskamp 91), specifically his assertion that

> [a]esthetic reading directs our attention to the interaction between
> text and reader and encourages us to explore how the text affects us.
> This implies that aesthetic reading includes a reflective element and is

characterized by the dialectic between involvement and detachment. (Bredella 18)

Weskamp pairs these remarks on the importance of a reader's involvement and detachment with a list of typical "productive tasks" that have been used in didactic adaptations of the reader-response approach: in these tasks, students are encouraged to re-create the text, for instance, by turning a short prose narrative into a dialogue or into an interview with prominent characters. Finally, Weskamp mentions the "reception-aesthetic talk" (*Rezeptionsgespräch*) as a potential method that could guide the students to focus on their experiences after reading a literary text and to modify their views through a discussion with fellow students, during which a teacher would act as moderator (Weskamp 191). I felt greatly encouraged by these suggestions because they promote the students' own activities, emphasize personal experience, and allow for the intellectual development of an individual by measuring his or her thoughts against the perceptions of others.

The advantage of using Weskamp's first theoretical pairing of involvement and detachment for my purpose was clear. No teacher would want to stop students from first getting involved in a text by bringing in their own cultural and intellectual experience. Why not let them approach this "romantic" story on the basis of their romantically defined cultural background. Let them close in on Fortunato and collect all the Romantic themes in their first reading, when they are also groping with strange Latinized words. Then, according to Weskamp, they should come to realize a need for detachment, an awareness that there might be more to the story. A brief discussion of the silly death of a Romantic figure could help shift their attention toward Montresor's objective and strategies. Even the mere realization that they may have missed something in this story could help to promote detachment.

This is where Weskamp's second suggestion—that is, his list of practical tasks such as role-playing or interviewing, could be brought into the discussion, since a re-creation of a text from a new perspective might indeed force a reader or actor to reconsider the strategies of primary characters. The experience of acting itself may lead an actor to question how that character is to be acted vis-à-vis another actor. In fact, the narrative text of "The Cask of Amontillado" is already punctuated by passages written in direct speech. Thus, it would be easy for the students to collect "relevant" dialogic exchanges and present them in role-play. But I did not want to leave the selection or the play completely up to the students. If Montresor's ironic approach was to be conveyed through the playacting, then the dialogic re-creation would have to be planned carefully. Instead of giving the dialogic task to all the students, I chose to split the task between various groups of students and myself. One group of four students (out of thirty-one) was to prepare the dialogue and to rehearse two good actors from the class to play their scene, but according to my directions. Two other students were to collect some props, such as a picture of a crypt, a jester's hat and bells, a bottle of wine, some rocks, a coat of arms, and a trowel. The remaining students were to be given the dialogic text before the enactment and were to act as critical spectators. I thought that the division into actors and viewers would prevent uniformity in views and would justify my own greater interference. In fact I told them what English actors had told me, after performing Oscar Wilde's *The Importance of Being Earnest* in my town: "Foreigners don't laugh at the right points. We have to make extra pauses and support each joke with gestures and intonation. It's frustrating." I therefore insisted that the dialogue must contain clearly separate scenes, repetitions of important phrases, and accentuation of relevant words or syllables through tone and gestures. The following conversation between Fortunato and Montresor takes place in the Montresor vaults. The text is adapted from Poe and was enacted by the students; it therefore contains repetitions and textual additions (here capitalized):

MONTRESOR.   My dear Fortunato, you are luckily met (*pause*) today. How fortunate and happy you look (*pause*) today!

FORTUNATO.   Thank you, my friend. But what worries you? You wear no costume in the middle of the carnival.

MONTRESOR.   Oh, I received a cask of wine of true Amontillado, but I have my doubts. Would YOU like to test it and decide whether it is an Amontillado or not?

FORTUNATO.   Indeed. Come, let us go.

MONTRESOR.   Whither?

FORTUNATO.   To your vaults.

(*Pause.*)   (*In the vaults. A picture of the catacombs.*)

FORTUNATO.   (*He is coughing.*) Ugh. Ugh. Ugh.

MONTRESOR.   Come, we will go back; your health is precious.

FORTUNATO.   Enough, the cough is a mere nothing; it will not kill me. I shall not die of a cough.

MONTRESOR.   (*Laughter aside.*): True—true.

(*Pause.*)

MONTRESOR.   (*He picks up and offers a bottle of Medoc wine to an already tired Fortunato.*) Here, this will give you strength: A long life to YOU!

FORTUNATO.   Thanks.

(*Pause.*)

FORTUNATO.   Let's go slowly. These vaults are really extensive.

MONTRESOR.   Well, the Montresors are a large family.

FORTUNATO.   I forget their coat of arms.

MONTRESOR.   It's a huge human foot that crushes a serpent. (*Now looking at Fortunato.*)

FORTUNATO.   Good.

(*Pause.*)

FORTUNATO.   So, you are not of the brotherhood, but you are a mason?

MONTRESOR.	Yes, yes, yes, YES. And I love it.
FORTUNATO.	You? Impossible? A mason?
MONTRESOR.	Yes, a GOOD mason.
(Pause.)	*(Montresor picks up a trowel and some rocks.)*
FORTUNATO.	The Amontillado! The Amontillado! Let us be gone.
MONTRESOR.	Yes, let us be gone and GONE.
FORTUNATO.	For the love of God, Montresor!
MONTRESOR.	Yes, Fortunato, FOR THE LOVE OF GOD!

Weskamp's third point of advice, the use of a "reception-aesthetic talk" at the end of class, in which the students are given a chance to review their own interpretations in a discussion with the other students, also seemed reasonable to me. First of all, it would give the students a chance to express their views on the effect and effectiveness of the play performed by their fellow students. Potentially, it could also raise the question of why such a strange ironic method was needed in terms of foreshadowing or what negative irony reveals about a person's character.

Report Following Class Activities

The first didactic method, that is, the phases of involvement and detachment, were exactly what the EFL students needed. My deliberate withdrawal from the first stage of individual involvement gave them a chance to follow their own ideas. They listed the Romantic features that they detected—the carnival and the drinking, the dressed-up clown, the revenge theme, a dark path through the catacombs, the walling up, as well as the pleasant and noble dialogue. And, as was expected, the main point, the foreshadowing of death through the narrator, was not seen. The students had to be told to look for phrases that are a premonition of Fortunato's death, like a repetition of a death knell. Then, someone mentioned that the bells could be ambiguous; they could in fact announce the fool and herald his death. But verbal citations were missing. The discussion raised the question of whether the story is a horror story or a revenge story, such as *Hamlet*. There must be clues foreshadowing the murder. Where are they?

The use of Weskamp's second suggestion, the playacting, was then motivated by the need for further investigation, and a search for new methods of investigation ensued. I pointed out that the text contains larger sections of dialogue, and it would be interesting to see how some students present that dialogue. When I worked with the small group of students who prepared the dialogue and discussed the first ironic example with them, I noticed how quickly they caught on and found the remaining examples. But they needed guidance. The highlighting of features in the text and the playacting were more difficult, since we were not actors. During the performance in front of the whole class, some students smiled at the "pun" about Fortunato, fortunate and "lucky," but then everybody grew quiet. Thus, the direct sequence of separate scenes with identical impact fulfilled the anticipated purpose of tightening the atmosphere into foreshadowing Fortunato's death: first the acting out of the reference to Fortunato not dying of a cough, then the crushing by the serpent (underscored by Montresor's holding the coat of arms over Fortunato), finally the masonry underscored by the rocks and the trowel. I realized that our exaggerations had shortchanged Poe, because the exaggerated and somewhat clumsy emphases and markers that we had loaded into the dialogue would certainly have raised Fortunato's awareness too in real life. Thus, Poe did indeed depend on the dual strategy of both making Fortunato drunk and stupid so that he would not grasp the ironies and raising the reader's or spectator's awareness through the chain of Montresor's kind and simultaneously negative responses and clarifications. It also struck me that the repetition of the address "my friend" in the dialogue quoted above and, somewhat strangely, in Montresor's narrative directed only to the reader, had a great impact on the "spectators." In the performance, this obviously sardonic address revealed Montresor's true view of Fortunato as a villain.

In the third class session, I tried to moderate a "reception-aesthetic talk"— that is, a talk in which the students discussed their reading experiences and insights from our activities. I was pleased to hear that the concentration on the ironies did allow the students to recognize the foreshadowing of Fortunato's death. But then I had to dig deeper. How about the story as a whole? Did we misrepresent Fortunato's stupidity? Is he really guilty? Was he seen by Montresor as being simply stupid? Why does Montresor always speak to him and talk about him as a friend, except for the opening passage of the story? Did he mean to say that he is Fortunato's friend? At this point, everyone agreed that the friendliness was only a trick. But why does Montresor use such a trick?

There were a number of interesting responses to this last question:

> "People like him enjoy seeing that the opponent does not recognize what
>   they are up to."
> "They see the opponent as an enemy, no matter what he is really like."
> "An enemy who boasts that he is the real expert does not deserve to live
>   (in Montresor's view)."
> "They feel they are always greater than the others."
> "Do they want to tell their opponent what they feel about him?"
> "Not necessarily, if the plan could fail."

I realized that I was overstepping the rules of the "reception-aesthetic talk" by engaging the students in a question-and-answer chain. Nevertheless, I felt the students had grasped some elements of horror, such as the unpredictability of the perpetrator's motivation with respect to the victim and the planned giving of information to readers. Irony was understood as a strategy by which Montresor creates his own negative image of his opponent but withholds clues from the victim. He insinuates friendship to the victim but communicates his true intention to kill him to the reader. Thus, irony derives its impact from a negative evaluation of another person that leads to a negative action, but its apparent Romantic language makes it undetectable to the victim. It seems to be more than a strategy since it precludes a change of mind.

NOTE

[1] There are other interpretations of the story, which are not thematized here: for instance, that Poe was constantly being taunted by Thomas English and wished to retaliate satirically by predicting the opponent's medieval immolation and attributing stupidity to this arrogant critic. The story might also be read as a joke or game, in which Montresor proves to the reader that he can kill someone with impunity and finishes the story (apparently retold after fifty years) with a proud and merry *requiescat in pace*. See Cunliffe for these and other possible interpretations of the story.

CLASSROOM CONTEXTS

The Red Death's Sway: Teaching Poe and Stephen King in the American Literature Classroom

Tony Magistrale

One of the joys of including work by Edgar Allan Poe on the curriculum of an American literature survey course is that his poetry and fiction present such a contrast to his canonical contemporaries, Ralph Waldo Emerson and the other transcendentalists, or to those writers that preceded him historically, the federalists and the colonialists. While some students necessarily struggle to make sense of the bizarre and mysterious death-haunted obsessions typically affiliated with Poe's aesthetic, most undergraduates welcome his narratives as a genuine reprieve—a blessed draught of foul air, if you will—from the moral righteousness of the transcendentalists and the smug complacency of the Enlightenment. Poe's poems and fictions are a constant reminder to readers that life is often not neatly ordered, rational, or divinely inspired. His violent themes—featuring passionate, out-of-control protagonists whose irrational behavior transforms them into monsters and victims simultaneously—end up, ironically, connecting to the lives of contemporary students in ways that are intimate, disturbing, and remarkably timely.

Whether teaching Poe in a survey of American literature or in my genre-specialty course tracing the evolution of gothic art, I always stress the affinity Poe maintains with other writers, visual artists, and filmmakers who have been directly influenced by his fiction and poetry. For example, I have often deliberately subverted the chronological order of an introductory-level American literature survey course to follow a section on Poe with a viewing and discussion of

Alfred Hitchcock's *Vertigo*, a film that aptly portrays the disquieting masochism of many Poe males while illustrating the master director's effort to "put into [his] films . . . what Poe put in his stories: a perfectly unbelievable story recounted to readers with such a hallucinatory logic that one has the impression that this same story can happen to you tomorrow" (Hitchcock 143). On other occasions, I have assigned work from a contemporary popular writer—for example, Joyce Carol Oates, Peter Straub, Thomas Harris, or Stephen King—to illustrate for students the range of Poe's influence on American culture.

There are a myriad of opportunities to establish Poe's line of descent. Students might read short story selections from Oates's gothic grotesques to consider how the complex gender dynamics that represent such an important element in Poe's short stories are reinterpreted and reconfigured by a contemporary feminist who is also writing tales of psychological terror. I typically assign the following Oates-Poe pairings: "Where Are You Going, Where Have You Been?" with "Berenice" and "Ligeia"; "The Premonition" with "The Cask of Amontillado"; "Martyrdom" with "The Oval Portrait"; and "The White Cat" with "The Black Cat." If a teacher desires to emphasize the ratiocinative dimension that Poe was first to introduce in his detective tales, Harris's *Red Dragon* or *The Silence of the Lambs* as well as Straub's novels *Mystery* and *The Blue Rose* offer appropriate parallels for illustrating the evolution of the intuitive detective's crime-solving skills in the face of disquieting criminal activity. Straub, Harris, or Oates represents an excellent addition to any course curriculum that includes the study of Poe; the interrelation between Poe and other writers helps impress on students Poe's significance as arguably the most influential writer in American literature. An awareness of Poe's unique line of descent also helps young readers to understand Poe's place as an artist who transcends his own historical context. Indeed, Poe's aesthetic has at least as much in common with a postmodern sensibility as it does with anything written before 1850.

While I have experienced great success in juxtaposing Poe's fiction with the aforementioned contemporary popular authors and filmmakers, my most interesting classes have traced Poe's influence on selected novels and short stories by King. Many students are immediately attracted to King's literary accessibility, so those readers who find Poe's convoluted prose difficult to digest may be more engaged when reading the colloquial King; such readers often then return to Poe with a greater level of enthusiasm. King's fiction helps invite otherwise reluctant students into the world of books and encourages them to understand and enjoy more-canonical writers. What few of these students realize, at least initially, is the pervasive degree to which Poe has enriched the American literary canon—from mainstream authors influenced by his fiction, such as William Faulkner, Flannery O'Connor, and Richard Wright, to many of the most popular writers in the world, including King. Assigning a King narrative on the syllabus of an American literature survey class also generates an excitement in undergraduate readers similar to that which they evince when Poe's work follows several class sessions on Emerson or selected colonial American writers.

The match between certain King and Poe works depends on the selected texts and thematic emphases of the individual instructor. In the pairings that follow, King either alludes directly to the specific Poe text with which it is aligned or provides enough intertextual parallels to inspire an active classroom discussion. On different occasions and in various courses, I have explored the following Poe-King pairings:

> "The Raven" and *The Dead Zone* (King's novel and David Cronenberg's film adaptation are both effective, but the film works best), *Gerald's Game, The Girl Who Loved Tom Gordon*
> "The Cask of Amontillado" and "Dolan's Cadillac"
> "The Fall of the House of Usher" and *The Shining, 'Salem's Lot*
> "The Masque of the Red Death" and *The Shining*
> "The Black Cat" and *The Shining*
> "William Wilson" and *The Dark Half, The Shining*
> "The Murders in the Rue Morgue," "The Purloined Letter" and *Needful Things*

As these pairings indicate, *The Shining* offers the most provocative comparison with Poe's fiction, and it remains the selection that I include most often in classes that feature or include Poe. (Limited space precludes me from commenting here on the other Poe-King textual relations listed above, but teachers who wish to pursue them should especially consider the intriguing points of similarity that connect "The Cask of Amontillado" and "Dolan's Cadillac.") Because *The Shining* relies heavily on the rich gothic history of ghosts and haunted houses, it remains one of King's most "literary" and "teachable" books. This is also the novel that best intersects with Poe's earlier tales of an infernal biology of place—where physical structures are mysteriously animated to invoke terror—most notably present in "Usher," "The Masque of the Red Death," and "The Pit and the Pendulum." The Overlook Hotel is the ultimate embodiment of the haunted-house tradition as it was first established in the eighteenth-century European Gothic castle and later embellished in Poe's American landscape.

A teacher wishing to emphasize the parallels that link *The Shining* to works of Poe might simply begin by asking the class to generate a list on the blackboard of general similarities (and contrasts) among the texts. This initial list will certainly contain topics worthy of further exploration—for example, a shared gothic milieu, the degree to which each writer relies on supernatural inclusions—and might mention King's deliberate referencing of "The Masque of the Red Death" throughout *The Shining* and the reimposition of many of the core symbols found in Poe's story, such as a clock of doom and a sequestered building divided into highly symbolic rooms. I eventually steer our classroom discussion to the first of *The Shining*'s many direct allusions to "The Masque of the Red Death." While perusing a scrapbook containing selected illustrations of decadence and greed from the past history of the Overlook Hotel, Jack Torrance, the protagonist of King's 1977 novel, discovers an invitation to a masked ball held at the hotel in 1945. After reading the invitation, Torrance is motivated to paraphrase the last line of Poe's tale: "The Red Death held sway over all!" Since I wish my students to focus on this specific moment in both texts, before a general classroom discussion I ask them to spend three to five minutes writing a reaction in their journals or notebooks to Torrance's response to Poe:

> He frowned. What left field had that come out of? That was Poe, the Great American Hack. And surely the Overlook—this shining, glowing Overlook on the invitation he held in his hands—was the farthest cry from E. A. Poe imaginable.   (157)

If the students fail to mention key words from this quotation in their reactions, which are read by several members of the class, I ask for direct commentary on why King deliberately and ironically uses phrases such as: "the Great American Hack," "this shining . . . Overlook," and "the farthest cry" from the "imaginable" Poe. Most of all, I wonder aloud, why does his recollection of Poe inspire Jack Torrance to "frown"?

Some of the most important issues that should emerge from the ensuing classroom discussion of this excerpt are the false assumptions Torrance makes in failing to recognize the connections that link "this shining" repository of ghosts at the Overlook with Poe's own haunted psyche. Poe's influence on *The Shining* is most discernible in King's use of gothic characterization and setting. Like Prince Prospero in "Masque," sequestered inside a fortress that eventually becomes both prison and tomb, Torrance is haunted by both his own past and the hotel's, as well as, finally, by Poe himself. Prospero shares much in common with King's protagonist: they are both supremely selfish men consumed with their own worldly success and social status. In fact, both narratives coalesce around the issue of encroaching madness, perhaps the inevitable consequence of any obsession focusing on complete domination. In "Masque," the prince creates a decadent milieu where "[t]here was much of the beautiful, much of the wanton, much of the *bizarre*, something of the terrible, and not a little of that which might have excited disgust" (487–88). In this self-enclosed microcosm, Prospero remains oblivious to the suffering of his dominion and subjects, "[T]he Prince Prospero was happy and dauntless and sagacious. . . . The external world could take care of itself" (485). Prospero creates a "voluptuous scene" (485) that is echoed in the allure of King's hotel. Party central for "the richest men in America and their women" (157), the Overlook's guests are similarly self-absorbed, concerned exclusively with their own pleasures; they, too, wear masks that separate them from less fortunate men and women and from moral responsibility for the care and maintenance of others. In both worlds, perhaps reflecting the inevitable consequences of too much money and power, there is an omnipresent admixture of beauty and disgust.

A class well versed in the gothic doublings and dualisms that characterize Poe texts such as "The Black Cat," "William Wilson," "The Fall of the House of Usher," "The Tell-Tale Heart," and "The Purloined Letter" will discover another literary character in possession of a divided self in King's Jack Torrance. Torrance's love of family is pitted sharply against forces—some of them external, some of them psychological—that lure him into the solipsistic desire for fame, independence, and the self-destruction associated with addiction and violence. Poe's tales and King's novel feature characters that transform monstrously; these narratives, when juxtaposed with each other, illustrate for students the fluid, shape-changing dynamic that is an important element of gothic horror.

When students encounter Poe for the first or even for the last time in an American literature curriculum, his biography remains a source of endless fascination and speculation. Poe's themes—particularly alcoholism, drug addiction, dead and dying beautiful women and their inconsolable men—and how closely they parallel the writer's life are topics readers pursue with great zeal, and most teachers and scholars recognize them as relevant to an accurate understanding of his canon. Indeed, any teacher of Poe's fiction needs to be attuned to how often significant use of alcohol and alcohol-driven behavior motivates his plotlines.

The Shining is a novel of ghosts, history, and a nuclear family under siege. It is also a story of alcoholism. King saddled his protagonist with many of the real-life problems he himself had encountered before the swift success that attended the sale of the paperback rights to *Carrie* in 1975: his fear of never making a living as a writer, his anxiety at suddenly finding himself the breadwinner for a young family, his financial desperation exacerbated by gambling, and a tendency to turn to alcohol as a means of escape. Jack Torrance's situation in Colorado, in essence, bears disturbingly close parallels to King's own life when he was writing *The Shining*. As the author acknowledged later in an interview with *Playboy* magazine:

> I wish I could say today that I bravely shook my fist in the face of adversity and carried on undaunted, but I can't. I copped out to self-pity and anxiety and started drinking far too much and frittering money away on poker and bumper pool.　　　　(King, *Bare Bones* 30–31)

Students are captivated when they learn this history; few of them realize that this famous and successful man was once on the verge of financial and psychological collapse. In addition to connecting the author to his protagonist in *The Shining*, this information may open classroom discussion to important topics such as, What personal price must an artist pay to produce his art? How closely aligned are self-respect and monetary success in America? And why do people frequently turn to alcohol and gambling as a response to depression and financial stress?

All the issues discussed above are of course immediately relevant to the career of Edgar Allan Poe and serve to establish even closer bonds among Poe's literary career, his destitute protagonists, and Jack Torrance and Stephen King. While an undergraduate at the University of Virginia, Poe took up gambling to obtain money. As he lost greater amounts, he continued to wager still more. During these early years of financial struggle, Poe initiated what would become a lifelong problem with alcohol. He established a pattern similar to the one Jack Torrance follows in *The Shining*: extended periods of sobriety, followed by the urge to seek release from intolerable circumstances through drink, and then the inevitable relapse into public intoxication and boorish conduct. Economic desperation compounded by domestic crises were among the demons that confronted Poe. Like Torrance and King, Poe wondered if he would ever be appreciated as a "serious" writer, and, like them, his penchant for self-pity, argumentation, and violence was only exacerbated each time he turned to alcohol.

In the end, Jack Torrance comes to have more in common with Poe and his doomed male protagonists than he does with his creator, Stephen King. King emerged from his early penury to become the famous author that Torrance and Poe could only dream of someday becoming themselves. And while King has learned to regulate his predilection toward substance abuse, alcohol only pushed Poe and Torrance further from reality and toward their ultimate isolation in death. These facts speak to the biographic and literary correspondences that deepen the connection between Poe and King, but teachers may also discover that this discussion will frequently extend personally and directly to the students in their classroom, who have their own stories to tell.

The King novels included on the syllabus for my American literature survey course inspire more student writing and more lively class discussions than the works of any other writer the class studies, with Poe usually a close second. While most members of the class are already familiar with King's best-seller reputation, few of these students have ever read his fiction as "literature"—that is, as work that is serious enough to be included on the syllabus of a university English class and that is written by an author whose canon is part of a larger tradition that includes Poe as a progenitor. Reading King in a course that includes selected Poe tales opens undergraduates to the possibility for appreciating both these writers on a different level than when they are studied independently. It also helps students realize that the arguments many literature teachers raise to distinguish "popular" writers from "serious" writers are often specious and arbitrary. It is always worth remembering that *popular* does not necessarily mean "subliterary" and that Poe himself—now firmly entrenched in the literary canon—was once considered beneath scholarly attention. King may not yet possess the academic pedigree associated with Poe, but an American literature teacher interested in providing a distinctly contemporary slant to Poe's aesthetic vision or simply seeking to continue the enthusiasm for literature that typifies classroom discussions of Poe, would be well advised to include a work by Stephen King in the course curriculum.

Teaching *Pym* in a Survey of
American Literature

James R. Britton

In some ways, *The Narrative of Arthur Gordon Pym of Nantucket* may seem an odd choice for an American literature survey course. After all, much of Poe's other work, both poetry and short fiction, generally has been considered artistically superior. Moreover, the generic innovation of some of his short stories underscores their significance in nineteenth-century American literature and beyond. For some, the short fiction marks Poe as America's first literary innovator. Given the demands of a typical survey course, including *Pym* and some of these more often studied works would likely prove difficult to manage and justify. Nevertheless, *Pym* is an excellent choice in a survey of American literature. As Toni Morrison has noted, "No early American writer is more important to the concept of American Africanism than Poe," and she makes it clear that this is largely because of *Pym* (*Playing* 32). Morrison's perspective, which emphasizes the intersection of aesthetic and cultural concerns in literature, suggests that there are compelling reasons to teach Poe's only novel in a survey of American literature, including its problematic representations of race and American identity, its use of whiteness and blackness in racial terms and as symbols, and its unconventional and experimental narrative form—all of which can provoke a wide-ranging consideration of American literature and culture.

In my experience teaching *Pym*, students find the latter parts of the novel, beginning with chapter 18 when the *Jane Guy* reaches Tsalal, both intriguing and confusing. First, the racially charged depiction of the Tsalalians merits consideration and, second, the meaning of the looming white figure and the vortex, along with other seemingly significant symbols leading up to this point and the subsequent note, demand interpretation. Understandably, students often see these as disparate elements of the novel, so it is essential for an instructor to lead discussions and craft class work that integrates the formal and the cultural in a way that places Poe within the literary and cultural histories of the United States. In this essay, I discuss the importance of integrating an exploration of the formal elements of Poe's novel with an examination of the author's representation of racial identity. As a work that reveals an author who is at once visionary regarding literary form and, at best, indifferent to the plight of African Americans, *Pym* allows students to investigate the forms American literature can take, the ideology of antebellum American culture, and the intersection of the two.[1]

Familiarizing students with some of the period's history, particularly regarding race, slavery, and abolition, provides them with the background meaningfully to examine the latter chapters of the novel. Poe wrote *Pym* during a crucial period in the history of race in America. Beginning in the late 1820s, the debate over slavery's place in America became increasingly contentious. In 1829, David Walker published his *Appeal to the Coloured Citizens of the World*, and Nat Turner led his rebellion in 1831, signifying an active African American challenge to slavery. In 1831, William Lloyd Garrison began the *Liberator*, the most influential abolitionist newspaper in American history, and in 1833 the American Anti-Slavery Society appeared, and England formally abolished slavery. The combination of African Americans demanding and fighting for freedom and the largely white abolitionist organizations challenging the place of slavery in American society posed what was perceived as a very real threat to the Southern way of life. In this context Poe wrote *Pym*, a novel that obliquely addresses contemporary concerns about race and authority in America. One way to expose students to the cultural history not directly represented in the narrative is to provide excerpts from works like Walker's *Appeal*, early issues of the *Liberator*, or newspaper accounts of Turner's rebellion and the trials that followed. These texts can do more than simply establish a historical context for reading *Pym*: they can also help students understand the mind-set of readers who would have feared the contemporary challenges to slavery as an institution and to white political dominance. Both Walker and writers for the *Liberator* contested the racial hierarchies of 1830s America, presenting a philosophical challenge to white political dominance, while the actions of Turner and his compatriots represent the threat of a slave revolution, something white Southerners feared. For students, even those entirely unfamiliar with this period of American history, materials like these can begin to provide an understanding of what Poe's contemporaries believed was at stake and how those beliefs helped shape the novel.

For most students, the Tsalal chapters of *Pym* represent the novel's first consideration of race, particularly of African identity. Because of this it is important to discuss how the earlier images or invocations of blackness and racial identity establish a context for the latter parts of the novel. To accomplish this, I encourage students to explore how race informs the narrative before the Tsalal chapters. Either group work or a short in-class writing response can work well to initiate this line of inquiry. Once students have read the entire novel, I ask them to consider the significance of race before chapter 18. If they find themselves stymied, I suggest that they begin by considering the appearance or mention of race early in the novel. Typically, students will identify the presence of the black cook and of mixed-race Peters as important, although they are often uncertain about these characters' significance. This can also provide the opportunity to discuss Poe's use of white identity, which is at the heart of the novel but nonetheless remains invisible to many readers. Poe's use of the black cook aboard the *Grampus* is particularly important. While to students he may initially appear little more than a peripheral character, his role assumes greater importance when his behavior is considered on a continuum with that of the Tsalalians. As Pym presents it, the cook helps lead the uprising aboard the

Grampus, acting more viciously than any other mutineer. Once the rebellious crew takes over the ship, Poe writes that, "a scene of the most horrible butchery ensued. The bound seamen were dragged to the gangway. Here the cook stood with an axe, striking each victim on the head as he was forced over the side of the vessel by the other mutineers" (1042). Here and elsewhere, the cook represents unrestrained violence, the kind of behavior imagined in racist conceptions of African American identity. John Carlos Rowe has observed that

> like Nat Turner, the Black Cook strikes his victims on the head, testifying to the symbolic danger to reason posed by the emergence of the irrational savagery so many Southern whites imagined would accompany slave rebellion or even legal emancipation.   ("Poe" 128)

From this perspective, particularly when we consider Poe's description of the Tsalalians, the crew's mutiny is related to the corruption introduced by the only identified black crew member. The cook, whom Pym describes as a "perfect demon" (1043), thus foreshadows the racial characterization of the Tsalalians Poe elaborates on later in the novel, when Pym identifies them as "the most wicked, hypocritical, vindictive, blood-thirsty, and altogether fiendish race of men upon the face of the globe" (1174).

Once students have begun to consider the centrality of race in the novel, many develop a sense that Poe's use of race is connected to the symbolism he employs. Because Poe links racial blackness with blackness as a metaphor in his representation of the Tsalalians, it is important also to identify how images of darkness function figuratively earlier in the novel. As the encounter with the *Flying Dutchman* suggests, the color black represents the potential corruption of the white body. When the remaining members of the *Grampus* spot the approaching ship, Pym pays particular attention to the man who seems to be gesturing to them, describing him as having "very dark skin" (1085). This "very dark skin" gains thematic significance when juxtaposed with the skin of Pym's companions, which becomes "paler than marble" after they realize that their potential rescuers are in fact decaying corpses (1085). Of course, men exposed to the sun for as long as they have been could not have skin "paler than marble," but, as in the chapters on Tsalal in which racial whiteness and the color white overlap, Poe uses the relative whiteness of European skin for symbolic emphasis. The whiteness of Pym and his companions contrasts with the dark skin of the deceased and decaying bodies aboard the *Flying Dutchman*. In terms of prefiguring the Tsalal chapters of the novel, the encounter with the *Flying Dutchman* also underscores the limits of interpretation that Pym and his companions experience, as Pym's description of the approaching ship and the seemingly living crewman suggests:

> He seemed by his manner to be encouraging us to have patience, nodding to us in a cheerful although rather odd way, and smiling constantly so

as to display a set of the most brilliant white teeth. As his vessel drew nearer, we saw a red flannel cap which he had on fall from his head into the water; but of this he took little or no notice, continuing his odd smiles and gesticulation. I can relate these things and circumstance minutely, and I relate them, it must be understood, precisely as they *appeared* to us. (1085)

Pym and his companions are unable, or perhaps better put, unwilling, accurately to interpret what they see. As with the Tsalalians later, there is ample evidence that something here is amiss, that these people, the man's repetitive movements, and the erratic course of the ship are not what they initially appear to be, but Pym finds it difficult to penetrate appearances. Moreover, Poe provides symbolic connections between this encounter and the later encounter with the Tsalalians. The man's "brilliant white teeth" can be connected to the Tsalalians all-black teeth, while the red flannel cap perhaps reappears transmuted as the bush "full of red berries" and the "singular looking land animal" with "long claws of brilliant scarlet" that the *Jane Guy*'s crew recovers just before they make contact with the Tsalalians (1135). Using these passages, an instructor can identify the continuity between the Tsalal section and earlier parts of the novel, where blackness is associated with corruption and decay in both racial terms and symbolically and where Pym finds meaningful interpretation difficult if not impossible.

Poe's desire to keep the level of tension high throughout clearly drives much of the narrative. To maintain this level of tension, Poe taps into the racial stereotypes and fears that would register with many of his readers. As the novel progresses, the situations Pym confronts become increasingly sensational, requiring Poe to create even more extreme predicaments for Pym. Teresa Goddu observes in her discussion of Poe's short fiction that "Poe trades on the discourse of slavery to manufacture the terror of his tales and to make them sell even as he reveals the conventions to be market productions" ("Poe" 107).[2] From this perspective, Poe produces a sensational effect by providing his white audience with terrifying images of a world dominated by blackness. After offering multiple near-death situations in the *Grampus*'s hold—the bloody mutiny, the encounter with the *Flying Dutchman*, and cannibalism, among other astounding scenes—Poe grounds the sensationalism of the Tsalal section in contemporary racial fears pervading the antebellum South and much of the antebellum North.[3] To create and maintain a climate of terror, Poe offers a vision of black savagery that would resonate with many of his readers. As a society run by black-skinned people, Tsalal represents an imagined black savagery unfettered by the "civilizing" influence of whites. It is a place not exactly untouched by whiteness but defined in opposition to it, as the Tsalalians' reaction to all things white suggests. Of course, the "civilizing influence" familiar to Poe's readers would have been slavery. When presenting this to students, my goal is not to argue that Poe's representation of the Tsalalians tacitly supports the enslavement of Africans; instead, I emphasize that Tsalal represents Poe's vision of an all-black society rooted in racially coded savagery and that he is using that savagery as a means of advancing a sensational effect. At this point, students understand that this conception of race would have been familiar to Poe's readers, who would have Turner's rebellion and Walker's *Appeal* in their recent memory, as well as visions of the bloody Haitian revolution as a cultural reference point. Moreover, with the rise of an active abolitionist movement in the early 1830s, fears of black freedom would have been on the minds of many whites, especially white Southerners.[4]

While Poe predicates his depiction of the Tsalalians on contemporary racist beliefs and fears of black power that the narrative appears to reinforce, instructors should acknowledge the complexity of the depiction.[5] The Tsalalians clearly embody stereotypes associated with Africans that Americans would have recognized, including the simplicity of their living conditions, their nudity, their superstitious nature, and their brutality. Instructors can use this depiction as a departure point to explore how these racist stereotypes hold up in the narrative itself. First, it can be interesting to ask students whether the Tsalalians share traits with any other characters. Clearly, their brutality, violence, and treachery are behaviors engaged in by others in the novel, most notably by those aboard the *Grampus*. Of all the characters in the novel, Dirk Peters is perhaps the most violent, and, while Poe may attribute that violence to his Native American half, by the time they arrive at Tsalal Pym clearly identifies Peters as a white man. It is also evident that Pym survives because of Peters's readiness to kill others, often brutally; without Peters's brutality, Pym would not survive. Ultimately, it is the Tsalalians ability to deceive that defines their treachery and hypocrisy for Pym, but throughout the novel deception is often Pym's own modus operandi. The connection students make between the Tsalalians behavior and that of whites at other points of the novel underscores that the novel's representation of race is ambiguous when it aligns white with good/civilization and black with evil/savagery. As Joan Dayan has observed, because of the "scenes of butchery, drunkenness, treachery, and cannibalism" that occur before Pym arrives at Tsalal, "when the explorers finally visit the island village, the common racist divisions between 'civilization' and 'barbarism,' good and evil, black and white, are no longer operative" ("Romance" 108).

Another way to complicate Pym's straightforward representation of racial identity is to have students carefully consider the perspective of the Tsalalians. This may be difficult for some students, since Poe's use of the first person engages them, and they thus are sympathetic to Pym; most tend to accept his version of the events. However, if an instructor can make connections to texts representing early cultural encounters in the Americas, then students can begin to develop a critical reading of *Pym* that will more readily allow them to understand the behavior of the Tsalalians. I ask my students to submit short responses to their reading throughout the semester, and one area I suggest they explore is the cultural encounter. When applied to Pym, students connect the contact between the *Jane Guy*'s crew and the Tsalalians to a range of other encounters, including Bernal Diaz del Castillo's description of Cortés's devastation of the Aztecs in *The True History of the Conquest of New Spain*, William Bradford's *Of Plymouth Plantation*, and Mary Rowlandson's *Narrative*. Making these kinds of connections encourages students to notice the elements of economic colonialism associated with the purported story of exploration they are reading. Pym's statement that in Tsalal "we established a regular market on shore, just under the guns of the schooner" points to the implied violence associated with the *Jane Guy*'s mission, just as the use of Tsalalian labor to harvest bêche-de-mer and the crew's sexual use of the Tsalalian women, whom Pym describes as "especially . . . obliging in every respect," suggest qualities associated with American slavery (1146, 1150). As Dana Nelson has observed:

> The Jane Guy's encounter with the Tsalalians calls to mind the colonial exploitation of Native Americans. Europeans invade Tsalal and exploit the Tsalalians, bartering, as did the early North American Anglo settlers, with trinkets and beads. The scene has suggestive links as well to the colonial and antebellum South. Captain Guy, we are told, "was a gentleman of great urbanity of manner, and of considerable experience in the southern traffic."   (98)

The Tsalalians are thus both the potentially colonized and the potentially enslaved, and despite Pym's reflections on their general ignorance, they are clearly aware of what Captain Guy and his crew has planned for them. From this perspective, their actions can be understood as a means of self-defense.

This does not suggest, however, that Poe advocates such self-defense but that he develops a cultural reading of a racial encounter according to terms his readers would have readily understood. From our perspective today, the crew of the *Jane Guy* engages in a racist enterprise built on the subjugation of a racial other. Pym, however, sees the Tsalalians as different, inferior, and naturally and necessarily subordinate to whites, a perspective compatible with the slavery, westward expansion, colonialism, and African exploration of the time. Whites may be corrupt, but that is related more to their behavior than to their core identity, at least as Poe offers it. Tsalal represents one antebellum vision of what a black society would look like, and it is something many of Poe's contemporaries would have feared.

Beyond the Tsalalian land of blackness, Pym discovers a region of even more pervasive whiteness, which has proved to be the most perplexing part of the novel for student readers and scholars alike. A reader might here expect an examination of whiteness that parallels the use of blackness in chapters 18–22, but instead Poe offers absence rather than presence. While the whiteness does represent a counterpoint to and in some ways an antithesis of the blackness, the enveloping whiteness Pym, Peters, and Nu-Nu experience and the huge "shrouded human figure" colored "the perfect whiteness of snow" resist stable interpretation (1179). Morrison's discussion of whiteness in *Playing in the Dark* is particularly relevant here. She refers to images of whiteness throughout American literary history, but Poe and *Pym* are central to her examination:

> These images of impenetrable whiteness need contextualizing to explain their extraordinary power, pattern, and consistency. Because they appear almost always in conjunction with representations of black or Africanist people who are dead, impotent, or under complete control, these images of blinding whiteness seem to function as both antidote for and meditation on the shadow that is companion to this whiteness—a dark and abiding presence that moves the hearts and texts of American literature with fear and longing.   (33)

I would suggest that the cultural and historical contextualizing I discuss earlier in this essay could begin an inquiry into the presence of this seemingly "impenetrable whiteness" at the end of *Pym*. Throughout the novel, readers are offered the concept that blackness and whiteness, as symbols and as racial identities, are opposing forces, yet, as a close reading demonstrates, the behavior of whites and blacks is more alike than different. In terms of the narrative itself, the white Pym is accompanied by both the mixed-race Peters and the all-black Tsalalian Nu-Nu, complicating the meaning of this journey toward what Pym purports to be all-encompassing whiteness. In my experience, students not surprisingly want to know what all this means, and their questions range from, What happened to Pym? to, What does the white figure represent? to, What is Poe saying about whiteness? I encourage my class to work through such issues, but I also suggest to students that the lack of real narrative closure not only is part of Poe's narrative strategy but also points to the difficulties in representing a stable form of white identity distinguishable from the identities of racial others. Pym can thus offer a facile definition of black identity, but we never learn what the whiteness he discovers means, perhaps because it is a literary and cultural fiction to begin with. The ambiguities are thus grounded in Poe's aesthetic design and the culture of antebellum racial attitudes. I also tell students that this ending has vexed literary scholars for decades, some of whom have attributed this to Poe's failings as a novelist. Yet G. R. Thompson has sharply observed that "[d]espite the astonishing range of readings, what emerges from all the critical attention is that there is in Pym a coherent and symmetrical structure of events that generates a haunting ambiguity" ("Edgar" 274). It is this ambiguity, growing out of the novel's many artistic and cultural complexities, that helps make *Pym* such an excellent addition to a survey of American literature.

NOTES

[1]Many critics have labeled Poe's depiction of the Tsalalians as racist, a charge that is difficult to deny. However, recent critics have questioned the value of such labels, including Dayan, who in works such as "Romance and Race" and "Poe, Persons, and Property" has argued that Poe often critiques American racist ideology and offers a complex exploration of race far more nuanced than simple racism typically associated with many antebellum whites. In *Edgar Allan Poe and the Masses*, Whalen takes a different approach, arguing that Poe's perspective on race reflects what he calls the "average racism" of the period but that critics have "in the rush to denounce Poe's racism" obscured "the peculiar formal and historical determinants of Pym" and have, as a result, offered skewed readings (139).

[2] Instructors interested in discussing Poe's use of the gothic to explore race should see chapter 4 of Goddu's *Gothic America*.

[3] Peeples offers an alternative method of understanding Poe's use of the sensational, which can prove useful in a class discussion. He writes, "These nearly continuous hair-breadth escapes seem 'too much,' even for an adventure novel, but their very implausibility could be satiric, parodying through hyperbole the sensationalistic plots of exploration narratives, both fictional and nonfictional" (*Afterlife* 62). See chapter 3 of Peeples for an extended discussion of the various literary forms Poe employs in *Pym*. A discussion of Poe's use of parody or satire is beyond the scope of this essay but can work well in the classroom, particularly in terms of Poe's relation to modernism and postmodernism.

[4] Perhaps the most nuanced discussion of Poe's relation to the literary marketplace, particularly useful for instructors teaching *Pym*, is Whalen's *Edgar Allan Poe and the Masses*. Whalen argues that "Poe's calculating approach to the mass literary market complicates the political meaning of *Pym* and his other fictional writing" (145). In chapters 5 and 6 of his book, Whalen offers a particularly fine exploration of Poe's racial and political attitudes while addressing what he regards as questionable claims of recent Poe scholarship.

[5] There's a wide range of interesting interpretations of *Pym* that investigate race, colonialism, and related issues that an instructor could use to shape a classroom discussion or lecture. In "Edgar Allan Poe's Imperial Fantasy and the American Frontier," Rowe argues that in *Pym* Poe reveals an "imperial fantasy" that is rooted in an "American rhetoric" of imperial power (77). Offering a very different perspective in "Romance and Race," Dayan argues that Poe, as his career progressed, attempted "to screen his increasingly subversive concerns" and that the conclusion of *Pym* has apocalyptic resonances related to the presence of slavery in the South, revealing "the fears of some southerners, like Jefferson and Poe, that God's judgment could not be stayed, that the inevitable catastrophe is at hand" (109). In chapter 5 of *The Word in Black and White*, Nelson develops the argument that "while on one level *Pym* is a racist text, on another the text provides a reading that counters racist colonial ideology, and the racialist, scientific knowledge structure" (92). Whalen, offering perhaps the most nuanced reading, finds in *Pym* what he calls "average racism" and emphasizes not colonialism but commercial imperialism, which he distinguishes from "full-scale colonial occupation of South America and the Pacific Rim" (*Edgar* 182).

Trust Thyself? Teaching Poe's Murder Tales in the Context of Transcendental Self-Reliance

Paul Christian Jones

In American literature survey courses (e.g., a survey of American literature from its beginnings to the Civil War), the writings of Edgar Allan Poe—especially stories like "The Fall of the House of Usher," "The Black Cat," or "The Tell-Tale Heart"—often strike students as being out of place, as gruesome (though entertaining) aberrations from the other readings in the course. Thus one of the challenges facing any teacher who introduces Poe's fiction in historical survey courses is to find a way to connect his depictions of murderers, addicts, and madmen to the themes and concerns of the literature that surrounds these stories in the syllabus—issues such as national identity, democracy, and liberation. This essay describes one approach that I have successfully used to make this connection for my students between Poe's work and the cultural debates of his day. By encouraging my students to read Poe's stories as contributions to the discussion about the issue of individualism, I have been able to get them to make connections between the tales and antebellum Romantic texts that celebrate the potential of the self-reliant individual and the texts that we have read much earlier in the course (e.g., disagreements between Puritans and Quakers) about human nature. Students often come to see Poe not as irrelevant but as a vital—even a very persuasive—voice in this crucial argument of his time.

The context in which Poe's work is introduced to students is crucial to how they will think about his writing. In my historical survey courses, Poe's texts are usually introduced after the class has read the writings of transcendentalist authors, such as Ralph Waldo Emerson, Henry David Thoreau, and Margaret Fuller, and those writers influenced by them, such as Walt Whitman. The striking juxtaposition of these very disparate views of human potential and human nature provides the foundation for a more developed discussion about issues of self-reliance and extreme individualism in American culture. Works such as *Nature*, "Self-Reliance," *Walden*, *Woman in the Nineteenth Century*, and "Song of Myself" present readers with an exhortation to break from their socially imposed shackles and revel in their own individuality. These texts, which encourage people to live deliberately, to choose their beliefs and actions consciously, rather than sleepwalking through a life of routine, become exemplars of the values of American Romanticism and its celebration of extreme individualism over the authority of obsolete institutions. In "Self-Reliance," Emerson famously urges his reader to "trust thyself" and to "accept the place divine providence has found for you" with the belief that "the absolutely trustworthy [is] seated" in the human heart (260). The consequence of such a philosophy is the discrediting of tradition—all institutions, whether religious, legal, or political—in favor of individuals who, in the words of Fuller, begin to "unfold [their rule] from within" rather than "from without" (22).

While most of the students in an American literature survey find much to admire in these romantic celebrations of individualism, there will almost always be a couple of students in each class who express cautious concerns about too quickly throwing off all tradition, institution, and law in favor of individuals being guided by self-reliance. They suggest that a world, like that envisioned by Thoreau in *Walden*, in which every individual marches to "a different drummer" and steps "to the music which he hears, however measured or far away" ([ed. Rossi] 217), might be an invitation to disorder and even utter chaos. They also wonder whether everyone should be trusted to be self-reliant or whether there are certain people in the world—specifically, the evil or the insane— whom society would prefer did not follow the impulses of their hearts. Even the fans of these liberating texts usually admit that these writers are putting a great deal of faith in human nature and that their romantic vision relies entirely on the assumption (perhaps in the face of strong evidence against them) that people are essentially good.

These skeptical students are usually pleased to find that criticisms similar to their own were being raised about this radical individualism in the 1830s and 1840s. I typically present the students with some excerpts from negative reviews and hostile responses to the transcendentalist movement and its writings, printed in newspapers and journals of the time (a number of reviews of this type have been usefully included in Myerson). For example, the *New York Review*'s 1841 review of Emerson's *Essays* questions self-reliance because this philosophy perceives "every man as utterly independent of all other men" and "places each individual in a proud and selfish solitariness . . . and checks kind sympathies and tender affections" (Myerson 78). William Silsbee, writing in the *Christian Examiner* in 1844, argues that the "faith in *self*" is dangerous because "there is a limit to the power of the human faculties" (338). Silsbee worries that a person who "push[es] the transcendental ethics to an extreme, would own allegiance to no human government, because it seemed to them a usurpation of the authority of conscience," and he predicts that "unrestrained individualism would be the destruction of the State, not less than of the Church" (340). An 1849 *Literary World* review of another Emerson volume containing "Self-Reliance" asks whether "those who are little minded" can "be trusted thus to confide in the resources of their own reason" (Rev. of *Nature* 375). This writer believed Emerson's teachings to be in direct opposition to Christianity, which tells believers to "[b]eware thy inclinations [and] trust not thy heart," and he reminds his readers to "remember thy weakness in following what thou knowest to be good" and to "remember that evil is in the world" (375). Students usually find most of their own objections to transcendentalism and radical individualism somewhere in these critiques.

The piece from the *New York Review* is useful for my class discussion because it draws readers' attention to a passage in Emerson's "Self-Reliance" that is often extremely troubling to some of my students. This passage early in the essay presents Emerson's response to a friend who questions his intention to be self-reliant, "to live wholly from within," by reminding the author that "these impulses may be from below, not from above." To this, Emerson responds, "They do not seem to me to be such; but if I am the Devil's child, I will live then from the Devil" (262). While Emerson himself seems unbothered by this possibility and does not return to it in the remainder of his essay, his reader is likely to be unsatisfied with this answer. As the *New York Review* critic points out, Emerson's "answer is proof enough that the rule [of self-reliance], alone, cannot be a safe one" (Myerson 79). This disagreement is part of the larger debate about the nature of man taking place in the 1830s and 1840s between religious leaders and transcendentalists, a debate best exemplified by texts written by the Unitarian minister Andrews Norton (*A Discourse on the Latest Form of Infidelity* [1839]) and the transcendentalist George Ripley (*"The Latest Form of Infidelity" Examined: A Letter to Mr. Andrews Norton* [1839]), from which I also distribute brief excerpts included in Perry Miller's *The Transcendentalists* to my class. Once this cultural debate has been sufficiently illustrated for students, it becomes easy to get students to begin to consider Poe's writings as making a contribution to this dialogue and to read his nightmarish stories of horrific murders as imaginative illustrations of the concerns expressed by Emerson's critics. In this context, Poe becomes a strong voice of opposition to unrestrained self-reliance since his stories portray the philosophy of self-reliance as an actual license to kill for certain individuals (the "Devil's children") who exhibit a firm belief that their impulses, whatever they might be, should be followed regardless of the harm that may come to others.[1]

A number of Poe's tales can be presented to students as responses to this specter of doubt that a person might be "the Devil's child," the figure who acts on diabolical impulses and consequently proves to be a threat to society at large. "The Imp of the Perverse" (1845) is a good place to start if a teacher wants to present Poe's writing as a dialogue with Emerson's work, and in fact it is helpful to read this story alongside selected passages from "Self-Reliance" since it employs similar rhetoric. Poe's story examines human nature's tendency toward "perverseness"—that primitive impulse "to do wrong for the wrong's sake" (827). Like Emerson, Poe's narrator evokes the heart and soul as his authority on the issue of human nature. Whereas Emerson claims that "the absolutely trustworthy [is] seated in [people's] hearts" (260), Poe's narrator suggests "an appeal to one's own heart" as proof of human perversity: "No one who trustingly consults and thoroughly questions his own soul, will be disposed to deny . . . the propensity in question" (828). The narrator gives the reader examples of this propensity, ranging from procrastinating and missing deadlines to pondering throwing oneself off the edge of a precipice. It is also easy to get students to brainstorm for additional examples from their own or their peers' behaviors (which they are usually more than happy to provide) that would provide even further evidence of the perverseness described. After getting students to agree that this impulse does seem to be part of human nature, I encourage students to return to Emerson's essay to find any reference to this quality (other than the vague possibility of being the "Devil's child"), and they usually come up empty-handed, which highlights how the juxtaposition of the two pieces can expose for students important omissions in Emerson's doctrine. With this story, I also suggest to my students that Poe refers implicitly to Emerson's "Devil's child" and his resolve to "live then from the Devil" as the "Imp" narrator confesses his own crime, which involves using a poisonous candle to murder a man, and proposes that this perverse impulse might be "a direct instigation of the Arch-Fiend" (829).

Because "The Imp of the Perverse" is mostly composed of the narrator's treatise on perverseness (which, for Poe, is an undeniable element of human nature), it allows students to get a sense of the criticism that might be detected in Poe's work of the transcendental view of human nature and the dangers Poe imagines coming with unfettered and universal self-reliance. Other well-known stories by Poe can also be introduced to build on this discussion. The narrator in "The Black Cat" (1843), for example, similarly blames his crimes on "the spirit of PERVERSENESS" (599). He kills his beloved pet cat Pluto after first attacking it in a drunken rage and cutting one of its eyes from its socket. Afterward, perverseness pushes him to complete the destruction of the animal. He claims that "of this spirit philosophy takes no account" but asserts that it is "one of the primitive impulses of the human heart—one of the indivisible primary faculties, or sentiments, which give direction to the character of Man" (599). The narrator claims that this impulse is responsible for an individual "committing a vile or silly action, for no other reason than because he knows he should *not*" and "violat[ing] that which is *Law*, merely because [he] understand[s] it to be such" (599). The narrator argues that it is "this unfathomable longing of the soul *to vex itself*—to offer violence to its own nature—to do wrong for the wrong's sake only" that guides him (599). Certainly, this impulse, as the narrator claims, is one for which transcendental philosophy, as articulated in "Self-Reliance" and *Walden*, makes little or no account. Yet surely, as Poe suggests, this impulse must be considered part of human nature and might govern those who abide by the policy of self-reliance. As this tale progresses, the narrator attempts to murder a second cat (possibly a reincarnation of the first), kills his loving wife with an axe, and conceals her body within a brick wall in a basement. Even after this, he manages to sleep "soundly and tranquilly . . . even with the burden of murder upon [his] soul" (605).

"The Tell-Tale Heart" (1843) can be used to make similar points, since Poe yet again gives his readers a horrifying narrator confessing dastardly deeds. Like the others, he is a dark figure of self-reliance, trusting his impulses to an awful extreme, regardless of what reason, custom, or social norms would tell him. With the writings of the transcendentalists fresh in their minds, students often detect possible additional references to the transcendental project in this story. For example, I ask them to consider the connection between the narrator's extraordinary sense of hearing ("above all was the sense of hearing acute" [555]) and the transcendental assertion of the human capability to transcend— whether literally or figuratively—the limitations of the human senses. While Thoreau's poem "Inspiration" describes his ability to "hear beyond the range of sound" and to "see beyond the range of sight" (*Collected Poems* 231), I usually ask students to look closely at the more famous example from Emerson's *Nature*, where heightened senses become crucial to enlightenment. As Emerson explains, "few adult persons can see nature," or "at least they have a very superficial seeing" (10 [ed. Porte]). Through an intimate, direct relationship with nature, he posits, men can transcend the limits of their senses in a way that surpasses the superficial. In his image of his own transformation into "a transparent eye-ball," he offers his best depiction of the individual surpassing these corporeal limitations: "I see all. The currents of the Universal Being circulate through me; I am part or particle of God" (10). I encourage the students to compare this passage with the opening paragraph of "The Tell-Tale Heart," where the narrator similarly claims that his senses have been abnormally sharpened (some of my students have read the narrator's claim that his victim's eye is the motivation for his crime as an even more explicit connection to *Nature*). Like Emerson, this narrator proclaims that his heightened senses give him connection to the universe and to God; he tells us, "I heard all things in the heaven and in the earth." Yet because he is part of Poe's project of presenting readers with "the Devil's child," the more negative possibility of these beliefs, the narrator further adds that "I heard many things in hell" (555), providing students with another example of how Poe's stories fill in the silences and omissions of Emerson's texts. Although the narrator tells us that what we "mistake for madness" in him is merely "over acuteness of the senses" (557) and attempts to make the case that all of his actions are completely reasonable, the reader is left horrified by this self-reliant, hypersensitive figure who claims, impossibly, that he can hear the beating of a dead man's heart.

    With all three of these murder tales, the class continually comes back to certain questions: should these narrators be trusted to practice self-reliance? If not, what flaws do the examples presented in these tales expose in the philosophy of self-reliance? When thinking about the answers to these questions, students are not certain about how to approach the intriguing resolutions of the tales, each of which features the murderer confessing his crimes to police and submitting himself again to society's judicial system. Because these conclusions feature the diabolical figures incarcerated and awaiting execution, usually because they have impulsively exposed themselves as lawbreakers, they do appear to give some credence to the assertion made by the narrator of "The Imp of the Perverse" that "perverseness" has been "occasionally known to operate in furtherance of good" (829). The "Imp" narrator's own actions following his successful crime are used to illustrate this possibility. Years after murdering his victim and not being implicated in the crime, the narrator one day thinks, "I am safe . . . if I be not fool enough to make open confession!" Despite his belief that he is not "fool enough," he does confess when he cannot resist "the maddening desire to shriek aloud" (831). Similarly, the narrator of "The Tell-Tale Heart" implicates himself ("I admit the deed!" [559]) and submits to the custody of the police officers who interrogate him. And, in a different way, the murderer in "The Black Cat" also reveals his guilt to police investigators, when he confidently taps on the wall concealing his wife's body only to discover that he has sealed the live cat inside as well. The cat's cries alert the police to the evidence of the narrator's crime.

Considering these specifics, some of my students have argued that these endings could reflect Poe's belief that self-reliance ultimately will lead all individuals, even these misguided fiends, to good. While I consider in our discussions that this might be a feasible reading of these three tales, I emphasize that this is hardly an endorsement of self-reliance because, even if it can be credited with the confession and subsequent punishment in these tales, it also must be seen as the cause of the murders in the first place. To raise further questions about this reading, I present students with later stories, like "The Cask of Amontillado" (1846) and "Hop-Frog" (1849), in which the murderous figures do not make confessions and appear to go unpunished for their deeds. While it could be argued that Montresor, the narrator of "Amontillado," at least confesses his crime as he relates to the reader his murder of his enemy Fortunato a half century earlier, Hop-Frog, the vengeful dwarf who kills a king and his seven courtiers, does not confess his crime to readers at all (he is not the story's narrator), nor does he suffer any punishment. Instead, he and his accomplice Trippetta "effected their escape to their own country" and "neither was seen again" (908). Taking these works into account, it becomes more difficult to make the case that Poe argues that people will always—eventually—follow their impulses toward good acts.

I close this essay with brief comments about a way in which another much anthologized tale, "The Fall of the House of Usher" (1839), could be discussed in the context of debates about individualism, even though it strays from the pattern seen in the previously discussed stories of murder. In "Usher," the self-reliant figure is not the tale's narrator, but his childhood friend, Roderick Usher, who, like the killer in "The Tell-Tale Heart," is suffering from "a morbid acuteness of the senses" (322). In this tale, Poe further develops parallels to transcendental figures as we hear Usher's abstract theories about the "sentience of all vegetable things" and about the connection between the natural world and human feelings that would not be at all out of place in *Nature*, *Walden*, or *Leaves of Grass* (327). Like Poe's other figures, Usher is also guilty of a dread crime, the premature burial of his sister Madeline. Whether he knew he was burying her alive as he did so or merely left her entombed after he became aware that she remained alive does not change the monstrosity of his actions. The actual narrator of the story, Usher's friend, is ultimately threatened by his association with Roderick, who makes him an accomplice to his crime. This difference from the previously discussed tales suggests Poe's view of the dangerous consequences involved for those who listen to the advocates of self-reliance, become persuaded by the theory, and begin to practice it in their own lives. Over the course of the story, the narrator begins to take on the characteristics of Roderick, as his own senses begin to heighten and he comes to share his friend's responses to the gloomy atmosphere of the house. His sanity is ultimately at risk as well. As Roderick and the narrator await Madeline's impending arrival in the chamber, Roderick begins shrieking at the narrator: "Madman! . . . *Madman! I tell you that she now stands without the door!"* (335). His disturbing assertion that it is the narrator who is mad is one of the most shocking moments in the tale. To preserve his sanity, the narrator flees from the siblings' final embrace, which results in the destruction of the entire house of Usher.

Because of its vision of the preacher of self-reliance threatening the mental health of his audience and destroying the social structures around him, the end of "Usher" is an appropriate conclusion for this discussion. Since they can be seen to dramatize the cultural anxieties about "the Devil's child" running amok and to echo the critiques made by those commentators skeptical of radical individualism, Poe's horror stories of self-reliance seem to illustrate to his readers that marching to the beat of their own drummer and trusting themselves completely can weaken and dissolve the very social institutions that support and protect American civilization. Thus, Poe's murder tales can be seen to present a warning to the world about the potential consequences of self-reliance, arguing for limitations to individualism and proposing that self-interest must end when it threatens social disruption.

NOTE

[1] As background to this debate, instructors might present students with some of the critical discussion of Poe's relation to transcendentalism and its leading advocates. They will be interested to hear of his public hostility toward the so-called Frogpondians. In "How to Write a Blackwood Article," for example, Poe condemns the transcendental tone as one that "hint[s] every thing, [and] assert[s] nothing" (283). In "Never Bet the Devil Your Head," when the character Toby Dammit begins to make a fool of himself, the narrator asserts that Toby has been "affected with the transcendentals" (463). In an 1847 review, Poe cautions Nathaniel Hawthorne to avoid the influence of the movement if he wants to improve his work (Rev. of *Twice-Told Tales*). Students will also be interested to know that some important scholars have differed from the general consensus that Poe was antagonistic to the movement and its proponents. These critics, most notably Eric Carlson (in "Poe's Vision" and "Transcendentalist Poe") and Ottavio Casale (in "Edgar Allan" and "Poe on Transcendentalism"), have argued strongly, using such texts as "Ligeia" and *Eureka*, that Poe shared essential beliefs with his transcendentalist contemporaries, including the connection between human spirit and the material world of nature and the primacy of intuition. Despite the merit of these studies, most scholars nevertheless hesitate to label Poe as a transcendentalist and usually assume a position similar to what Leonard Deutsch has argued, that "even if [we are] right to see Poe as having a great deal more in common with the transcendentalists than he cared to admit, the fact remains he *perceived* himself as opposed to them and consciously, deliberately, and frequently derided them" (20).

Loving with a Love That Is More Than Love: Poe, the American Dream, and the Secondary School Classroom

Alison M. Kelly

> The American Dream would have no drama or mystique
> if it were a self-evident falsehood or a scientifically
> demonstrable principle. Ambiguity is the very source of
> its mythic power, nowhere more so than among those
> striving for, but unsure whether they will reach, their
> goals. Yet resolution may not afford clarity, either. Those
> who fail may confront troubling, even unanswerable,
> questions: Do I blame myself? Bad luck? The
> unattainability of the objective? Such uncertainty may be
> no less haunting for the successful, who may also question
> the basis of their success—and its price.
>
> —Jim Cullen, *The American Dream*

> Living happily ever after is a possibility, but it is not the
> standard.
>
> —Ian O'Brien, high school senior

The concept of the American dream is an enduring theme explored in many high schools and some college American literature classes. However, Edgar Allan Poe takes his readers on journeys into worlds that do not typically represent aspects of the American dream popularized by Benjamin Franklin, Horatio Alger, and others, such as optimism, financial and personal success, and lasting love. Rather, Poe's dark fictions present the dream as a compelling siren song that not only lures its victims into self-destructive behaviors but also leads to the destruction of loved ones. As such, Poe's fictions present a powerful corrective to the naive optimism of proponents of the American dream, and this rejection of "happily ever after" resonates throughout later American works such as F. Scott Fitzgerald's *The Great Gatsby*, Vladimir Nabokov's *Lolita*, and Toni Morrison's *The Bluest Eye*. In all these texts, aspects of the American dream are embraced and sought, but the dream becomes a self-induced nightmare.

In this essay, I present an approach to Poe's work geared toward teenage readers that pairs his fictions with commonly taught high school texts as part of a thematic unit that might be referred to as the underside of the American dream. By reading Poe in conjunction with Fitzgerald, Nabokov, and Morrison, not only is Poe's influence over the development of the canon of American literature made plain to secondary school students but also larger issues, such as personal autonomy and the nature of the human psyche, are provocatively raised. Ultimately, Poe's fictions, particularly when read together with other texts manifesting a similar cynicism, raise the question of whether the American dream is nothing but an unrealizable fantasy that perniciously obscures darker human desires and impulses.

My Lady Love: Poe and The Great Gatsby

A commonly taught high school text that shares Poe's pessimism concerning the possibility of perfect fulfillment through romantic love is *The Great Gatsby*, which I have found pairs particularly well with Poe's "Ligeia." In both stories, financial success has been achieved, but there is a lasting and obsessive quest for love to complete the dream. When teaching "Ligeia" in conjunction with *The Great Gatsby*, it is crucial to approach these stories bearing in mind most teens' limited experiences with romantic love, as well as their ideas about the extent to which lasting companionship is a crucial aspect of the American dream. It is helpful to have them list the categories "crush," "love," "lust," and "obsession" on the blackboard to prompt a candid conversation before the actual textual analysis, especially when discussing the differences between desire and need. Which categories have overlapping qualities? How does one distinguish between love and lust? How does one know when it is truly love? What are the boundaries crossed when any of the first three emotions change into obsession? What are the dangers associated with obsession? And finally, what happens when the relationship ends? What Poe has done so skillfully in "Ligeia" is to thrust his readers into a gray area of emotion in regard to his male protagonist's desires and needs, as well as his capacity for love. We can argue that Ligeia's husband is capable of love, but his love becomes transmuted, paving the way to obsession and his emotional self-destruction, as well as to the physical destruction of Lady Rowena. In analyzing his behaviors, should students feel sympathy for him? Should they condone his behavior?

In "Ligeia," these themes are addressed as the narrator confesses that he does not know the surname of his beloved, although he will obsessively rhapsodize about her eyes. It is especially effective to have students read this paragraph out loud in order to hear the obsessive quality of the narrator's voice: "Those eyes! Those large, those shining, those divine orbs!" (264). Then, after focusing on this passage, I call attention to the fact that it is an eyeball that the narrator worships more than any other part of Ligeia. While not all high school students may be experienced enough readers to recognize the interesting resonances Ligeia shares with the "transparent eyeball" in Emerson's "Nature" (39 [ed. Ziff]), the strangeness of this fixation on Ligeia's eyes does suggest to them that the borders between love and obsession, as well as the boundaries between the natural and the supernatural, have been crossed.

In reference to eyeballs, the Scribner's paperback edition of *The Great Gatsby* features cover art by Francis Cugat, which provides a splendid visual link to "Ligeia." Before even beginning a study of the novel, I have my students analyze the cover art, from the use of color to the oversized eyes looming over the night landscape, with women reclining in the retinas. The women in the eyes are often initially overlooked by the students, but, once they know where to look, it prompts a detailed discussion of men whose women (the object of their obsessions) become a true part of them. Charles May writes:

> When one is obsessed, by definition, one's obsession becomes the center of one's experience and perception. As a result, everything the obsessed person experiences or perceives is transformed into an image of the obsession, and nothing is allowed to enter into the experiential framework of the person except those things that fit in with the obsession. (69)

In keeping with this description of obsession, the narrator of "Ligeia" becomes a slave to the power of his beloved's eyes, and Jay Gatsby (whose face could be depicted on the cover) can be read as having incorporated Daisy Buchanan into his very being. Another interpretation is that Daisy is the face on the cover, proving that her existence is an all-encompassing force. Everything that Gatsby is and does is for her, and her face, omnipresent in the night, hovers over every aspect of his life. The eyes are the windows to the soul, and she has claimed his. With this in mind, the famous green light at the end of Daisy's dock becomes a tangible beacon of unfulfilled promise and desire for Gatsby, with a power equal to Ligeia's eyes. This attention to the obsessive qualities of both protagonists allows my students to conclude that the identities of the two men are wholly wrapped up in defining themselves through the women they perceive as the loves of their lives.

Perhaps the most interesting link between "Ligeia" and *The Great Gatsby* lies in the characters of Ligeia and Daisy. For Gatsby and the narrator of "Ligeia," the American dream translates into monomania: both men seek complete fulfillment through romantic union and will stop at nothing to fulfill this goal. However, in their roles as the objects of desire, the women consciously play a large part in encouraging and fueling these men's pathological obsessions. Ligeia ardently refuses to stay dead; although some can argue that it is the narrator's strength of will that brings her back (as well as his willingness to allow Rowena to imbibe a drink into which "three or four large drops of a brilliant and ruby colored fluid" have been mysteriously dropped [273]), he has entombed Ligeia and adopts the facade of having moved on. However, Ligeia arguably reappears one night after having taken over the corpse of Rowena, Ligeia's black hair streaming as her beloved shrieks in wonderment at her return. His fidelity to her memory has become a tangible reality, but we are left wondering what will become of this new relationship; the fulfillment of the dream has taken on a nightmarish quality with a questionable future.

Similarly, Daisy Buchanan is a woman who has followed her own American dream by marrying into wealth and a life of hedonistic luxury. However, it becomes clear that she has not achieved her dream through marriage to Tom Buchanan; she has the life of wealth that she wants and a husband and daughter who earn her respect and admiration, but Daisy wants more: "I've been everywhere and seen everything and done everything" (22), she tells the narrator, Nick, indicating that she still feels as though there is something missing in her life: true love. For Daisy, this comes in the form of Jay Gatsby, the one man who worshiped and loved her as she desired.

In both "Ligeia" and *The Great Gatsby*, the women take advantage of the all-consuming love that the men feel for them; Ligeia's unwillingness to let another woman take her place brings her back from the dead, where she causes the physical death of her competition, and Daisy makes a conscious decision to engage in an affair with Gatsby, which results in his murder when he takes the blame for the death of Myrtle Wilson. For Gatsby, "Daisy does not exist in herself. She is the green light that signals him into the heart of his ultimate vision" (Stavola 141). She becomes less of a woman and more of a symbol of his heart's desire; his choice to remain in love with a memory and unwillingness to view Daisy as less than an ideal are what destroy him. Richard Lehan writes, "If Gatsby cannot seal the hole in time, cannot buy back the past, he also cannot commit himself to the future" (108). Gatsby's inability to imagine a future without Daisy—his refusal to give way on his desire—makes death unavoidable.

A paper topic I usually assign in this vein asks my students, Are the men in "Ligeia" and *The Great Gatsby* in love with their respective women, or are they in love with love? What is the difference? Answers will vary, and this topic prompts teenagers to examine their own experiences in defining the roles of the women in the two texts. Are they the masterminds in the failure to attain the American dream? Are the men mere pawns? Does obsession override love and self-preservation?

Timeless Lovers: Poe and Lolita

One of the most obvious connections between Poe and a twentieth-century American author—one that clearly demonstrates Poe's significance in directing the development of modern American literature—is that between Poe's poem "Annabel Lee" and Vladimir Nabokov's *Lolita*. Nabokov has named Poe as one of the great American writers he most admires (Morton 5) and even considered "The Kingdom by the Sea," an allusion to "Annabel Lee," as a possible title for *Lolita* (J. Meyers 54). Furthermore, Nabokov intentionally recycles Poe's language in the first chapter, referring to Humbert Humbert's seaside home as a "princedom by the sea" (9). "Annabel Lee," of course, is a poem about obsessive love, a love that is "more than love," and, when I teach the poem, I prompt my students to consider the narrator's mental state and whether there is something unhealthy in his melancholic attachment to his deceased bride. We then see this obsessive love mirrored in Humbert's proclamation of Lolita as "my sin, my soul" (9) and in his continued search in the "land of opportunity" for the spirit of his own love, Annabel Leigh, who he convinces himself has been reincarnated in the body of another little girl, Dolores "Lolita" Haze. As Humbert (Jeremy Irons) confesses in the 1997 film version, "The poison was in the wound, you see. And the wound wouldn't heal" (Schiff 5). This "poison" seems to be the grief and morbid attachment that afflict both the narrator of Poe's "Annabel Lee" and Nabokov's Humbert Humbert.

In "Annabel Lee," the narrator's beloved remains dead, which allows him to continue to mourn, but Humbert's dream is realized: Lolita initiates their first sexual encounter and engages in behavior that allows him to believe that he is her dream. As Humbert, our questionably reliable narrator, describes, "Lolita arrived, in her Sunday frock, stamping, panting, and then she was in my arms, her innocent mouth melting under the ferocious pressure of dark male jaws, my palpitating darling!" (66). Clearly, physical contact has been made, and Humbert has kissed his reincarnated Annabel, but it is not clear whether Lolita really kissed him, or if this is merely an attempt to convince himself (and the jury members) that he was the recipient of the kiss. I discuss this passage with my students in class, asking them if they believe Humbert's version of the story. Some argue that Lolita does kiss Humbert; some believe that he kissed her but wants to believe that she initiated the contact; and still others argue that the kiss is purely a figment of his imagination and that he is attempting to convince the jury and his readers of what he desperately wants to believe.

Adrian Lyne removes the novel's ambiguity in his film version of *Lolita* when Lolita leaves for camp. She throws herself into Humbert's arms, kisses him passionately, and then gazes at him through the open car window as her mother drives down the street. Humbert then enters her bedroom and finds a magazine ad tacked up over her bed depicting a smiling and waving mother in the background. In the foreground, a father and preadolescent daughter are smiling and hugging. Lolita herself has written "H. H" in a heart with an arrow pointing to the father figure. In Humbert's mind, there is tangible proof that Lolita is looking for both a father and a lover, and he fully believes that he can be both to her. His dream has come true. Yet his inability to be a father and her demanding nature lead readers to believe that everything would have turned out better for all involved if Humbert's Annabel had never come back to life.

It is especially helpful to study Lyne's film version alongside Nabokov's novel, since the novel's Lolita rarely speaks, and the entire basis of the story is Humbert's retelling of the circumstances leading up to Clare Quilty's death. In viewing the film, however, Lolita becomes a character that exists on her own and not only as a memory through Humbert's storytelling abilities. Students are able to see Humbert's anguish and delight, witness Lolita's game playing and hear her nightly sobs of pain and sorrow, and visually assess the controversial scenes depicting the physical nature of their relationship as Humbert achieves his American dream through the physical reincarnation of Annabel Leigh and as Lolita fulfills teen dreams of her own through American materialism.

My favorite lesson plan involves a simultaneous study of "Annabel Lee," *Lolita*, and the music video of Tom Petty and the Heartbreakers' "Mary Jane's Last Dance." The video features Tom Petty as an undertaker who steals a beautiful corpse, played by Kim Basinger, and brings her home to be his "bride." Despite Petty's attempts to bring her back to life (he dresses her in a wedding gown, makes an elaborate meal for her, and even dances with her), he is forced to come to the realization that while her body is there, her essence is gone. He then takes her body from the house and down to the beach on a moonlit night, where he lays her to rest in the water. As morbid as it is, Petty's video represents the healthiest resolution when compared with "Annabel Lee" and *Lolita*, since his character is able to let his love go. In the classroom, this juxtaposition prompts a discussion about what happens when we cannot let go, which establishes a kind of sympathy for the narrator of "Annabel Lee" and for Humbert Humbert and makes Humbert's relationship with the young Dolores Haze even more difficult to label and judge. A chart is helpful in comparing the three men and their circumstances during class discussions of the texts (see chart).

The pairing of the "Mary Jane's Last Dance" music video with "Annabel Lee" and *Lolita* is an effective tool in modernizing the two "classic" texts and increasing their accessibility in American literature. The video addresses the same themes that Poe and Nabokov used, but it provides a healthier response to the loss of this aspect of the American dream: the loss of a cherished loved one. In all three texts, the dream is lost, a variety of coping mechanisms are exhibited, and the protagonists must deal with the consequences of their actions and decisions. When their loves die, the men either try to re-create the women in the bodies of others or allow their hearts, minds, and souls to be

	NARRATOR OF "ANNABEL LEE"	HUMBERT HUMBERT	MARY JANE'S ADMIRER
Their Women	Annabel Lee	Annabel Leigh	Mary Jane
Trauma	Early death caused by a chilling wind	Early death caused by typhus	Unnamed early death
Coping Mechanism	Nights shared in her tomb	Reincarnation through Lolita; lust for nymphets	Morgue robbing; brings her home as a companion
Consequence	Dissociation from reality (monogamy with a dead woman)	Criminal behavior (pedophilia and murder)	Returns her to the sea (learns to heal)
Our Response?	Unhealthy (living in denial)	Unhealthy (takes Lolita's childhood and kills Quilty)	Healthy (shows the ability to grieve and move on)

Comparison of Three Male Characters and Their Circumstances

drained by the memories of their lost loves. Petty's character is the only one who learns to accept the death of his loved one and the death of his dream and relinquishes the past in favor of the future.

Students may best respond to the similar role of teenagers in these three texts: the lovers in "Annabel Lee" are described as children but were probably in their early teen years during their relationship; Lolita's story is traced from age 12 to 18 (Lyne purposely cast 13-year-old Dominique Swain to play Lolita in the film); and "Mary Jane's Last Dance" is analyzed in class in its music-video format. This focus on teens as worthy characters and a legitimate and important audience shows that Poe's influence has surpassed the written word and entered into the video generation.

Skeletons in the Closet: *Poe and* The Bluest Eye

The death of the American dream resonates throughout what many perceive as Poe's masterpiece: "The Fall of the House of Usher." In creating a story about a dying family and questionable relationships between a brother and sister, Poe alludes to an even darker side of the American dream: sexual perversion. This is mirrored in *The Bluest Eye*, where Toni Morrison takes Poe-esque themes, such as the trauma of alcoholism and incest, and creates a story with an ending that is significantly less tidy than those in Poe's stories. Instead of a murderer being apprehended or a house caving in on itself and burying its inhabitants, she asks, What happens after? What happens if the murderer is not caught? What happens if the house does not collapse and allow its victims a release through death? Morrison skillfully and grimly addresses the themes that Poe successfully veils in his story of Roderick Usher and Madeline Usher.

Poe depicts the Usher siblings as the final two in a family that belongs to a fallen world. Their home and grounds are described as being pervaded by "an atmosphere which had no affinity with the air of heaven, but which had reeked up from the decayed trees, and the gray wall, and the silent tarn—a pestilent and mystic vapor, dull, sluggish, faintly discernible, and leaden-hued" (319). Poe has created an atmosphere that matches the shame, frustration, and sickness of a family tree that, seeking to maintain its strong, pure, and aristocratic bloodlines, has dwindled into the final remaining members of the family who are analogous to the decayed trees that surround the property. Roderick, who suffers from an undisclosed mental disorder and an "excessive nervous agitation" (321), arguably makes the decision to entomb his ill sister prematurely and enlists the help of his friend, the narrator, to complete the task.

I suggest to my students that Roderick in "The Fall of the House of Usher" and Cholly Breedlove of *The Bluest Eye* commit the sins they do in the hopes of escaping the past. Roderick knowingly keeps a living Madeline entombed in the hopes that her death will end his unnatural obligation to a long line of Ushers and allow him to break free, despite his own inevitable death in the near future. As Tony Magistrale points out, "In the end, [Roderick's] final madness is precipitated by his guilt over the premature burial of his sister Madeline, and equally as significant, his refusal to aid in releasing her, despite his knowledge of her struggles within the coffin" (65). In class, we take it one step further by examining Roderick's statement, "I *now* tell you that I heard her first feeble movements in the hollow coffin. I heard them—many, many days ago—yet I dared not—*I dared not speak!*" (334–35). This passage usually prompts a discussion of whether Roderick knowingly entombed Madeline alive in his desperate attempt to leave his family behind and start over. Similarly, Cholly accidentally rapes his daughter, Pecola, for the first time in the hope of regaining an earlier version of himself as a loving husband and provider, *not* as an alcoholic father and a failure.

Unfortunately for Roderick, Madeline—like Ligeia—will not go quietly into death and comes back to claim her brother. In her final act, she "fell heavily inward upon the person of her brother, and in her violent and now final death-agonies, bore him to the floor a corpse, and a victim to the terrors he had anticipated" (335). There is no place for the Usher family in the American dream; ultimately, the collapse of the house signifies the collapse of the family and the end of the polluted, too-pure bloodline. In relation to this conclusion, Magistrale writes, "Perhaps the onus of guilt associated with that [secret] sin erodes both their spirits, making death and madness welcome releases from the daily reminders of their shared burden" (65).

The "welcome releases" are what Morrison denies her main character, Pecola, in *The Bluest Eye*. In what is perhaps the clearest rendering of what the American dream has become, Morrison opens her novel with the use of the Dick and Jane series of books as a representative of the American dream from a child's perspective. These are the stories that America's schoolchildren read for several decades in the middle of the twentieth century, thus teaching them of what to dream: a structured, clean, organized, attractive, controlled, two-parent white world of happiness and promise. Unfortunately, this is not what many people in twentieth-century America actually experienced. Rather, it is a world that many want to believe can exist, and it does exist for some, but it is completely foreign to the African American family in Morrison's novel, the Breedloves.

The repercussions of the impossibility to realize the American dream in *The Bluest Eye* are far crueler than the fates of Madeline and Roderick, whose sins die with their bodies and remain secret—even to the readers, who can only assume that they shared an incestuous bond. However, Cholly repeatedly rapes Pecola; Pauline, her mother, remains in denial about the incidents; and Pecola is left to handle the traumas of rape, incest, and pregnancy on her own. Pecola's friend, Claudia, tells us, "The damage done was total. She spent her days, her tendril, sap-green days, walking up and down, up and down, her head jerking to the beat of a drummer so distant only she could hear" (204). In this passage, according to Madonne Miner, "Claudia's description of the mutilated Pecola leaves no doubt that she no longer exists as a reasonable human being" (89). Unable to comprehend what has happened to her, Pecola descends into madness, talking to a little blue-eyed girl in the mirror who she believes is her pretty, new best friend. Only in her insanity does Pecola find her American dream: she becomes the white girl she has always wanted to be, one deserving of parental love and society's acceptance. Meanwhile, her closest relatives are systematically destroyed through the power of gossip and the family's dysfunctional nature: Pecola's brother, Sammy, leaves town; her father dies in a workhouse; and her mother rejects her in favor of continuing her job cleaning for the white upper class. Meanwhile, Pecola herself is alive and homeless—a constant reminder that her family believed too strongly in false promises and what America has to offer them.

The Breedlove family's inability to live up to their name and their subsequent self-destruction correspond with Maurice Beebe's comment: "[W]hether or not Roderick Usher wills his fate is less important than that the fate does occur. . . . Roderick Usher is both the agent of his fate and its object" (129). This notion of our becoming our fate through our will implies not only a matter of choice but also a deadly cycle. On the Web site for the 1997 film version of *Lolita*, Jeremy Irons describes his portrayal of Humbert as follows: "It's about a man who fell in love with a dream he lost, and who remained in love with it" (*Lolita*). What Poe and his successors may be trying to prove to their readers through their works is that an obsessive desire to achieve any or all of the aspects of the American dream might not only destroy us, but may even make us criminals. Is moderation or a more pessimistic view of our dreams the key? Or, as Jim Cullen points out in *The American Dream: A Short History of an Idea That Shaped a Nation*, does the "unattainability of the objective" make it that much more desirable (7)? If we acknowledge the possibility of failure and remind ourselves that it is only a dream, then is that enough to maintain sanity and achieve happiness? Reading Poe together with Fitzgerald, Nabokov, and Morrison raises these and other powerfully unsettling questions and prompts provocative discussion concerning the political realities of the American dream. Young adults are at the perfect age to discuss these themes, since they are approaching adulthood, developing their own dreams, and coming to terms with what their own realities might be. Through his stories and poems, as well as through his profound influence on America's more modern literary staples, Edgar Allan Poe has aptly proved the harsh and frightening repercussions of listening too closely to the false promises of the siren song in the quest to make an impossible dream a reality.

Poe, Literary Theory, and the English Education Course

Donelle Ruwe

This essay describes an undergraduate course, Seminar in the Teaching of English, in which I use the works of Edgar Allan Poe to teach prepracticum students how to incorporate literary theory into secondary school classrooms. The qualities of Poe's works make him particularly well suited to a theory-oriented pedagogy class. His tales and poems are rich in imagery and accommodate a range of critical lenses. His works are familiar to students, so they can easily move from simple understanding of texts to the more complex issues of creating successful lesson plans. And, finally, my students appreciate the practical opportunity to create lesson plans about an author whom, in all likelihood, they will be teaching in the future.

The works of Poe are paradigmatic of the American pedagogical canon, which is made up of the classics of the secondary school classroom. It takes no more than a quick glance at the table of contents of major junior high and high school textbooks to demonstrate that Poe appears at almost every grade level (see chart).[1]

Most of the students in English 404, Seminar in the Teaching of English, have already taken a battery of methodology courses offered by the Department of English and the College of Education at Northern Arizona University. English 404 is an open-topics course, and faculty members take various approaches to the class, such as gender studies, grammar in the classroom, poetry, or bridging from young-adult literature to the classics. My choice to have students master the teaching of literary theory in the 6–12 classroom was inspired by my sense that English-education majors, though lovers of literature and potentially gifted pedagogues, have inadequate knowledge of literary theory. In preparing lesson plans, they default, time and again, into either reader-response or New Critical modes without even understanding what these approaches are. There is some justification for these default modes: adolescents are notoriously self-centered, so helping them find personal connections to texts is a consistently successful classroom approach. Likewise, mastery of the New Critical technique of close reading is practically de rigeur in today's high schools, given the ways in which our education system is driven by our movement toward nationalized tests and demands that schools be held accountable for student progress.[2] Close reading emphasizes skills that are measurable—vocabulary, literary terminology, reading comprehension, and text-based interpretation.

However, both reader-response and close-reading techniques have limitations and should be only two out of many modes of textual analysis.[3] Though close reading is an essential basic skill for all readers of literature, students need to learn to use it as a means not to a single end but to many possible ends. Teachers

	LANGUAGE TO LITERATURE (McDougal 2002)	TIMELESS VOICES, TIMELESS THEMES (Prentice 2005)	ELEMENTS OF LITERATURE (Holt, Rinehart 2003)
Grade 6		"A Dream within a Dream"	
Grade 7		"Annabel Lee"	"Annabel Lee"
Grade 8	"The Tell-Tale Heart"	"The Tell-Tale Heart"	"The Tell-Tale Heart"
Grade 9	"Annabel Lee" "The Bells" "The Cask of Amontillado" "Letter to Maria Clemm"	"The Bells" "The Cask of Amontillado" "The Raven"	"The Cask of Amontillado"
Grade 10	"The Pit and the Pendulum"	"The Masque of the Red Death"	"The Pit and the Pendulum"
Grade 11	"The Fall of the House of Usher" "The Masque of the Red Death" "The Raven"	"The Fall of the House of Usher" "The Raven"	"The Fall of the House of Usher" "The Raven"

Poe Selections by Grade Level in 6–12 Literature Series

who use reader-response criticism (as it is so often misapplied in middle schools and high schools) ask their students to find personal connections to literature but do not ask them to consider why they misread texts. Deborah Appleman writes that school teachers and teenagers oversimplify reader response as follows: "What does this book mean *to me*?" (45). If reader-response criticism is to help adolescents become stronger readers, it must help them gain a critical self-awareness so that they can understand how their preconceptions and preferences lead to misinterpretations. Even more crucially, adolescents need to avoid making judgments about a text's value merely based on whether it appeals to them personally. In the case of multicultural texts, students misread worst when they, out of good intentions, desire to affirm that others are just like them—therein doing violence to the essential differences between nations, cultures, and texts.

In English 404, I require my students to consider four different critical theories: New Criticism, reader response, gender studies, and cultural studies. I consider these literary approaches to be the most accessible to secondary school students. As we study frequently taught 6–12 texts such as Lois Lowry's *The Giver* and Nathaniel Hawthorne's short stories, we discuss how different critical approaches open new avenues of questioning and interpretation. I want the prospective teachers in my class to understand their own instinctive preferences for approaching literature and to develop a wider repertoire of text-analysis techniques. I also want these prospective teachers to create lesson plans that make their future students flexible readers who understand different ways to approach literature.

In addition to novels, essays, and poetry, I selected two textbooks for English 404: Deborah Appleman's *Critical Encounters in High School English: Teaching Literary Theory to Adolesecents* and Charles E. Bressler's *Literary Criticism: An Introduction to Theory and Practice*. Many elements of my course are inspired by Appleman's book, the only sustained discussion of teaching literary theory in secondary schools. Appleman is an experienced high school teacher, and her book includes excellent case studies and a useful appendix of theory-oriented lesson plans. However, Appleman's chapters are uneven in their presentation of different approaches, so Appleman's book should be supplemented with a theory text. I selected Bressler's book from the many good introductory theory texts because it contains sample student essays, literary selections that are frequently taught in high schools (including Poe's "The City in the Sea"), an extensive glossary, a survey of Web sites for further exploration, and a valuable, straightforward list of questions and guidelines to be used by readers in the process of applying different literary methods to texts.

The seminar is divided into four sections, one unit on each of the four literary theories we cover during the semester: "Creative and New Critical Approaches: Getting at Form and Content"; "Reader Response: Helping Students Connect and Question Their Connections"; "Gender Studies: Understanding the Pressures of Being a Man, of Being a Woman"; and "Cultural Studies: Living in a Middle-Class, White, Capitalist, Nationalistic Society." At the end of each unit, students select a "chestnut" school text, one that is frequently assigned in grades 6–12, and create an extensive, theory-oriented lesson plan adopting a particular critical lens. For each of the four lesson plans, students complete the following tasks:

> Summarize the selected schoolroom classic.
> Provide an MLA citation for it.
> Identify and discuss its key themes.
> Overview the particular literary critical approach that is being used.
> Provide a narrative description of the day-to-day classroom activities.
> Include sample handouts and formalized lesson plans.

"The Raven" and "Annabel Lee" were popular selections for lesson plans adopting New Critical approaches. Several of my students crafted close-reading assignments around these poems—reading the poem aloud, identifying difficult vocabulary words, and then identifying repeated images and phrases and exploring how an accumulation of detail can be used to create suspense and tension. One student used a close reading of "The Raven" as a springboard for creative writing work for junior high school students. This student's lesson asks the class to divide the poem into dialogue and action sections. Next, the class brainstorms information about a favorite animal, a favorite room, and a word that is ambiguous in that it "represents many things but not one thing."[4] The junior high school students then create and share original, modernized versions of "The Raven." These new versions keep the dialogue and action format intact but replace the raven, the place, and the word "nevermore" with new material.

Various students selected "The Tell-Tale Heart" for a gender studies unit. Angela, for example, developed a five-day lesson plan that incorporates a blend of close reading and gender studies approaches. The lesson, designed for a ninth-grade class, requires students to create an initial reading of the tale and then to listen to an Iggy Pop recording of it from *Closed on Account of Rabies: Poems and Tales of Edgar Allan Poe.* Once the ninth graders are familiar with the tale, the teacher introduces simple techniques for examining gender in texts: in particular (following Bressler's and Appleman's suggestions), to change the gender of a narrator from male to female or vice versa to see what new insights might be gained. The ninth-grade class divides into small groups to reread the tale, identifying passages that gain new importance when the narrator's gender is questioned. As Angela notes in her lesson-plan overview, "*nowhere* in the text does it specify that the narrator is male." When Angela herself attempted to read the tale with a gender switch, she was excited by the many new insights that she gained. She noted that Poe at first appears to link the narrator to mad*men*: "You fancy me mad. Madmen know nothing," but the subsequent sentence separates out the narrator from the category of madmen: "You fancy me mad. Madmen know nothing. But you should have seen *me*." Once Angela began to play with gender, all sorts of interesting possibilities appeared: Does the narrator's statement "I loved the old man" suddenly suggest a romantic love rather than a friendly or paternal one (555)? Might the narrator's obsession with the old man's eye indicate a woman's "pan[ic] when she feels she is being observed, or watched by men"? Does she feel compelled to speak to the policemen because, as a woman, she feels powerless in the face of patriarchal authority? On the final day of Angela's lesson plan, students compare their initial readings with their new ones and discuss the insights gained by a gender-switching technique. The unit culminates with a comparison of narrators in Poe's tale and Charlotte Perkins Gilman's "The Yellow Wall-Paper." Although Angela's analysis lacks the sophisticated psychoanalytic apparatus found in important feminist rereadings of Poe's tale, such as Gita Rajan's "A Feminist Rereading of Poe's 'The Tell-Tale Heart,'" Angela is able to arrive at many of the same insights. For example, Rajan, like Angela, reinterprets Poe's unmarked narrator as a woman, noting that the narrator "deeply resents the scrutiny of [the old man's] eye" and that the narrator's attack represents her desire to "rid herself of the male gaze, or domination" (295).

Another of my students, Ben, applied gender studies to his lesson plan on "The Tell-Tale Heart." Ben's lesson is for an eleventh-grade honors class, and his plan is scheduled to appear in the middle of a gender studies unit. Ben decided that "the story lends itself better to issues of masculinity" than a feminist reading. Ben's lesson divides the class into four groups, each with a different assignment, as follows:

> Group 1: Assume the narrator is male. Analyze the story according to the homosocial-homoerotic continuum and ideas about homophobia. Why might the narrator have decided to kill the old man?
>
> Group 2: Assume that the narrator is female. Analyze the story as a woman's triumph over an oppressive male, paying particular attention to the significance of the evil eye.
>
> Group 3: Assume the narrator is male. Analyze the old man as the narrator's doppelganger and pay particular attention to the symbolism of the eye and heart.
>
> Group 4: Make no assumption about the narrator's gender. Analyze the story as a metaphor for the struggle between id, ego, and superego.

Ben's groups are required to present their findings to the class, and the class then evaluates the effectiveness of the various readings.

Ben crafted his lesson plan in direct response to the most provocative article we read in English 404, an analysis of the negative effects of reader-response classroom approaches on gay and lesbian adolescents. Jim Reese's "Creating a Place for Lesbian and Gay Readings in Secondary English Classrooms" contends that when secondary school teachers ask teenagers to speak about their personal responses to a text, they cause unintended harm to gay and lesbian students. For a gay teenager, to be open about a personal response to a text is tantamount to being forced to "come out." Rather than risk harassment or public exposure of a private feeling, gay and lesbian adolescents learn to present deceptive, untrue responses. Teachers frequently ignore the fact that a significant (and vulnerable) subset of the student population feels alienated by the overwhelmingly heterosexist culture of high school and by culturally accepted high school literary texts. Ben's lesson plan for "The Tell-Tale Heart" requires his class to create four readings and does not privilege one over the others. Ben's lesson thus acknowledges the validity of a queer-theory reading without having individual students present this reading as a personal response. Further, in setting up four divergent readings for his class, he validates the diversity of student responses and encourages his students to think about texts as possibilities rather than as works with a predetermined, monolithic meaning.

As my seminar progressed, the students became more and more comfortable in creating lesson plans that encouraged divergent thinking, and students, such as Angela and Ben, were able to create truly ambitious lesson plans. Once my students understood the rudiments of literary theory, they began to think about Poe as an author to be challenged rather than revered. In *Cultural Capital*, John Guillory notes that the relation between value and the literary work is keyed to the level of the educational system (22). The lower levels are characterized by a rhetoric of great works, but, at the level of the graduate school or professional conference, cultural capital is signaled by questioning the rhetoric of the great work and the canon. My students had learned to play the "game" with Poe: they had learned to value questions more than adulation.

Guillory also notes that, in the early nineteenth century, a canon of texts emerged that was specific to the primary levels of the education system, texts that were considered "minor" in relation to high canonical writing (29). These texts of the "pedagogical canon" were explicitly intended to create a standard language of scholarship, culture, and aesthetics. In other words, these texts were to be read with an instrumental function in mind—they were presented as rhetorical models of superior written and spoken language, and students were to learn rhetorical strategies from these model texts. The Holt, Rinehart, and Winston eighth-grade reader containing "The Tell-Tale Heart" is marketed along with multiple ancillary materials, and these supplementary worksheets and student activities indicate that the texts of the pedagogical canon are still being used with an instrumental function in mind. "The Tell-Tale Heart" worksheets draw vocabulary items, spelling words, and grammar exercises from Poe's tale. By contrast, my students used theory to enliven their classroom approaches to Poe and to move beyond using Poe for vocabulary lists. Those students who used Poe in lesson plans informed by New Criticism or reader response did so with some sophistication and creativity, and those who adopted gender studies approaches found that, in the words of one student,

> [T]he results were overwhelming. "The Tell-Tale Heart," a story I have read countless times, and one that has always been a personal favorite, read as though it were now in a different language. *Everything* about the story had changed for me. . . . Instead of designing a study guide or worksheets for this unit as I have done in the past, I would like to experiment with various activities [so that] by the time students finish they have made discoveries for themselves.

NOTES

[1] Most twelfth-grade literature texts have a British or world literature focus, so Poe's works are not represented in these publishers' senior readers. However, senior-level college prep classes often adopt *Perrine's Literature: Structure, Sound and Sense*, which contains "Dream within a Dream" and "Cask of Amontillado" (Arp, Johnson, and Perrine).

[2] The national advanced placement exam requires students to provide a written analysis of a prose and a poetry passage on the spot, a task that suits a New Critical approach to text analysis. In Arizona, the test that holds high school students accountable is the AIMS (Arizona's Instrument to Measure Standards) test. Arizona's Standards-Based Teaching and Learning program has adopted the Six Trait Analytical Writing Rubric (developed by the Northwest Regional Educational Laboratory) as a standardized rubric of criteria to be used in grading student writing samples from the AIMS test. The

six traits are ideas/content, organization, voice, word choice, sentence fluency, and conventions. See www.ade.az.gov/sbtl/6traits/. I thank Jean Boreen for explaining the politics of the AIMS test.

[3] Student teachers are not the only secondary school practitioners who default to reader-response and New Critical approaches. In a survey of fifty-five practicing English teachers, the poetry editor of the *English Journal*, James Brewbaker, found that when given the same cluster of poems to present to their classes, eleven teachers focused on student interests, eighteen emphasized poetic conventions and language, and twenty-one focused on meaning or theme; most of these teachers chose "theme convergent" approaches (in other words, by utilizing close-reading techniques and directed questioning techniques, they led the class into discovering the same, or convergent, theme). Five teachers used uncategorized methods.

[4] The quotations from student essays are from classroom assignments submitted in my fall 2004 seminar in teaching English. I thank the students for their graciousness in allowing me to quote from their work. Although I covered New Criticism, reader response, gender studies, and cultural studies approaches, none of my students selected Poe for a cultural studies unit.

Teaching Poe in the Disability Studies Classroom: "The Man That Was Used Up"

William Etter

The critical examination of the historical experiences, social identities, and cultural representations of persons with disabilities—both real and fictional—lies at the heart of the scholarly field known as disability studies. An interdisciplinary field that can encompass areas of study from history to feminist studies to literary studies to sociology, disability studies has emerged in the late-twentieth and early-twenty-first centuries as a significant area of scholarship. Like gender and ethnic studies, disability studies turns its attention to a crucial element of human experience that has typically been ignored in our history, society, and culture. At the same time, disability studies scholars—again like their colleagues in gender and ethnic studies—have encouraged us to see disability not as a peripheral element of historical events, culture, or literary texts but as central to them. Indeed, some of the best scholarship and teaching in disability studies examines the relationship among persons with disabilities, cultural assumptions about human differences, and the broader social and historical milieu in which they exist. Social visions of how bodies should "normally" function or appear and how society treats individuals with bodies imagined as "normal" or deviating from "normality" are therefore a central concern of this field.

At the present time, colleges and universities are including disability studies courses in their curricula with increasing frequency; the University of Iowa; the University of Wisconsin; the University of California, Los Angeles; the University of Michigan; Syracuse University; and various California state universities are just some of the institutions that have recently added course offerings and programs of study in disability studies (Davidson and Siebers 498). Furthermore, in 2004 the Modern Language Association and Emory University sponsored a conference, Disability Studies and the University, to highlight the importance of teaching disability studies and explore its pedagogical future.

Because many concepts and methodologies of disability studies are complex, instructors of disability studies often search for new ways to make class material more accessible. Alternatively, instructors who teach literature courses that encourage students to examine texts through the lens of disability studies often look for useful primary source material on which to apply the analytic approaches of the field. Other instructors of literature who are not familiar with disability studies but are interested in learning more about the field or instructors who wish to incorporate different critical approaches in their classes seek literary works that are provocative and relevant to disability studies but that can function in an introductory capacity for teacher and student. Any or all of these instructors will find in Edgar Allan Poe's writings valuable classroom resources. Even teachers of Poe who have never taught texts, concepts, or methods of disability studies can find that approaching Poe's tales from a disability studies perspective offers fresh insights, additional richness, and increased enjoyment for readers.

Students who read Poe's commonly taught tales ("The Fall of the House of Usher," "The Masque of the Red Death," "Hop-Frog") and less frequently taught tales and poems ("Loss of Breath," "The Premature Burial," "For Annie") readily appreciate that images of nonnormal—damaged, grotesque, or ill—bodies are prominent elements of these texts. However, Poe also stresses the social significance of physical normality and privileges the drive to attain what society accepts as a normal body. Like other United States writers of the antebellum era (for example, Emerson, Lowell, and Hawthorne), Poe used literary discourse to create and reinforce cultural visions of the sorts of bodies society should consider normal and thus legitimate, pleasing, and useful, as well as what sorts should be classified as deviant and thus denied these classifications.

In this essay, I focus on the use of Poe's fiction to help students understand one crucial concern of disability studies: what Lennard J. Davis, in his book *Enforcing Normalcy*, calls "the construction of normalcy." This concept can be defined as the processes by which society determines, maintains, and regulates individuals' value based on culturally determined physical standards. A primary goal of this critical approach may be summed up as the attempt to "understand . . . the body-images of 'normal' subjects" as a means of critically examining "what is and is not tolerable or incorporable into normality" (Grosz 56).

As theorists of disability teach us, normality only appears to be a naturally occurring, unmarked status when it is in reality a social construction of the majority culture. Disability studies scholars have demonstrated that bodies are constructed as normal through interrelated material, personal, social, linguistic, and historical elements, to name some of the most prominent. It should not surprise us that college students of all levels have a great deal of difficulty understanding and applying these challenging concepts. I have found, however, that many of Poe's short stories can serve as useful tools for teaching this important aspect of disability studies. In this essay I discuss the story I believe to be the most valuable in this regard: "The Man That Was Used Up."

Students generally find this short tale engaging and, at times, comical. It describes the temperamental narrator's fascination with a former Indian fighter, General A. B. C. Smith. Intrigued by the praise lavished by friends on the general's physical endowments, the narrator learns the general was seriously mutilated by "Bugaboo and Kickapoo Indians" (309); among other injuries, he is scalped, his teeth knocked in, and a leg is cut off. Now he rebuilds his body each day using the finest American prosthetics. Characters in the tale who know Smith regard him as a legitimate member of their society, and his body as socially acceptable.

In short, General A. B. C. Smith's body—despite its unusual and extensive injuries—is constructed as normal throughout the tale. At first glance, however, students typically are inclined to see him as yet another of Poe's physically fantastic characters. I begin to encourage students to see this character in a different way by asking them to consider the protagonist's laughably ordinary name, just one marker of Smith's normality. When students are open to this possible reading of the tale, the class can begin to analyze the complicated ways in which Smith's body achieves normal status.

Specifically, it is useful to structure class work on this tale through an exploration of how the body that is "Smith" is a construction of three major elements: his mechanical and organic body components, his social circle and its language, and his historical period. Because these elements builds on one another and it is important for students to understand the relationships among them, I have found it is most effective to teach them in the order given.

Smith's Mechanical and Organic Components

The first of these—Smith's mechanical and organic components—is the most salient in the tale and thus the easiest for students to grasp after an initial reading. Smith's injuries, as well as his prosthetics, are alluded to frequently, either by Smith or by his friends. The Indians Smith fought are described as a "bloody set of wretches" (311), and conflicts with them in swamp battles as "Horrid" and "dreadful business" (313). Smith himself describes how a "Big Bugaboo rammed [him] down with the butt end of his rifle," bashing out all his teeth, and how some Kickapoos carved out part of his tongue (315). Similarly, there are references to such prosthetics as Smith's "capital cork leg" and the "singular-looking machine" that is his artificial palate (312). In constructing a composite frame of mechanical and fleshly parts to produce the general's body that enters the public realm, Poe's tale invites us to consider the way in which one's socially accepted "body" is a construction.

Students can readily grasp the important contribution Smith's prosthetics makes to the construction of his material body. Instructors can then build on this understanding to encourage them to consider that Smith's personality helps these material elements operate effectively to create a socially valuable body. The tale indicates that the general's personality is defined by a "high reputation for courage" sustained in the manner in which he interacts with his social circle (309). I have found it helpful to challenge students to explain how the general uses his prosthetics to create this heroic persona. In response, students often point to references in the tale that depict Smith as "[b]owing stiffly, but profoundly" and speaking in a "strong" voice (309). Indeed, Smith's imposing will combines the stiff movements of his reconstructed shoulders and legs and the alterations of his voice produced by a mechanical palate with a rugged bearing, thus helping him play the role of a heroic veteran.

In addition, because the intersection of technology and disability is often a focus of discussion in disability studies classrooms, the tale relates well to scholarly texts on present-day reconfigurations of how we imagine the human "body."

Such reconfigurations are based on assessments of how people with disabilities come to imagine wheelchairs, prosthetics, hearing aids, and computer-assisted communication devices as part of their "selves."[1]

In a course on disability and literature, this approach to the tale promotes the use of close reading to develop a consistent interpretation and emphasizes the importance of storytelling in establishing an individual's social identity. All the general's friends know of the "Horrid affair" of his battle with the Indians because the soldier has regularly related the story to them in striking detail (311), just as he relates it to the narrator at the end of the tale. Smith's personal memories help socially "re-member" his body, just as his prosthetics do. In a disability studies course, this line of discussion offers a point of entry into one approach to the study of disability prominent in the work of sociologists since at least the 1960s: the critical examination of disabled individuals' drives to control the "impression" of themselves in social situations, sometimes called the "dramaturgy" of interpersonal interactions involving individuals with disabilities. Smith is a disabled person performing a role, the sociopolitical parameters of which are delineated by mainstream society, in order to be socially accepted. His success is evident in the comical Cognoscenti sisters' expression of their delight in Smith's well-managed act, praising it as "so just an appreciation of stage effect" (311).

When students view Poe's story through the lens of disability studies, they can appreciate that prosthetics serve aesthetic and social as well as functional purposes. General Smith's physical disabilities are widely known, while his prosthetics are regarded as aesthetically pleasing. Virtually everyone the narrator encounters knows about "the tremendous events *quorum pars magna fuit* ["of which he was an important part"], during the Bugaboo and Kickapoo campaign" (310). In many ways, that is Smith's primary social virtue: his abnormality is never ignored yet all the while he is a figure who epitomizes the drive to be normal. A somewhat older, but still frequently referenced, work in the field of disability studies—the sociologist Erving Goffman's short book *Stigma*—is not only accessible to college students of all grade levels but, when paired with "The Man That Was Used Up," also offers useful material for teaching students to apply theoretical work on disability to primary texts. Goffman's concept of the "gentleman deviant," for example, aptly describes General Smith, who validates normality as something all individuals, no matter how physically damaged, are obligated to strive to attain. The general and his social circle thus conserve status-quo beliefs regarding human physical difference by committing themselves to an endeavor Goffman terms "normification": "the effort on the part of [an abnormal] individual to present himself as an ordinary person, although not necessarily making a secret of his failing" (31).

Smith is successful in his diligent efforts to assimilate and to avoid making his abnormality troublesome or aesthetically offensive to others. He makes what Goffman terms a "good adjustment" and is celebrated for the same reasons some disabled individuals are celebrated in the mainstream media culture of our day: they conserve dominant ideologies of normality by giving the impression they are earnestly struggling to "overcome" their disabilities, all the while keeping the idea that they remain "different" before the public eye. According to the historian Paul K. Longmore, this social arrangement "involv[es] an implicit bargain in which the nonhandicapped majority extend[s] provisional and partial tolerance of the public presence of handicapped individuals so long as they demonstrate . . . continuous cheerful striving toward normalization" (48).[2]

Along these lines, I have successfully developed discussion topics, analytic and research essay assignments, and examination questions by challenging students to use "The Man That Was Used Up" (sometimes in conjunction with excerpts from Goffman's book) to discuss questions like, Do prosthetics conceal or testify to physical differences? What end do their manufacturers intend? What end does mainstream society intend? What end does the individual who uses the prosthetics intend? Can prosthetics serve all or some of these ends simultaneously, and, if so, what are the personal and social effects that result?

Smith's Social Circle and Its Language

When students are exposed to Smith's social existence as a performance, they are learning about how Smith's body is public knowledge and serves the mainstream culture's ideology. Because disability studies asks us to consider how physical normalcy and physical disability are not natural, preexistent conditions but are formulated in different ways by various societies at various historical periods, it is particularly important for students to interpret General Smith's body in the context of his social interactions.

Because the narrator of the tale repeatedly encounters acquaintances of Smith's who are eager to discuss the general, students have ample opportunities to consider how Smith's society views him. A class discussion of the complimentary statements made by Smith's friends can lead to a detailed consideration of how these friends choose to envision him as a "person." For example, the third paragraph of "The Man That Was Used Up" offers a vision of a body deemed socially acceptable by consensus: "Every connoisseur in such matters admitted the legs to be good" (308).

One particular mode of analysis in disability studies—the consideration of the symbolic and linguistic representation of human physical differences—fits very well with the analysis of Poe's tale in courses on literature. Persons with disabilities both inside and outside academia have repeatedly called attention to the same thing that many teachers of literature stress in the classroom: the crucial role language plays in the construction of individuals' sociopolitical identities. For example, when examined through the lens of disability studies, there is a profound difference between labeling an individual "lame," with its accompanying suggestion of weakness, and referring to her or him in a far more humanizing way as a "person with a disability." Similarly, the term *midget*, with its fairy-tale connotations, is now understandably rejected in favor of the more neutral "short-statured person." In teaching "The Man That Was Used Up," it can be very productive, therefore, to work with students to examine how individuals are constituted as valuable social entities by virtue of how they are referred to by their society.

Once again, close reading proves a productive approach to teaching this tale because language plays an important role in the constitution of Smith as normal by his social acquaintances. I ask students to reread the tale and note repetitions of phrases and statements that describe Smith. While students typically find this task tedious, the activity helps them notice the ways in which Smith's friends make similar, often identical, statements such as "fought like a hero," "did you ever behold a finer figure?" (311), "that leg!" (312). At this point some students will even criticize the tale for wasting time with characters and comments that do not seem to offer any new information about the general. They are absolutely right. As it turns out, Smith's social figure is perpetuated largely by clichés, which provide a model for how Smith's body is socially constructed. Clichés produce a stable identity ossified by the repetition of approving statements about his body. Most strikingly, as most students note in their survey of repetition in the tale, the sources the narrator interviews conclude their discussion of Smith by referring to him as "the man," continually coding him as a normal, unmarked, and thus socially valuable individual.

Alternatively, instructors may choose to teach this concept in a more focused way by asking students to look closely at the language of the tale's final scene. When the narrator intrudes into the general's private apartment, he initially cannot recognize the "exceedingly odd looking bundle" of wounded organic flesh and simply denigrates it by referencing the flesh as "it" and "the thing" (314). Poe depicts the injured body as disrupting signification; the "bundle" of flesh is an uncategorizable, shapeless mass of abnormality that must be corrected and made meaningful. That is precisely what occurs. When Smith, with the help of his African American servant, assembles his organic and mechanical parts into a unified collection, his body becomes recognizable as an individual who can then be named "he," "the general," and a "man" (316). In this scene of physical reconstruction where the narrator gradually shifts pronouns from "it" to "he," the reader witnesses normalization in progress. In addition, students can better appreciate a point stressed in disability studies: individuals who physically deviate from established norms may be dehumanized through language ("it" and "thing"), while individuals who are imagined as fulfilling, or coming close to fulfilling, these norms are rewarded with appellations that grant them human status ("general" or "man").

By approaching the language of the story in this manner, an instructor can also use it to emphasize the crucial premise of disability studies I have been addressing in this essay: normality is not a stable, much less a natural, condition. It therefore needs to be continually referenced and reinforced—linguistically, for instance—in order to exist as a social reality.

As readers of this essay have no doubt gathered, I generally teach Poe's vision of disability in this tale and many others as an intolerant one because it demands that bodies be—or at least strive to be—normal. However, it should also be noted that in depicting the construction and constant reiteration of the normal, Poe's tale offers us a foundation for a critique of this social phenomenon. In this regard, I have sometimes used this tale as a way of introducing students to important connections that theorists of disability have forged between feminist and disability studies. In courses for advanced undergraduate or graduate students, the idea that normality must be reinforced and reiterated in order to exist as a social reality may be introduced in "The Man That Was Used Up" and further studied by reading Judith Butler's *Bodies That Matter* alongside recent works in disability studies that address issues of physical difference with respect to language and literature, like Davis's *Enforcing Normalcy*, Brenda J. Brueggemann's *Lend Me Your Ear: Rhetorical Constructions of Deafness*, and Jay Dolmage's "Between the Valley and the Field: Metaphor and Disability."

Smith's Historical Period

Such connections between disability studies and other scholarly fields show us that disability is not a marginal concern in culture, literature, and history. Rather, it intersects with numerous other topics that are currently taught as important elements of American literature and history. For example, many teachers of American literature make nationalism, race, and Native American history a central component of their courses. In "The Man That Was Used Up," all these important topics are directly related to the constructions of Smith's wounded and normalized body.

Once students have considered the importance of the technological and social elements in the composition of General A. B. C. Smith, they are equipped to pursue the relation between the social construction of normalcy and the history of United States–Native American relations highlighted in the tale by the damage the "horrid savages" wrecked upon Smith in fierce swamp battles with United States soldiers. Instructors who wish to deal with this context concisely can point out to students that "The Man That Was Used Up" was first published in 1839, near the close of a decade-long historical period during which peoples like the Choctaws, Seminoles, and Cherokees were driven west under federal and state governments' brutal Indian-removal policies. Consequently, this period also witnessed extensive armed conflict between United States soldiers and resisting Native Americans like the Second Seminole War, an event that was covered extensively in the newspapers of the time and with which Poe is believed to have been familiar (Silverman, *Edgar* 148). Alternatively, instructors who wish to cover this period in more detail may consult Francis Paul Prucha's abridged edition of *The Great Father* or Peter Nabokov's

Native American Testimony, both of which offer discussions of these historical conflicts, and both of which students find accessible and informative.

Regardless of the extent to which instructors choose to cover this historical context, I believe it is important to stress that, materially as well as ideologically, these conflicts between the United States and Native Americans are presented in the story as participating in the construction of Smith's body. Given that disability studies helps us interrogate the relation among physical differences, political and social institutions, and cultural representations, this perspective can help us further understand the function of Smith's wounding and prosthetics. The general's violent engagement with Native tribes results in a severely damaged white male body. What is ultimately given to the reader of the tale, however, is an intact, socially acceptable body, produced by American prosthetic technology and "civilized" social interactions, which symbolizes the idea that the threat of Native violence can be controlled. The redemption of this American soldier's body is celebrated as an expression of the United States' military, intellectual, national, and racial power. The nation creates a triumphantly white, male, normalized body in response to the nonwhite peoples who mustered all their "savage" violence to render it abnormal.

Teachers can therefore teach Poe's story as closely related not only to United States history but also to disability history. Students are typically surprised to learn, for instance, that several decades ago Cornelia Varner proved that many of the proper names referenced in "The Man That Was Used Up" as the sources for Smith's prosthetics were actual antebellum physicians, inventors, and dentists. Students enjoy Varner's brief article because it teaches them some unique facts about the historical context of the tale. Smith's comic pun, "Thomas is decidedly the best hand at a cork leg," for instance, refers to John F. Thomas, who advertised in periodicals like the *Philadelphia Public Ledger* as "a manufacturer in New York for 20 years . . . for LEGS, ARMS, HANDS, or the COMMON WOODEN LEG" (qtd. in Varner 78). In addition to dovetailing nicely with the technological and political context of Poe's short story, Varner's historical information offers students one illustration of what historian Douglas Baynton calls the recovery of the "hidden history" of disability, the often-ignored history of people who used artificial limbs, crutches, and other assistive devices.

Poe's tale celebrates the authority of the white, male American over African Americans and Native Americans. Written during a historical period on the cusp of a significant increase in the United States slave population as well as expanded calls for abolition, the story simultaneously promotes physical normality and white American power as they are enacted through the carefully controlled exploitation of debased nonwhite Americans. Every day, Smith's severely damaged flesh is transformed into a socially acceptable being with the assistance of a black servant who positions and adjusts the general's prosthetics. As Pompey works, Smith reviles him with curses: "Now, you dog, slip on my shoulders and bosom!"; "Now, you nigger, my teeth!" (315). The ability to claim a normal body is thus a mark of, and a route to, social and racial power in the antebellum United States even as nonwhite individuals contribute significantly to the achievement of this power. Teaching this element of "The Man That Was Used Up" is also valuable for disability studies courses, I believe, because it encourages students to recognize the participation of ideologies of physical normality in the operations of politics and historical conceptions of race. As a result, students can appreciate more fully the ways in which disability studies can help us investigate other crucial concerns of humanistic inquiry.

In fact, some of the richest uses of "The Man That Was Used Up" I have encountered in my classes have originated with students themselves, who have applied insights gained from studying the tale to present-day issues in disability studies. Some students have chosen to write research papers comparing General Smith with modern obsessions with plastic surgery. Others have come up with the idea of comparing the social reception of the former Indian fighter with that of disabled Vietnam veterans. One student wrote a fine paper exploring images of wounded masculinity in "The Man That Was Used Up" and contemporary works of fiction, like Rick Bass's short story "The Fireman." These students' work illustrates what I have suggested in this essay: "The Man That Was Used Up" is pedagogically valuable both because it is a unique consideration of the social construction of physical normality and because it offers inspiration for exploring a variety of topics commonly addressed in disability studies courses.

NOTES

[1] Two expressions of this scholarly interest are Donna J. Haraway's *Simians, Cyborgs, and Women* and Irving Zola's *Missing Pieces: A Chronicle of Living with a Disability*.

[2] Longmore's *"Why I Burned My Book" and Other Essays on Disability* includes analyses of representations of people with disabilities in contemporary media. Students can learn a lot about these representations by applying Longmore's discussions of television and film characters to characters in Poe's short stories such as Roderick Usher and Madeline Usher, the short-statured Hop-Frog, the sickly narrator of "The Man of the Crowd," and the blind devil in "Bon-Bon."

Rediscovering Poe through the Eyes of World Authors: What Do They See in Him?

Lois Davis Vines

As a professor of French who has given Poe workshops for high school teachers and seminars for college students in English, I offer an approach to the study of the American author that transcends national boundaries. My approach is based on my own rediscovery of Poe during a year-long graduate course on the French poet and essayist Paul Valéry in which my professor praised Poe's "lucidity of intellect" and described his influence on several renowned French writers. Was he talking about our own Edgar Allan? For me, a native-born American, Poe was part of my childhood reading and a melancholy face on a card in the game called Authors. Jinglelike phrases such as "in a kingdom by the sea . . . the beautiful Annabel Lee" and Halloween images inspired by "The Fall of the House of Usher" constituted the remnants of Poe's work in my mind. I soon became obsessed with learning more about writers in France and in other countries who adopted Poe as their mentor. This voyage of literary discovery eventually took me from Europe to Latin America and as far away as Japan and China. Along the way I could not help imagining Poe's great pleasure had he known that his work would be admired on a truly global scale.

Although it would be a pleasure for me to give a series of lectures on Poe's influence throughout the world, a more effective approach is to engage students in their own explorations with a guiding framework that I provide. Students work in small groups to prepare their research, which they present to the whole class. Since students often do not know one another, I have them draw numbers to form groups of three. I give them a few minutes in class to get together, exchange e-mail addresses, and plan a time to meet. As I explain to the students, the goal of each small group is to become a community of scholars on their research topic. After reading and discussing the texts in their group, they prepare a twenty-minute oral presentation followed by a question-answer exchange with their fellow classmates. Each student also prepares a ten-page paper, which I will explain below after giving the outlines for the research topics.

Each group is assigned a subject along with specific references to use as the basis for the presentation. I carefully plan the topics, taking into account three considerations: (1) Each research topic includes a text (translated into English) written by the foreign author. My goal is for the students to study a text by a world-renowned author who was influenced by Poe and not just read about the author and the text. (2) To make the research assignments more or less equal in length and complexity, I have selected texts that students can master on their own. (3) I make sure the texts are available either online or on reserve at the library. At my university, the academic year is divided into ten-week quarters, which do not allow much time for obtaining books through interlibrary loan.

I want to avoid a situation in which students embark on a topic only to find that the texts they need are not available. Although additional areas of inquiry concerning Poe's influence are fascinating, such as his role in the literary development of writers in Russia, Japan, and China (see Vines, *Poe Abroad*), my own research reveals the difficulty of finding texts in English that are accessible, which is the reason I prefer to plan the basic structure of the oral presentation. On their assigned topics, students are also encouraged to find additional related material. They are very adept at using electronic resources and presenting their themes using *PowerPoint* to illustrate the main ideas. Below I give six examples of presentation topics along with essential texts, all of which are in English.

Poe and Baudelaire

Poe learned in 1846, just three years before his death, that his "Murders in the Rue Morgue" had been mentioned in a Paris newspaper. He was unaware that a budding writer by the name of Charles Baudelaire, who would become one of France's greatest poets, published a translation of "Mesmeric Revelation" in 1848 and was preparing a major article on Poe that would appear in 1852. Although Baudelaire's biography of Poe contains several errors, he gives a sympathetic account of the poet condemned to live in the puritanical culture of America. For Baudelaire, Poe was a literary genius who understood the mechanism of artistic creation. Baudelaire's long article was later used as the preface to his translation of Poe's tales published in 1856. A revised and condensed version became the preface to Baudelaire's second volume of translated tales in 1857.

Baudelaire's discovery of Poe has become legendary in literary history. The French poet recalled the excitement that led to his Poe obsession: "In 1846 or '47 I came across a few fragments by Edgar Poe. I experienced a singular shock. . . . I found poems and short stories that I had thought of, but in a vague, confused and disorderly way and that Poe had been able to bring together to perfection" (Baudelaire qtd. in Lloyd 148). Baudelaire also found parallels between his life and Poe's, although they had grown up in very different cultures. I recommend the following texts to students as preparation for their presentation: early Poe translations that led to Baudelaire's first reading and his Poe obsession (Bandy, Introduction);[1] similarities between Poe's life and Baudelaire's (Vines, "Poe in France" 10–11); Baudelaire's article on Poe that was used as a preface to his translations (Carlson, "New Notes"); lines of poetry that appear to be Baudelaire's borrowings from Poe (Wetherill); letters written by Baudelaire in which he talks about Poe (Lloyd).

Poe, Stéphane Mallarmé, and Paul Valéry

Baudelaire's fascination with Poe was communicated to his successors, Stéphane Mallarmé and Paul Valéry. Mallarmé, a leading figure in the symbolist movement in France, took on the task of translating Poe's poems into French. Poe's poetry and views on literary creation inspired Mallarmé's attempt to achieve perfection through the constant refinement of language. The French poet envisioned a poetic language that would be purified of everyday meaning through the creation of new usage, rhythms, rhymes, and even the positioning of the words on the page. Mallarmé found the origins of modern poetry in Poe's work. The image of Poe that Mallarmé bequeathed to future poets is summed up in his poem "The Tomb of Edgar Poe," written to commemorate the twenty-fifth anniversary of Poe's death. The poem immortalizes Poe as a misunderstood artist who achieved recognition only after his death. Reading for the students' presentation should include background on Mallarmé, his interest in Poe, and his poem about Poe (Vines, *Valéry* 29–42).[2] Valéry took up the banner for Poe after Mallarmé's death in 1898. In an essay titled "The Place of Baudelaire," Valéry describes Poe's influence on Baudelaire while expressing his own admiration for the American poet. Although Valéry admired Poe's poems and poetics, he was directly influenced by Auguste Dupin, the main character in three of Poe's crime tales. Valéry transformed Poe's detective into Monsieur Teste. A close examination of Valéry's prose piece, *The Evening with Monsieur Teste*, reveals numerous similarities between his main character and Poe's detective. The aspect of Poe's character that captured Valéry's imagination was the detective's ability to observe his own analytic faculties. In Monsieur Teste, Valéry created a superbrain, a mind that was not only intelligent but also capable of understanding its own mental operations. As in Poe's Dupin tales, Valéry uses a narrator to describe and react to the main character. But unlike Dupin, Teste does not need to show off his superior intellect. His greatest pleasure is observing the functioning of his own mind. To prepare the presentation, students need to read Valéry's "The Place of Baudelaire" and *Monsieur Teste* plus the chapter on the Dupin-Teste connection in Lois Vines, *Valéry and Poe*.

Poe and Jules Verne

Among the many French writers and poets influenced by Poe, Jules Verne wrote fiction that reveals the closest connection. Verne expressed great admiration for Poe and admitted that his own work was a direct descendant of several stories written by his favorite American author. The students' presentation on Verne should be divided into two parts. Since each part is rather long, the topics could be assigned to two groups:

Group 1

Verne wrote a sequel to *The Narrative of Arthur Gordon Pym* (1838), which he titled *The Sphinx of Ice* (1897). Verne was so captivated by the story that he decided to pick up where Poe had left off. Poe's tale ends rather abruptly with a mysterious apparition:

> And now we rushed into the embraces of the cataract, where a chasm threw itself open to receive us. But there arose in our pathway a shrouded human figure, very far larger in its proportions than any dweller among men. And the hue of the skin of the figure was of the perfect whiteness of the snow. (1179)

Poe added a "note" on the following page saying that Pym had died suddenly while preparing the narrative, and the remaining chapters of his adventure had been lost. Poe then adds: "This, however, may prove not to be the case, and the papers, if ultimately found, will be given to the public" (1180). It was perhaps this suggestion of a sequel that inspired Verne to write his own tale. Verne makes a direct connection to Poe's story by creating a narrator, an American naturalist by the name of Jeorling, who signed on board the schooner *Halbrane*, which just happened to belong to Captain Len Guy, the brother of Poe's William Guy, who rescued Peters and Pym at the end of chapter 13 of *The Narrative of Arthur Gordon Pym*. Len Guy tells Jeorling that he tried unsuccessfully to find Pym and even Poe himself. The captain then recounts (in about twenty pages) Pym's experience based on Poe's tale. On board the *Halbrane* is a mysterious sailor who turns out to be none other than Dirk Peters. *Quelle coïncidence!* The adventures that follow as the *Halbrane* heads toward the South Pole share numerous similarities in style and events with Poe's novel. The main readings for the presentation are Poe's *Pym* and Verne's *The Sphinx of Ice*. In addition to simply recounting Verne's sequel, students are encouraged to present elements of style, techniques used to convince the reader that the story is true, and the similarities in the use of images. Their research should also include critical studies of *Pym*, such as those found in Richard Kopley's collection of essays, and a discussion of points from those analyses that also apply to Verne's sequel.

Group 2

The second part of the Verne topic deals with his interest in balloon flight. Two of Poe's tales, "The Balloon-Hoax" (13 pages) and "The Unparalleled Adventure of One Hans Pfaall" (51 pages), inspired Verne's first successful novel, *Five Weeks in a Balloon* (1863). The presentation should include similarities in style between the two authors' texts, which include numerous scientific explanations to make the stories more believable. It is interesting for students to do research on the invention of the hot-air balloon by the French brothers Joseph Michel Montgolfier and Jacques-Étienne Montgolfier in the latter half of the eighteenth century and the fascination with this type of air travel, including recent attempts to circumnavigate the globe in a hot-air balloon without descending.

Poe's Influence on Latin American Authors

Through their reading of Baudelaire, many writers in Latin America learned about Poe and were, in turn, influenced by his prose and poetry. For student presentations, I have chosen two major literary figures: Jorge Luis Borges and Julio Cortázar. Born in Argentina, Borges read Poe at an early age and proclaimed his indebtedness to the American author throughout his lifetime. He was especially captivated by Poe's detective stories, "Murders in the Rue Morgue," "The Mystery of Marie Roget," and "The Purloined Letter." As background preparation for Poe in Latin America, students read Susan F. Levine and Stuart Levine; for an introduction to Poe and Borges, the six-page essay by Graciela Tissera in Vines's anthology is very helpful. After reading the three Poe stories just mentioned, the students are prepared to appreciate two tales by Borges that show Poe's influence. In "Death and the Compass," Borges compares one of the main characters, Lönnrot, to Poe's detective: "He thought of himself as a reasoning machine, an Auguste Dupin, but there was something of the adventurer in him, even something of the gambler" (147). It is not difficult for students to discover parallels between Borges's crime story and Poe's tales of ratiocination. These connections can also be seen in Borges's eight-page tale "Ibn-Hakam al-Bokhari, Murdered in His Labyrinth," which has a surprise ending. Early in the story, the two main characters, Dunraven and Unwin, are trying to solve a mystery. When Dunraven suggests a complicated explanation, Unwin interrupts him saying: "Please, let's not multiply the mysteries. Mysteries ought to be simple. Remember Poe's purloined letter" (256). After reading Borges's stories, it is helpful for students to consult John T. Irwin's study on Borges and Poe, *The Mystery to a Solution*.

Since the student presentation on Borges tends to be complex, it would be a good idea to assign the study of Cortázar to another group. Cortázar was born in Belgium but spent many years in Argentina before moving to France in 1951. He is sometimes called the Spanish-language Baudelaire because of the extraordinary affinity he felt for Poe and his five volumes of Poe translations into Spanish. I recommend that students begin their research on Cortázar by reading Mary G. Berg, who mentions numerous stories influenced by Poe and a couple of English-language studies analyzing the connections. Cortázar's nine-page tale "We Love Glenda So Much" shares a theme with Poe's "The Oval Portrait." On the surface, the stories are very different, but the underlying theme deals with the transformation of a living woman into an obsession with pure art. In the process, the real woman is sacrificed to a higher ideal.

For each of the presentations I have described above, students first give a brief overview of their writer's biography and contributions to literature, since the authors might not be familiar to many students in the class. The presenters prepare for their classmates a one-page handout with the most important points of the oral presentation. For their final paper in the course (about ten pages), students are given the option of choosing a theme from their research topic: for example, a comparison of images used by Poe and Verne. The paper provides the opportunity for a more in-depth analysis than can be given in the oral presentation.

Studying Poe's influence on outstanding authors in other cultures provides an excellent introduction to world literature. Students can be encouraged to read the authors in the original version. At Ohio University, I have collaborated with a colleague in history, Benita Blessing, who has initiated an interdisciplinary approach in her courses that engages students who have studied a foreign language for three or four years. Students in her contemporary history classes partner with faculty members in modern languages, who work with them on texts in the foreign language that complement the subject of the history course. We have dubbed this initiative the "foreign language option," with the acronym FLO, suggesting connections between disciplines. In the approach to teaching Poe that I have outlined, students with advanced foreign language skills could read the texts in the original and work with a language professor for a one-hour independent study. I have worked with three students recently and have been very pleased with the outcome. After studying texts in French with me, they present their research in English to the history class, which I attend for the presentation. It is rewarding for both the student and teacher to use the foreign language to enrich learning that is not limited to the English language. Edgar Allan Poe's poetry and prose connect us with major world authors whose creative endeavors can best be appreciated in their own languages. The works by authors that I have suggested for presentations can be read in the original language by students who have had at least three years of French or Spanish.

NOTES

[1] The title of Bandy's edition is in French but the introduction is in English.
[2] These pages include the text and an analysis of Mallarmé's poem dedicated to Poe.

Teaching Poe's Influence on Hitchcock: The Example of "Murders in the Rue Morgue" and *Psycho*

Dennis R. Perry

I teach a literature and film course on Poe and Hitchcock, the genesis of which was inspired by the director's admission that "very probably, it's because I like Edgar Allan Poe's stories so much that I began to make suspense films" (143). Because so many of Poe's stories and Hitchcock's films share plots, character types, and thematic and generic obsessions, the pairing provides new insights—not only on Hitchcock but also on the meaning and significance of Poe's art. Poe's influence on Hitchcock and countless other writers and filmmakers has made Poe an archetypal figure whose narrative paradigms have entered the collective consciousness and unconsciousness of nearly all subsequent artists of dark fantasy, suspense, horror, and detective fiction. In this essay I will summarize the objectives, organization, assignments, and texts I use in the Poe and Hitchcock course, followed by the example of teaching "Murders in the Rue Morgue" alongside *Psycho*.

The film and literature course at Brigham Young University is a 300-level course aimed at juniors and seniors, the focus of specific sections varying with instructors. My course objectives reflect the complex, double nature of both literature and film and Poe and Hitchcock. These objectives include students being able to be conversant on major critical works and trends of both Poe and Hitchcock, know and use the basic vocabulary of the cinema, analyze and write about film, understand the creative theories of Poe and Hitchcock, and generate useful insights in comparing their works. The course is organized around pairings of Poe and Hitchcock works that explore similar thematic or genre concerns such as doubles, voyeurism, ratiocination, inexplicability, perverseness, and apocalypse. Among the important ways students demonstrate their knowledge and skill is to write several "film logs" in which they analyze a frame and a sequence and then develop a point of comparison between two works around a relevant theme (such as "The Tell-Tale Heart" and *Rope* in terms of the imp of the perverse or "The Masque of the Red Death" and *The Birds* in terms of the apocalypse). In addition, students write a long paper in which they analyze an original pairing of a Poe tale (or poem) and a Hitchcock film (often one we have not discussed in class). Course texts will usually include a Poe anthology (Thompson's *Selected Writings of Edgar Allan Poe*), a basic introduction to film (Corrigan's *A Short Guide to Writing about Film*), and my own study of Poe and Hitchcock (*Hitchcock and Poe: The Legacy of Delight and Terror*). These choices, of course, can vary. Ultimately, the class highlights both the astonishing similarities and inevitable differences between Poe and Hitchcock, helping students generate insights back and forth between them.

The following account of a class discussion comparing works of Poe and Hitchcock is an exemplum only, not a transcript from the course. An example pairing, "Murders in the Rue Morgue" and *Psycho,* are two stories of horrifying graphic violence, detective work, and a surprise killer. I first ask students to identify similarities. The list we derive includes shocking murders of women; inexplicability of the crimes, including lack of motive; incompetent police; two people together discovering and trapping the murderer; isolation and alienation; and a superior analyst who fathoms and explains the heart of the mystery, uncovering the unexpected nature of the murderers. With so many correlations evident I next ask the class to compare certain similar features in these narratives and draw conclusions that illustrate how Hitchcock treats this somewhat analogous material differently: How are the audiences engaged? How do we feel about the victims? How much information is given to the audience? At what point does the narration begin? How do we identify with protagonists?

The results of this exercise lead students to three main conclusions: First, Poe engages the reader intellectually, while Hitchcock's focus is on audience emotions. Second, Poe's readers never know the murder victims and thus have no sympathy for them. Hitchcock's audience, however, gets to know both Marion and Arbogast enough to feel sympathy for them, increasing the shock and horror of their murders. Third, Poe provides readers with what the papers and the police know about the crime, and then what Dupin unfolds during his investigation and analysis. Hitchcock lets his audience partially see what happens to Marion and Arbogast, although, as in Poe's tale, the real murderer is only revealed in the end. "Murders in the Rue Morgue" begins with a lengthy introduction to Dupin and his eccentricities and then reveals the murder after the fact, as reported in the papers. *Psycho* begins by unfolding the frustrating life of Marion Crane, then presents her theft and murder. This is a key difference, not least because we believe the story is about a theft rather than a murder and are shocked that this star vehicle kills off its star almost halfway through the film. Dupin is too weird and brilliant for most of us to identify with, leaving us to identify instead with his everyman sidekick-narrator. With Marion's death Hitchcock complicates this issue, forcing us to try and identify with Sam and Lila, two much less sympathetic characters. Near the end, however, we begin to bond with the vulnerable Lila searching the Bateses' house.

After the class makes these comparisons, what have we learned of Poe? At least in this inaugural detective story, Poe privileges the intellect over emotions, keeps the violence offscreen (so to speak), makes his protagonist primarily an unsympathetic thinking machine, and withholds from the reader everything until Dupin unveils it. But in addition to these conclusions, I ask students to write a short paper about how reexperiencing Poe's tale in the context of *Psycho* changes their thinking on "Murders in the Rue Morgue." Their insights include the following: the Norman-Mother doubling suggests new ways to perceive the protective sailor-ape relationship; the psychiatrist's analysis of Norman lets us see into the proto-psychoanalysis of Dupin's reasoning through identification; Marion's brutal murder gives students a better sense of the horrific nature of the L'Esplanaye murders—as well as a striking soundtrack to accompany it; the violent murder of the women highlights issues of violence against women; and the psychotic dream life of Norman puts fellow dream reveler Dupin in a less heroic light. Thus, *Psycho* enables a rereading of Poe's tale, more clearly showing what it is and is not, what it does and does not do.

Perhaps during a subsequent discussion period, to take the comparison a level deeper in terms of audience participation, we do a cross-criticism exercise, reading an analysis of *Psycho* (Telotte's "Faith and Idolatry in the Horror Film") and seeing how it might apply to "Murders in the Rue Morgue." In short, J. P. Telotte asserts that the realistic horror film presents a rupture in the audience's perceptually created "real" world, leading to a cathartic recognition of the roots and hazards of voyeurism and other forms of alienation from society. I further point out how Robin Wood also notes how Hitchcock draws us into the film and implicates us in the action through specific cinematic means— the apparent random selection of shots: "it could be us" in the dark hotel room of the opening scene (Wood 142). Thus we feel our reality and complacency undermined after the shower murder (146). To set the stage in the class for considering "Murders" as a horror as well as detective tale, I begin by quoting Hitchcock on Poe's tale:

> I still remember my feelings when I finished "The Murders in the Rue Morgue." I was afraid, but this fear made me in fact discover something that I haven't since forgotten. Fear, you see, is a feeling that people like to feel when they are certain of being in safety.   (143)

We then try to identify what in "Murders" may have seemed scary to Hitchcock or to us. Inevitably students refer to the gothic, Usheresque atmosphere of Dupin's mansion and of Dupin himself; the graphic violence of the murders; the suspenseful buildup to a solution one almost does not want to know; the confrontation between Dupin and the Maltese sailor; and, most important perhaps, an atmosphere of dread—the feeling that something is terribly wrong or unnatural, a randomness that yields no apparent evidence or motive, as if perpetrated by a supernatural fury.

Having established as a class a common ground of realistic horror for the two stories, we consider Telotte's examination of alienation by comparing Marion and Dupin, beginning with the question of what alienates Marion from society. Students immediately point out that by stealing the $40,000, Marion has alienated herself from her immediate circle of work and family relationships and from society as a whole. We next consider what motivates her to so alienate herself from society. Clearly she needs money to marry Sam and live a happier, less lonely life. But we then probe beyond motivation into the question of what allows her to act on her positive desires in such a negative way. That is, we con-

sider the irony in Marion's at once wanting to participate in society's norm of fulfillment, marriage, and violating society's moral code to achieve it. Evidently,
students note, the balance between her perception of self and others is skewed
such that for selfish ends she willingly sacrifices social values. This leads us to
Owen Barfield's visual theory of "idolatry," discussed by Telotte, which suggests
Marion's "tendency to abstract the sense data from the whole representation [of
her social and self perception] and seek that for its own sake" (Barfield qtd. in
Telotte 149). In other words, Marion removes herself from "vital participation"
in society by blinding herself to it (Telotte 149). That is, as in idol worship, Marion's focus is on something lifeless. This insight takes us to Telotte's reading of
Marion's failing vision during her drive to Fairvale, where she is no longer able
to "see her way" (Telotte 150). The end of the shower murder, as Lesley Brill
adds, completes the picture of Marion's blindness, her dead eye superimposed
over the drain becoming an "emblem of final hopelessness" (*Hitchcock Romance*
224). Finally, I quote Paula Marantz Cohen that we, as cinematic voyeurs, like
Marion, watch life (film) with a dead, or complacent eye (*Alfred Hitchcock* 149).

   The class is next invited to turn its attention to Dupin, beginning with examining a number of passages I put on the board to indicate his alienation from his
society: "Dupin ceased to know or be known in Paris"; "we existed within ourselves alone"; "we admitted no visitors"; "our seclusion was perfect" (401).
Adding to these, students might note how Dupin prefers dreams to reality
(401), speaks as if in soliloquy despite others being in the room (415), and has
no qualms about abstracting other people into mere objects of observation and
analysis (402–04). Asked if his "seclusion" is perfect then, or if there is some
tension between his desires for alienation and participation in society, as there
is for Marion, students refer to his nightly walk "amid the wild lights and shadows of the populous city" to enjoy "that infinity of mental excitement which
quiet observation can afford" (401). They find it telling that this passage presents contrasts in Dupin—the lights and shadows representing his desires to be
both a part of and apart from society. Asked what motivates him, the class mentions Dupin's hunger for social recognition in outwitting the police as well as his
propensity to narrate dramatically his analytic insights to highlight his bril-
liance. Hence, Dupin's self-perception is out of balance with his social perception, making society either an audience or the subject of analysis to serve his
intellectual and egotistical needs.

   Finally, I ask if students see similarities in Marion's and Dupin's alienation.
After some discussion, the class decides that at the root for both are financial
concerns: Marion needs money to marry Sam, and "poverty" causes Dupin to
cease "to bestir himself in the world" ([401] though money is certainly a more
explicit motive in "The Purloined Letter"). I pick up on this image of stepping
away from society, of becoming dead to it. I refer the students back to
Telotte's comments on Marion's failure of vision while driving in the rain and
to the image of Marion's dead, staring eyes during and after the shower murder (Telotte 149–50). To link Marion and Dupin further, I then ask if this

image is duplicated anywhere in "Murders." The answer, of course, is the image of the "resolvent" Dupin's "excited" intelligence when explaining his conclusions: "His manner at these moments was frigid and abstract; his eyes were vacant in expression." The passage continues with the idea that the detective is "a double Dupin—the creative and the resolvant" (402), which also reminds us of the double Marion who vascillates about her crime until she finally decides, too late, to return the money. Thus, blindness becomes an important image in both stories to embody alienation. Marion's focus on herself abstracts reality and blinds her to others.

With this comparison of Dupin to Marion we have established important thematic links in these stories between alienation and perception. We now turn to a central aspect of Telotte's article: how we as audience members and readers identify with these characters, and the significance of that identification. Asked with whom *Psycho* has us identify, students venture that the camera shows us a distorted reality from the point of view of both Marion and Norman, a view that itself becomes a primary subject of the film. Through our identification with them our sense of reality, which the film's mise-en-scène re-creates, is ruptured. Asked how we are made to identify with Dupin, students note that the narrator, who idolizes his detective friend, gives himself "up to [Dupin's] wild whims with a perfect *abandon*" (401). Thus, since the narrator gives Dupin much of the story to tell in his own voice, we are encouraged to make his reality ours. We come to share Dupin's mental excitement and pleasure in "disentangling" and analysis (397), and with him approach the murders as a means merely to "afford us amusement" (412). Students also note that in *Psycho*, we often see the world from Norman's distorted point of view, even rooting for him to escape detection as he cleans up after "Mother" and suspensefully sinks Marion's car in the bog.

In summary, the class concludes that the same lessons Telotte finds in *Psycho* and other realistic horror films apply to "Murders." As Hitchcock and Poe cause us to identify with the "diseased" intelligences of Marion, Norman, and Dupin, we are cautioned to realize our own potential for the idolatrous abstracting of others. Hence, realistic horror locates the horror within us by demonstrating the volatile nature of perception itself in us as well as in the fictional characters with whom we identify. The ultimate horror for us can be, as it is for Norman, a loss of our ability to participate in the world with unimpaired vision, "effectively [departing] from the living and [becoming] little more than an object [ourselves]"—the ultimate alienation (Telotte 151). Asked what is cathartic about this, students see the terror of our potential for alienation through idol worship of selfish ideas. And, as Telotte notes, we are cautioned "to guard our new-found sense of human participation" (152–53). Asked what we have learned about Poe in this comparative exercise, they observe that, contrary to the traditional wisdom on Poe, his horrors can be seen as more than art for art's sake, since Poe's art engages our perceptions of ourselves and reality, containing vital truths about our relationships to others.

Finally, this comparison helps us enlarge Hitchcock's statement about enjoying safe fear. As Telotte suggests, "the most horrific effect is often when we leave the theater [or the book] still partially in the grip of those dark forces" (153). We can now see that we not only enjoy—but learn from—what we fear is within ourselves. Enjoying horror in comfortable circumstances may make us feel safe but not really innocent.

Poe in the Comics

M. Thomas Inge

In his own time, Edgar Allan Poe was an important presence in the popular press and literature of nineteenth-century America, and he was never to leave the consciousness of the public for very long. In the twentieth century, his books were always in print in both hardcover and inexpensive paperback editions, as they are today. Thousands of illustrated editions of his books have appeared in more than thirty countries (Pollin, *Images*). Almost one hundred feature-length films have been based on his works and life, as well as countless radio, stage, and television adaptations (Smith). Few writers have so successfully made a claim to both popular and academic audiences by producing works that respond to reading for such a wide variety of reasons, from simple pleasure and entertainment to the complex practice of any mode of literary criticism or critical theory.

Poe has frequently been used as a source of humor in hundreds of magazine cartoons, from the *New Yorker* to *Playboy*, as well as newspaper comic strips, but he has had a particularly strong presence in the comic book and the graphic novel. According to one count, his stories and poems have been adapted to the comic book more than three hundred times, and research continues to find many more (Inge). The popular comic-book periodical *Classics Illustrated* alone used Poe in over sixty editions worldwide from 1944 to 1997 (W. Jones), the Warren comic magazines published at least twenty-five versions, and numerous others appeared in horror titles in the United States and abroad.

The very first comic books were devoted to reprinting favorite newspaper comic strips, but by 1935 publishers began to commission new material for the pages of their suddenly popular publications. For themes, they turned to the pulp and magazine fiction of the 1930s—science fiction, detective, mystery, western, adventure, and sports stories. The sixty-four-page comic books each contained six to ten different types of stories. In a sense, these books were pictorial short story collections, and the authors and artists naturally turned to short fiction as models in the use of limited reading time. Creators of comic books faced the same challenges as writers of short stories: how to develop engaging characters and then establish a conflict and bring it to a resolution in a few pages. Inevitably they turned to Poe, Washington Irving, Ambrose Bierce, Stephen Crane, O. Henry, and other widely read writers for inspiration and instruction. They often borrowed the content as well, sometimes without attribution, which frequently happened to Poe.

While studying the form and function of the comic book narrative as if it were a short story can be useful, it should be remembered that the comic book is a distinctive and discrete medium of artistic expression because it values the picture as much as the printed word. How then should one evaluate an adaptation from literature? One approach is to take a cue from film critics who have come to consider the question, How faithful is the film to the original work? as irrelevant. Instead of asking this question, one should ask, Is it a good film? Just as the film should be considered on its own merits in accordance with the aesthetic possibilities of film, so too should a comics adaptation be evaluated in terms of its success as a piece of comic art. Does it use or expand on the full range of visual and verbal techniques available to the comic artist, as outlined in such critical works as *Understanding Comics* by Scott McCloud and *Comics and Sequential Art* by Will Eisner?

Such questions provide stimulating topics for class discussion and essay assignments. How effectively has a particular adaptation captured or re-created the mood and emotional appeal of a story? What changes have been made on behalf of the limitations and possibilities of the new medium? Were they necessary, and do they contribute to a more effective artistic vision? What are the losses and what are the gains? Can an adaptation ever be better than the original (recall *The Godfather*, which many consider a better film than the novel)? What is there in Poe that has attracted so many comic book artists and writers? Why do they want to keep his work before the eyes of contemporary readers?

This is an approach of which Poe himself might have approved. Especially as a magazine editor, he was cognizant of what a good illustration could add to a printed story or novel. In reviewing an illustrated edition of *The Vicar of Wakefield* by Oliver Goldsmith, Poe once noted that the relevance of the illustrations to the printed text was less important than the quality of the art. What one looks for, he said, are the elements of good art, "the skillful grouping of figures, vivacity, *naivete*, and originality of fancy, and good drawing in the mass," rather than a "too continuous adherence to the text" (qtd. in Pollin, *Images* 2–3).

The problem with the first comic book adaptations in *Classics Illustrated* was just that. Established in 1941 by a Russian immigrant named Albert Lewis Kanter, it used the comics to lure young readers away from the superhero titles back to the classics. Kanter was convinced that a faithful adaptation would accomplish this; thus artists and writers were seldom allowed to embellish or expand on their sources (Sawyer). Most of the titles, then, were plodding, literal versions that seldom used the rich potential of the emerging styles of comic art and visual storytelling. Even so, they were enormously profitable and attracted a faithful following, mainly among young readers who were already intellectually inclined. This writer first encountered *Hamlet* and *Moby-Dick* in the *Classics Illustrated* versions, was inspired to read the originals, and eventually became a professor of literature. Students might be asked if they have had a similar experience of seeing a film or comics adaptation of a novel or play and then returning to the original as a result. Which did they prefer, and why?

The appearance of Poe in *Classics Illustrated* began in July 1944 with "The Murders in the Rue Morgue" in *Classics Illustrated: Three Famous Mysteries*, and the creators continued to contribute to a variety of anthology titles featuring adaptations of the best-known tales, most of them rather mundane in their

art and mechanical in their telling. The most striking of them may be "The Adventures of Hans Pfaall" in an August 1947 issue entirely devoted to mysteries
by Poe (*Classics Illustrated: Mysteries*). The artist, Henry C. Kieffer, lets his visual imagination slip loose along with Hans Pfaall's balloon, and his caricatures
of the Dutch and their addiction to pipe smoking, the fantastic cosmos
through which Pfaall sails, and Kieffer's vision of the moon and its populace
(borrowing a little from the Munchkins in the 1939 film version of *The Wizard
of Oz*), are a humorous treat that only effective comic art can convey.

Classics Illustrated was concluded in 1962, and copies are not easily available
for research. Some are rare and expensive on the collectors' market, but many
of them were reprinted in 1997–98 by Acclaim Books, including two Poe collections, *Classics Illustrated: Stories by Poe* and *Classics Illustrated: More Stories by Poe*. These make it possible for students to evaluate for themselves the
judgment that these adaptations feature unimaginative art and narration and
perhaps to argue for the qualities of some of the other stories as reflective of
Poe's intentions or as good examples of comic art on their own. They have an
added advantage of explanatory notes and study guides by academics, but only
comic-book shops are likely to have any of the back issues. This is true, of
course, of most of the comic books containing adaptations of Poe since libraries
until recently neglected to collect them.

Resourceful students could be encouraged to go in search of well-read
copies, which are less expensive than those in mint condition. They might seek
out the horror comics produced by the publisher EC—*Crypt of Terror, Vault
of Horror,* and *Haunt of Fear*, in which some of the best-written and best-
drawn titles in comic book history appeared and in which several striking
adaptations of Poe appeared. They could also find issues of the James Warren
publications—*Creepy, Eerie,* and *Vampirella*—with stories in black-and-white
and intended for an adult audience. A new generation of artists produced a
powerful series of Poe tales for Warren. One of the best is Richard Corben's
version of "The Raven" in *Creepy* number 67. Through the use of photographic realism, shifting camera angles, and three-dimensional figures that
seem to break free of the panels, Corben has reimagined and re-created Poe's
best-known and all-too-familiar poem and given it a new vitality. A fruitful
topic of discussion for students would be how these particular visual elements
make Poe's poem seem new again. In what ways, however, does the poem retain an integrity that cannot be duplicated visually?

Recent efforts to revive *Classics Illustrated* can probably be found more
easily. Berkley Publishing revived it in February 1990, and the first title was
Classics Illustrated: "The Raven" and Other Poems, with full-page illustrations
by Gahan Wilson. His macabre humor and gothic style as displayed in his cartoons for popular magazines made him an appropriate match for the fully
reprinted nine poems in the book. While Wilson never drew for the comic
books, his work is a clear example of a cartoonist whose entire oeuvre has been

shaped by the melancholy and ghoulish despair that characterizes Poe. The same could be said for Charles Addams and Edward Gorey, except that Wilson has frequently included Poe himself and allusions to Poe's stories and poems in his panel cartoons. Students might find it interesting to search through old issues of the *New Yorker* and *National Lampoon* in the library to find Wilson's Poe-related cartoons and consider how they serve as comments on the writer or reflect public opinion of his character.

In September of the same year *Classics Illustrated: "The Fall of the House of Usher"* appeared in the new Berkley series with script and art by P. Craig Russell and Jay Geldhof, who value design and color over action and narrative. The text, based mainly on Poe's own words, is minimal, but the art is so powerful that moving through the book is an unsettling experience in keeping with the mood of Poe's original melancholy terror. Artistically inclined students will especially want to discuss and consider the use of color symbolism. Despite a strong start, this series was concluded in 1991 after twenty-seven titles, only two of them based on Poe.

Another comic book periodical, which started in 2001 and still continues in 2008, is *Graphic Classics* from Eureka Productions. The first title was devoted to Poe, a collection of new and reprinted versions of his stories and poems by underground and alternative press artists and writers. Especially noteworthy are Rick Geary's "The Tell-Tale Heart," illustrations by Robert Crumb's brother Maxon Crumb, and an unusual commentary in comics form on "The Inheritance of Rufus Griswold" by Spain Rodriguez. The title was so popular that revised and expanded editions were published in 2004 and 2006, each with new stories. The easy availability of these titles makes them especially useful for essay and discussion assignments.

Poe often appears as himself in these comic books. One notable example is the collection by Jason Asala simply called *Poe*. Beginning with six self-published issues in 1996 (collected in one volume in 1998), *Poe* would run for another twenty-two issues through 2000. The first opens with Poe mourning the death of a fictional wife named Lenore. Confronted by an angel named Israfel, Poe is offered a challenge. If he can defeat twelve earthly demons, he will be reunited with Lenore. He sets off on his quest after being told to follow a raven. Joined by three companions who attend to his physical and spiritual needs, their path of adventure leads through Virginia, Pennsylvania, and Massachusetts.

Asala incorporates into his plotlines numerous elements from Poe's stories; the results are not in any sense adaptations but rather free-association spin-offs, often with the sense of improvisation one associates with jazz. Asala's work is a singular and passionate tribute to Poe, and readers versed in Poe's works will enjoy the many inside jokes and references scattered throughout. An ambitious student might be asked to read a Poe biography and a full selection of his works to detect how Asala uses this information and how it comments on Poe's life and works. Is the adaptation respectful of Poe?

The last few decades have witnessed a remarkable development in the area of comic art: the graphic novel. Based on the comic book in its use of words and pictures within panels, the graphic novel is a lengthier, sustained work that relates more complicated narratives and addresses more complex issues. Graphic novels are usually published in hardcover or substantial paperback editions and are not to be confused with the popular Japanese manga, near which they are often placed in bookstores. An example is Art Spiegelman's *Maus*, which relates through animal-fable imagery the experiences of his parents in the Holocaust and its influence on him as the child of survivors. It won a special Pulitzer Prize. Another is Chris Ware's *Jimmy Corrigan: The Smartest Kid on Earth*, an innovative and technically challenging work that reflects on the human condition and the loss of values in the modern world. Some consider its example and influence in the world of the graphic novel comparable to James Joyce's *Ulysses* in that of the novel.

Given the popularity of Poe, it would naturally follow that some artists would turn to him for graphic-novel material. Rick Geary's *The Mystery of Mary Rogers* is a carefully researched and detailed account of the events that inspired "The Mystery of Marie Rogêt." Poe even appears as a potential participant in the crime but is then exonerated. Geary has a heavy, bold style that is reminiscent of woodcuts and daguerreotypes and suitable to the sensational tabloid nature of the murder. His emphasis on the historic circumstances remind the reader that the line between fiction and fact is often a thin one and that truth is not always discernible. There may be more psychological truth in Poe's stories than Sigmund Freud would discover on his consulting couch. Separating fact from fiction and the meaning of Geary's changes would be a good topic for a research paper.

In the Shadow of Edgar Allan Poe is a collaboration between the writer Jonathon Scott Fuqua, the artist Steven Parke, and the photographer Stephen John Phillips. It is a dark and brooding graphic novel in which photographs are interwoven with digital illustrations and boxed text to provide a fictional biography based on the discovery of a long-lost diary kept by Poe. Borrowing from Greek drama, *Hamlet*, and Freud's notebooks, Fuqua tries to explain Poe's neuroses as demon-driven. The result finally says more about our romantic attachments to Poe than the man and displays the extreme extents to which he can stir our creative imaginations. Students might enjoy discussing this radical portrayal and whether one can credit it with any probability, given what we *do* know about Poe.

Ravenous is a graphic novel inspired by Poe. Written and illustrated by the Hollywood set designer turned comic book artist Dawn Brown, the plot concerns the terrorization of a small town by a serial killer who leaves the bodies of his victims sliced in two parts. The detective-narrator turns out to be more than an innocent bystander stumped by the case. Almost as if designed for classroom use, Brown reprints as a supplement and in full the four stories and one poem that influenced her novel, and she identifies the theme she has borrowed from each. Given the graphic violence portrayed, only mature students should be assigned the book.

After reading the stories, students might be asked to determine specifically how she has used the themes for her own purposes and what other elements of Poe come into play. They should note especially the way the narrative occasionally moves into verse and echoes phrases from "The Raven" and other poems. Another good discussion question is whether the gender of the author makes a difference in a field largely dominated by men. All of these graphic novels function as artistic critical commentaries on Poe's writings, displaying diverse reactions to Poe and offering insights into the ways comic artists have absorbed and responded to his powerful influence.

Fruitful discussion can come from asking what has been lost in any comic book adaptation. Certainly we lose the language and style of Poe's narratives, some of the most beautifully rendered prose in American literature, although some adapters do retain the original texts. Also lost in most cases is the effect of the first-person narrative voice, rational but insane, which seduces and plays on our sensibilities and primitive fears. What has been retained are the elements of plot and narrative in some of the best-told stories in our literature. While Poe has been granted canonical status by the very critics who earlier had banished him to the world of popular culture, it remains the engaging tales of terror and suspense that have kept him in print as one of the most widely read writers in the world. The comic books have contributed to that larger, more democratic reputation.

From Page to Stage: An Interdisciplinary Approach to Teaching "The Philosophy of Composition" through Performing "The Raven"

Rebecca Jaroff and Domenick Scudera

One of the biggest challenges to teaching Edgar Allan Poe's "The Raven" is finding creative ways to reintroduce students to a literary text so entrenched in popular culture. Students may have had countless encounters with the poem from grade school on, and can, in addition, watch versions of "The Raven" and its author's persona on at least five episodes of "The Simpsons"; cheer along with the Baltimore Ravens' mascots, who are three large birds named Edgar, Allan, and Poe; eat and buy souvenirs at restaurants named for the poem; and, well, you get the picture ("Footprints"). While they may love Poe and his famous poem, many students are at best jaded and at worst bored when the poem turns up in an American literature class. Such students can have a difficult time taking the poem, or its author, seriously.

Poe himself may be responsible for some of this overexposure. Often desperate for money, he was well aware of how to please popular audiences, sometimes churning out work he considered substandard. Nevertheless, Poe was also a serious writer who was dedicated to his craft, as he demonstrates in "The Philosophy of Composition," detailing how he wrote "The Raven" to "its completion with the precision and rigid consequence of a mathematical problem" (1375). Indeed, his contemporaries recognized the poem's intricate design; one critic noted "the impression of a very *studied* effect is always uppermost after reading him. And you have to study him to understand him" ("Brook Farm" 29–30). Ideally, today's students should *study* his meticulous process as well, in order to appreciate Poe the artist, while simultaneously having a bit of fun with their old friend, Poe, the pop-culture icon.

Of course, teachers may feel just as jaded and bored as their students when teaching Poe, or may have trouble taking him seriously. So teaching "The Raven" presents various challenges for both the instructor and the students, particularly in terms of approaching the poem from a new perspective. With that goal in mind, we developed an interdisciplinary classroom exercise for Rebecca Jaroff's American literature students, based on Domenick Scudera's play *Poe on Poe*, that we believe reinvigorates Poe's most well-known text.

Before we discuss our approach to teaching "The Raven" in the classroom, it might be helpful to discuss how the play inspired it. The innate dramatic quality in Poe's prose and poetry inspires performance, and, even more important, almost insists on it. As Poe states in his "Philosophy," "It appears evident, then, that there is a distinct limit, as regards length[:] the limit of a single setting," which "intensely excites, by elevating, the soul" (1375). Although Poe was talking about his poems and short stories, the same philosophy applies to the length and effects of successful stage performances. The play's title, *Poe on Poe*, reflects the premise of the play: Edgar Allan Poe appears as a character and addresses the audience directly, talking about his work and introducing other performers who present stage adaptations of those works. Poe's dialogue was culled in part directly from his essays, letters, and marginalia.

As the play opens, Poe (the character) is out to prove that his work is intentionally original and that he labored to write finely wrought creations. He tells the audience:

> My writing possesses earnestness, minute, not profuse detail, and fidelity of description. My style is clear and forcible. My aim is . . . ORIGINAL-ITY! Originality, either of idea, or the combination of ideas. I think it a crime to write unless I have something novel to write about. Most writers get their subjects first and write to develop it. *My* first inquiry is for a novel effect—then for a subject; that is, a new arrangement of circumstance, or a new application of tone, by which the effect shall be developed. Thus it is that I have produced works of the most notable character.
> (Scudera)

Shaping the play thusly gives student actors the opportunity to perform in different styles and genres in order to develop their acting skills, and, perhaps more important, demonstrates to the actors and the audience that Poe's work is so much more than horror stories.

In addition to performing short stories, such as "The Tell-Tale Heart" and "The Cask of Amontillado," the play also includes poems such as "Bridal Ballad," "The Bells," and, of course, "The Raven." For this poem, two actors, dressed identically, divide the lines of the poem into two distinct voices—a narrator who talks to the audience in the past tense, and the persona who is living the story in the present tense. Two more actors portray Lenore (set high above the stage in a picture frame) and the raven.

After "The Raven" is performed in the play, Poe reappears invoking sections of "The Philosophy of Composition" to display to the audience how carefully he crafted his poem. Poe describes the choices he made and how he rejected a number of ideas before hitting on the most effective way to write his poem. The actors in "The Raven" act out Poe's rejected ideas to show how the poem could have taken a very different path if Poe had changed any element in the poem. Here is an excerpt:

POE.   One of my first concerns in writing "The Raven" was the choice of an impression, or effect, to be conveyed. How should I render the work universally appreciable? *Beauty*, I decided, was to be the sole legitimate province of this poem. My next question referred to the *tone* of Beauty's highest manifestation. What tone best befit my poem? *Lights return to the actors in "The Raven."* (*They begin the scene in the same manner as before, but use different tones to convey different moods.*)

NARRATOR. Once upon a noontime sunny, while I pondered, cute and funny.

POE. Um, no. That is not the proper tone.

NARRATOR. Once upon a bright mid-day, while I pondered, happy and gay.

POE. I don't think so.

NARRATOR. Once upon a midnight dreary, while I pondered, weak and weary.

POE. Ah, yes. Melancholy is the most legitimate of all the poetical tones. Next, I thought, what will be the nature of my refrain? Since its application was to be repeatedly varied it was clear that the refrain itself must be brief. And what of the character of the word? It must be sonorous and susceptible of protracted emphasis. A long "o" is the most sonorous vowel when connected with the most producible consonant, "r," I reasoned. The sound of the refrain being thus determined, it became necessary to select a word embodying this sound: (*The actors play the scene in the same manner as they had done before, but use different words to replace "Nevermore."*)

PROTAGONIST. Take thy beak from out my heart, and take thy form from off my door!

NARRATOR. Quoth the Raven:

RAVEN. Down the Shore.

POE. No.

NARRATOR. Quoth the Raven:

RAVEN. General Store.

POE. No.

NARRATOR. Quoth the Raven:

RAVEN. Mary Tyler Moore.

POE. What? No! Absolutely not! The word with the fullest possible meaning in keeping with the melancholy tone is the word "Nevermore."

This is all played for comic effect, but Poe's point remains clear: his work was not created on a whim; it was created through careful planning and intent.

We required the American literature students to see the play, after reading most of the texts included in it for class, and then asked them to write about how the experience influenced their understanding of Poe. One student observed how the play "brilliantly tied together 'The Philosophy of Composition' and an eclectic array of his fictional works." In fact, student responses to the scene we discussed above were perceptive:

> Having Poe as the background voice made the poem come to life. Poe standing above in the balcony chimes in as needed, referring to "The Philosophy of Composition." To me, this actor/author combination really made each word take on a whole new meaning. By emphasizing the lines to signify their importance, Poe's thoughts could take center stage.

Another student observed:

> By seeing it on stage, I started to understand the importance of each of the words and ideas that Poe included in this poem. [The notes from "Philosophy"] gave me a greater understanding of the thought process of Poe himself, and consequently, "The Raven" now holds a greater meaning than prior to the play.

The play's division of "The Raven" using four characters not only demonstrates how "The Philosophy" actually worked in composing the poem but also solves an age-old problem when students read the poem out loud. As Richard Godden argues:

> "The Raven" would be eminently readable, were it not that its remorseless trochaic rhythm, extended through one hundred and eight predominantly eight-foot lines, displaces attention from the meaning. An iteration of trochees may cause us to hear, but not to listen to what the poem says. (997)

While perhaps a bit nit-picking, this observation does apply to how undergraduates tend to read the poem out loud, often distracting from the poem's emotional impact or, worse yet, eliciting giggles at the singsong performance. But breaking up the speeches helps, as one student noted, because it "allows the audience to identify with the human emotions that the poem was intended to elicit. Additionally, the separation of the lines destroys the songlike rhythm that the poem seems to produce when read by a single speaker."

We used these and several other responses to develop a classroom exercise designed to link "The Philosophy of Composition" with "The Raven" through an interdisciplinary student-centered learning experience. According to Liz Grauerholz, pedagogical approaches that "promote student learning and growth on levels beyond the cognitive [and] incorporate diverse methods that engage students in personal exploration" produce the deepest learning results (44). Susan Pedersen and Doug Williams point out that "[e]ssential to student-centered approaches is student ownership of their goals and activities. . . . their work is meaningful to them [when it] encourages depth of understanding and an intrinsic motivational orientation" (283). Accordingly, we devised a group exercise that combined close reading with performance using the following handout:

> Carefully reread "The Philosophy of Composition" looking for answers to these questions:
> How should I render the work universally appreciable?
> What tone best befits my poem?
> What will be the nature of my refrain?
> And what of the character of the word?
> What could be the pretext for the continuous use of the one word "nevermore"?
> Of all melancholy topics, what, according to the universal understanding of mankind, is the most melancholy?
> When is death, the most melancholy of topics, most poetical?
> Now, to understand how Poe's original choices affected the finished poem, try to answer the above questions differently and then rewrite a section of the poem in order to provide the new desired effect. For instance:
> Question: What tone would befit my poem?
> Answer: Joy
> Resultant line: Once upon a bright mid-day, while I pondered, happy and gay . . .
> You will be called on to share your new version, striving, as did Poe, to influence your audience in a specific way, conveying the desired effect through performance of the written word.

In theory, the exercise was designed with two goals in mind: to allow the students as a group to do a close reading of the "The Philosophy of Composition," which they generally find off-putting or read superficially, then to engage them in active ownership of their knowledge by directing them to try it themselves. Furthermore, current approaches to teaching Poe through provocative new-historicist readings of his texts may be more effective after first doing a close reading of a short work. Becoming involved with how the language works can destabilize a familiar text and lead students to see more complex layers in the writing, such as inferences of race and class, on their own.

Students did pay much closer attention to "The Philosophy," and, more important, when they tried to compose long lines of trochaic poetry with a particular mood, complicated internal rhyme, and extensive alliteration, they discovered just how difficult Poe had it. While they resisted a bit at the beginning, students turned to themes central to their own lives as sources of inspiration, just as Poe had. This worked because, as studies suggest, "Students become engaged in topics or units [when] a central theme . . . is the making of connections with students' own lives" (Graffam 13). Once engaged, resistance turned into creative energy, and students came up with some fairly witty, if not terrific, examples of what was uppermost on their minds. For some, since it happened to be Valentine's Day, love, or the lack thereof, provided motivation. Here are two of the most memorable attempts:

> Presently my wrath grew stronger, I'll celebrate this day no longer,
> "Damn," said I, "your Valentines! Your candy hearts I do despise them,
> But the fact that I am single, longing for my heart to tingle . . ."

And thoughts of love led to thoughts of love's possible consequences:

> Once upon a sleepless night, my uterus gave me quite a fright.
> Push the peddle a little more, he's tap tap tapping on my cervix door.

One student arrived at class upset because her boyfriend broke up with her that day. Her group decided anger would be her poem's central emotion and soon discovered, like Poe's sonorous long "O," how words ending in *ck* expressed anger most powerfully. We have not included the example, but it was effective, and the class was certainly engaged with that poem.

Now that the students were warmed up, feeling creative, and less inhibited, it was time to perform "The Raven" in the classroom. After we assigned specific stanzas to groups of four, we encouraged students to identify the different voices in the poem, pantomime or choreograph their parts, and find innovative ways to break up the rhythm, thus revealing the poem's emotional impact. After seeing the poem performed on stage, one student remarked, "Hearing [the actor] scream at the raven, 'Is there—*Is* there balm in Gilead?' made the hairs on the back of my neck stand up," and students were instructed to strive for the same effect for their classroom audience.

Student enjoyment of this exercise was unanimous. They not only had fun with Poe but also stated that they recognized the connection between a poem's composition and final product much better, had a greater appreciation of Poe's artistic struggle to create "The Raven," and, most important, experienced the dramatic emotional impact of a poem they only thought they knew well.

NOTES ON CONTRIBUTORS

James R. Britton is a lecturer in the Department of English at the University of Miami. He has published essays on suffrage in the United States and on antebellum social reform.

Leonard Cassuto is professor of English at Fordham University. He is the author of *The Inhuman Race: The Racial Grotesque in American Literature and Culture* and the editor or coeditor of three other volumes, including an anthology of Poe's literary theory and criticism. His *Hard-Boiled Sentimentality: The Secret History of American Crime Stories* is forthcoming in 2008 from Columbia University Press. Cassuto is also an award-winning journalist whose writing has appeared in popular periodicals ranging from the *Wall Street Journal* to *Salon.com*. He is currently serving as general editor of the forthcoming *Cambridge History of the American Novel*.

Marcy J. Dinius is assistant professor of English at the University of Delaware. She has published an article on Poe and hoaxing in *Poe Studies / Dark Romanticism* and is currently at work on a book about early photography and antebellum American literature.

William Etter is assistant professor of English at Irvine Valley College. He has published articles on Edgar Allan Poe's "Loss of Breath" and the disabled soldier Alfred Bellard's Civil War memoirs.

Duncan Faherty is assistant professor in the Department of English at Queens College, the City University of New York. He is the author of *Remodeling the Nation: The Architecture of American Identity, 1776–1858*. His work has also appeared in *American Quarterly*, the *Edgar Allan Poe Review*, and *Reviews in American History*.

Benjamin F. Fisher, professor of English, University of Mississippi, is a past president of the Poe Studies Association, is chairman of the Speakers Series in the Edgar Allan Poe Society of Baltimore, serves on editorial boards of *Poe Studies*, the *Simms Review*, *Victorian Poetry*, and *Gothic Studies*. His most recent publication on Poe is an edited volume, *Essential Tales and Poems of Edgar Allan Poe*.

Derek Furr is assistant professor of English in the Bard College Master of Arts in Teaching Program, where he teaches courses in historicism and postcolonial fiction and works closely with pre- and in-service public school teachers. He is working on a book about poetry readings and the archive of modern poetry recordings.

Lesley Ginsberg is associate professor of English at the University of Colorado, Colorado Springs. She has published essays in journals such as *American Literature* and *Studies in American Fiction* and in volumes including *American Gothic, Enterprising Youth*, and *Popular Nineteenth Century Women Writers and the Literary Marketplace*. She is completing a book manuscript, "The Culture of Pedagogy: Children's Literature and American Romanticism, 1820–1870."

Desirée Henderson is assistant professor at the University of Texas, Arlington. She is the author of articles about death and mourning including "The Imperfect Dead: Mourning Women in Eighteenth-Century Oratory and Fiction" in *Early American*

Literature. She is completing a book-length study of memorial genres such as funeral sermons and eulogies and their influence on American literature.

Diane Long Hoeveler is professor of English at Marquette University. She has served as president of the International Conference on Romanticism and is the author of *Romantic Androgyny: The Women Within* and *Gothic Feminism: The Professionalization of Gender from Charlotte Smith to the Brontës*, as well as articles on a variety of literary topics. She has coauthored a critical study of Charlotte Brontë, and coedited the MLA Approaches to Teaching volumes on *Jane Eyre* and the gothic. Her edition of Poe's *Narrative of Arthur Gordon Pym* (edited with Fred Frank) is being published by Broadview (2009).

M. Thomas Inge is Robert Emory Blackwell Professor of Humanities at Randolph-Macon College, where he teaches courses in American studies and Asian literature. He writes about American humor and comic art, film and animation, and southern literature and William Faulkner. Publications include the four-volume *Greenwood Guide to American Popular Culture* and *William Faulkner: Overlook Illustrated Lives*.

Rebecca Jaroff is assistant professor of English at Ursinus College. She is the author of "Charlotte Barnes: A Life in the Theatre," in *Women's Contributions to Nineteenth-Century American Theatre* and "Opposing Forces: (Re)Playing Pocahontas and the Politics of Indian Removal on the Antebellum Stage," in *Comparative Drama*. She is currently researching Elizabeth Oakes Smith's relationship with the newspaper editor Horace Greeley.

Paul Christian Jones is associate professor of English at Ohio University. He is the author of *Unwelcome Voices: Subversive Fiction in the Antebellum South* and articles on American literature in the *Journal of American Studies, Southern Literary Journal, ATQ, Critique, American Periodicals, Mississippi Quarterly,* and *Southern Quarterly.*

Alison M. Kelly is a member of the English department at Deerfield Academy. She teaches sophomore classes in British literature and a junior American literature elective entitled American Psyche. She has published essays on *The Exorcist, American Psycho,* and *Carrie.*

A. Samuel Kimball is professor of English and chair of the Department of English at the University of North Florida. He has published on Poe, Hawthorne, and Melville and on film (including *Twin Peaks, Chinatown, Pulp Fiction, The Matrix, Terminator 2, Alien Resurrection,* and *The Fog of War*). His book, *The Infanticidal Logic of Evolution and Culture* appeared in 2007.

Tony Magistrale is professor of English and associate chair of the English department at the University of Vermont. His publications on Poe include *The Poe Encyclopedia, Poe's Children: Connections between Tales of Terror and Detection,* and *A Student Companion to Edgar Allan Poe.*

Scott Peeples is professor of English at the College of Charleston. His publications include *Edgar Allan Poe Revisited* and *The Afterlife of Edgar Allan Poe;* he currently edits the Literary Criticism in Perspective book series for Camden House–Boydell and Brewer and coedits the journal *Poe Studies.*

Dennis R. Perry is associate professor of English at Brigham Young University specializing in American literature and literature and film. In addition to his articles on seventeenth- and nineteenth-century American writers in *Early American Literature*, *Walt Whitman Quarterly*, *Poe Studies Newsletter*, and *Studies in Short Fiction*, he is the author of *Hitchcock and Poe: The Legacy of Delight and Terror*.

Philip Edward Phillips is associate professor of English and the director of graduate admisions in English at Middle Tennessee State University, where he teaches European, British, and American literature. He is the author of *John Milton's Epic Invocations* and coeditor of *New Directions in Boethian Studies*.

Stephen Rachman is associate professor of English at Michigan State University and the former director of the American Studies Program. He is coeditor of *The American Face of Edgar Allan Poe* and annotated the Modern Library edition of *The Narrative of Arthur Gordon Pym of Nantucket*. He has written on Poe and popular culture and on the history of medicine and nineteenth-century literature. He is a coauthor of *Cholera, Chloroform, and the Science of Medicine: A Life of John Snow*.

Erik Redling is assistant professor at the University of Augsburg, Germany, where he teaches American literature and culture. He is the author of " 'Speaking of Dialect': Translating Charles W. Chesnutt's Conjure Tales into Postmodern Systems of Signification" and is working on cognitive aspects in jazz poetry.

Donelle Ruwe is associate professor of English at Northern Arizona University where she teaches British literature and English education courses and coordinates the graduate programs in English. She has published on women writers from the Romantic era and edited special issues of *Nineteenth-Century Contexts* and *Religion and Literature*. She is the editor of *Culturing the Child, 1690–1914: Essays in Memory of Mitzi Myers*.

Domenick Scudera is associate professor of theater and chair of the Department of Theater and Dance at Ursinus College. He has directed plays at the Philadelphia Shakespeare Festival, Azuka Theater, the Philadelphia Fringe Festival, Historic Philadelphia, Inc., and other Philadelphia-area theaters. He directed a production of his original play, *Poe on Poe*, at Ursinus College in 2004.

Lois Davis Vines, professor of French and James Reid Distinguished Teaching Professor of Humanities at Ohio University, is the author of *Valéry and Poe: A Literary Legacy* and *Poe Abroad, Influence, Reputation, Affinities*. She was named Chevalier dans l'Ordre des Palmes Académiques by the French government in 1993.

Jeffrey Andrew Weinstock is associate professor of American literature and culture at Central Michigan University and is the author of *Scare Tactics: Supernatural Fiction by American Women* and *The Rocky Horror Picture Show*. He has edited academic volumes on American ghosts, *South Park*, "The Yellow Wall-Paper," and *The Blair Witch Project*, and his work has appeared in journals including *American Literature*, *Studies in American Fiction*, the *Arizona Quarterly*, and *Pedagogy*.

Edward Wesp is assistant professor of English at Western New England College. His research on narrative form in nineteenth-century American literature focuses on time in structures of national identity. His work on digital media, written with Eric Hayot, appears in *Postmodern Culture* and *Comparative Literature Studies*.

Brian Yothers is assistant professor of English at the University of Texas, El Paso, where he teaches early and nineteenth-century American literature. He is the author of *The Romance of the Holy Land in American Travel Writing, 1790–1876*.

SURVEY PARTICIPANTS

F. R. Adams, Jr., *James Madison University* (emeritus)
Lesliee Antonette, *East Stroudsburg University*
Bob Brill, independent scholar
James R. Britton, *University of Miami*
Eric W. Carlson, *University of Connecticut* (emeritus)
Leonard Cassuto, *Fordham University*
John A. Dern, *Gwynedd-Mercy College*
Marcy J. Dinius, *Northwestern University*
William Etter, *University of California, Irvine*
Duncan Faherty, *City University of New York, Queens College*
Benjamin F. Fisher, *University of Mississippi*
Derek Furr, *Bard College*
Lesley Ginsberg, *University of Colorado, Colorado Springs*
Santiago Rodríguez Guerrero-Strachan, *University of Valladolid* (Spain)
Desirée Henderson, *University of Texas, Arlington*
Diane Long Hoeveler, *Marquette University*
M. Thomas Inge, *Randolph-Macon College*
Tiffany Itsou, *University of Connecticut, Storrs*
Rebecca Jaroff, *Ursinus College*
Jeff Jeske, *Guilford College*
Paul Christian Jones, *Ohio University*
Alison M. Kelly, *Deerfield Academy*
Tony Magistrale, *University of Vermont*
Urania N. Pack *Clarion University*
Scott Peeples, *College of Charleston*
Dennis R. Perry, *Brigham Young University*
Keith Polette, *University of Texas, El Paso*
Stephen Rachman, *Michigan State University*
Tatiani Rapatzikou, *Aristotle University of Thessaloniki* (Greece)
Erik Redling, *University of Augsburg*
Robert T. Rhode, *Northern Kentucky University*
Margarita Rigel-Aragón, *Universidad de Castilla–La Mancha* (Spain)
Donelle Ruwe, *Northern Arizona University*
Domenick Scudera, *Ursinus College*
Jan Stahl, *Wagner College*
E. Kate Stewart, *University of Arkansas, Monticello*
Lois Vines, *Ohio University*
Jeffrey Andrew Weinstock, *Central Michigan University*
Edward Wesp, *University of Wisconsin, Milwaukee*
Brian Yothers, *University of Texas, El Paso*
Michael Young, *La Roche College*

WORKS CITED

The Alan Parsons Project. *Tales of Mystery and Imagination.* Mercury, 1976.

Allen, Hervey. *Israfel: The Life and Times of Edgar Allan Poe.* 1926. Rev. ed. New York: Farrar, 1934.

Allen, Michael. *Poe and the British Magazine Tradition.* New York: Oxford UP, 1969.

Amper, Susan. "The Biographer as Assassin: The Hidden Murders in 'The Assignation.'" *Poe Studies / Dark Romanticism* 35 (2002): 14–21.

Appleman, Deborah. *Critical Encounters in High School English: Teaching Literary Theory to Adolescents.* New York: Teachers Coll. P, 2000.

Argersinger, Jana L., and Steven Gregg. "Subject Index to 'International Poe Bibliography': Poe Scholarship and Criticism, 1983–1988." *Poe Studies / Dark Romanticism* 24 (1991): 1–48.

Arp, Thomas R., Greg Johnson, and Laurence Perrine. *Perrine's Literature: Structure, Sound, and Sense.* 8th ed. Fort Worth: Harcourt, 2002.

Asala, Jason. *Poe.* Dover: Dogstar, 1998.

"Ax Radio Host for Racist Slur." *New York Daily News* 30 Sept. 2003: 2.

Bailey, J. O. "Sources for Poe's *Arthur Gordon Pym,* 'Hans Pfaal,' and Other Pieces." *PMLA* 57 (1942): 513–35.

Bandy, W. T. Introduction. Baudelaire xi–xlv.

Barker, Clive. "Introduction to *The Doll's House.*" *The Sandman.* By Neil Gaiman. 3 Apr. 1990. 22 June 2007 <http://www.oddball.net/endless/intro.html>.

Barnet, Sylvan, et al., eds. *Literature for Composition: Essays, Fiction, Poetry, and Drama.* 7th ed. New York: Longman, 2004.

Baudelaire, Charles. *Edgar Allan Poe: Sa vie et ses ouvrages.* 1856. Toronto: U of Toronto P, 1973.

Bausch, Richard, and R. V. Cassill, eds. *The Norton Anthology of Short Fiction.* 7th ed. New York: Norton, 2005.

Bayer-Berenbaum, Linda. *The Gothic Imagination: Expansion in Gothic Literature and Art.* Rutherford: Fairleigh Dickinson UP, 1982.

Baym, Nina, et al., eds. *The Norton Anthology of American Literature.* 6th ed. 5 vols. New York: Norton, 2003.

Baynton, Douglas C. "Disability and the Justification of Inequality in American History." *The New Disability History: American Perspectives.* Ed. Paul K. Longmore and Lauri Umansky. New York: New York UP, 2001. 33–57.

Beebe, Maurice. "The Universe of Roderick Usher." Regan 121–33.

Beegel, Susan F. " 'Mutiny and Atrocious Butchery': The *Globe* Mutiny as a Source for *Pym.*" Kopley, *Poe's Pym* 7–19.

Bell, Michael Davitt. *The Development of American Romance: The Sacrifice of Relation.* Chicago: U of Chicago P, 1980.

Benton, Richard P. "Is Poe's 'The Assignation' a Hoax?" *Nineteenth-Century Literature* 18 (1963): 193–97.

Berg, Mary G. "Julio Cortázar." Vines, *Poe Abroad* 227–32.

Bloom, Clive. *Reading Poe, Reading Freud: The Romantic Imagination in Crisis.* Basingstoke, Eng.: Macmillan, 1988.

Bloom, Harold. *The Anxiety of Influence: A Theory of Poetry.* New York: Oxford UP, 1973.

———. Introduction. *Edgar Allan Poe.* Ed. Bloom. Modern Critical Views. New York: Chelsea, 1985. 3–15.

Bly, Mary. "A Fine Romance." *New York Times* 12 Feb. 2005: A17.

Bonaparte, Marie. *The Life and Works of Edgar Allan Poe: A Psycho-analytic Interpretation.* Trans. John Rodker. London: Imago, 1949. Rpt. New York: Humanities, 1971.

Bondeson, Jan. *Buried Alive! The Terrifying History of Our Most Primal Fear.* New York: Norton, 2002.

Borges, Jorge Luis. *Collected Fictions.* Trans. Andrew Hurley. New York: Viking, 1998.

———. "Death and the Compass." Borges, *Collected Fictions* 147–56.

———. "Ibn-Hakam al-Bokhari, Murdered in His Labyrinth." Borges, *Collected Fictions* 255–62.

Bredella, Lothar. "The Anthropological and Pedagogical Significance of Aesthetic Reading in the Foreign Language Classroom." *Challenges of Literary Texts in the Foreign Classroom.* Ed. Bredella and Werner Delanoy. Tübingen: Narr, 1996. 1–29.

Bressler, Charles E. *Literary Criticism: An Introduction to Theory and Practice.* 3rd ed. Upper Saddle River: Prentice, 2003.

Bretzius, Stephen. "The Figure-Power Dialectic: Poe's 'Purloined Letter.'" *MLN* 110 (1995): 679–91.

Brewbaker, James. "Fifty-Five Teachers, Poems in Hand, Approach the Cruelest Month." *English Journal* 94.4 (2005): 18–22.

Brill, Lesley. *The Hitchcock Romance: Love and Irony in Hitchcock's Films.* Princeton: Princeton UP, 1988.

"Brook Farm." *The Complete Works of Edgar Allan Poe.* Ed. James A. Harrison. Vol. 8. New York: AMS, 1965. 27–32.

Brown, Dawn. *Ravenous.* Toronto: Speakeasy Comics, 2005.

Brueggemann, Brenda Jo. *Lend Me Your Ear: Rhetorical Constructions of Deafness.* Washington: Gallaudet, 1999.

Buell, Lawrence. *Literary Transcendentalism: Style and Vision in the American Renaissance.* Ithaca: Cornell UP, 1973.

———. *New England Literary Culture: From Revolution through Renaissance.* New York: Cambridge UP, 1986.

Burton's Gentleman's Magazine and American Monthly Review. Philadelphia: Burton, 1839–40.

Butler, Judith. *Bodies That Matter: On the Discursive Limits of "Sex."* New York: Routledge, 1993.

Byron, George Gordon. *The Works of Lord Byron: With His Letters and Journals and His Life by Thomas Moore, Esq.* London: Murray, 1832.

Canny, James R., and Charles F. Heartman. *A Bibliography of the First Printings of the Writings of Edgar Allan Poe*. Hattiesburg: Book Farm, 1943.

Carlson, Eric W. *A Companion to Poe Studies*. Westport: Greenwood, 1996.

———. "New Notes on Edgar Poe." *Critical Essays on Edgar Allan Poe*. Ed. Carlson. Boston: Hall, 1987. 63–77.

———. "Poe"s Vision of Man." *Papers on Poe*. Ed. Richard Veler. Springfield: Chantry Music P, 1972. 7–20.

———. "The Transcendentalist Poe: A Brief History of Criticism." *Poe Studies / Dark Romanticism* 34 (2001): 47–66.

Casale, Ottavio. "Edgar Allan Poe." *The Transcendentalists: A Review of Research and Criticism*. Ed. Joel Myerson. New York: MLA, 1984. 362–71.

———. "Poe on Transcendentalism." *ESQ* 50 (1968): 85–97.

Cassuto, Leonard. "The Cultural Work of Serial Killers." *Minnesota Review* 58-60 (2003): 39–51.

———, ed. *Edgar Allan Poe: Literary Theory and Criticism*. Mineola: Dover, 1999.

———. *Hard-boiled Sentimentality: The Secret History of American Crime Stories*. New York: Columbia UP, 2008.

Charney, Hanna. "Lacan, Don Juan, and the French Detective." *L'esprit créateur* 26.2 (1986): 15–25.

Charters, Ann, ed. *Literature and Its Writers: An Introduction to Fiction, Poetry, and Drama*. 2nd ed. Boston: Bedford, 2000.

Chase, Richard. *The American Novel and Its Tradition*. Garden City: Doubleday, 1957.

Clark, Elizabeth A., ed. *History, Theory, Text: Historians and the Linguistic Turn*. Cambridge: Harvard UP, 2004.

Classics Illustrated: "The Fall of the House of Usher." Adapt. P. Craig Russell. Classics Illustrated 14. New York: Berkley, 1990.

Classics Illustrated: More Stories by Poe. Notes and guide by Gregory Feely. New York: Acclaim, 1997.

Classics Illustrated: Mysteries. Classics Illustrated 40. New York: Gilberton, 1947.

Classics Illustrated: "The Raven" and Other Poems. Classics Illustrated 1. New York: Berkley, 1990.

Classics Illustrated: Stories by Poe. Notes and study guide by Gregory Feely. New York: Acclaim, 1997.

Classics Illustrated: Three Famous Mysteries. Classics Illustrated 21. New York: Gilberton, 1944.

Closed on Account of Rabies: Poems and Tales of Edgar Allan Poe. Mercury, 1997.

Cohen, Paula Marantz. *Alfred Hitchcock: The Legacy of Victorianism*. Lexington: UP of Kentucky, 1995.

Connors, Thomas G. "The Romantic Landscape: Washington Irving, Sleepy Hollow, and the Rural Cemetery Movement." *Mortal Remains: Death in Early America*. Ed. Nancy Isenberg and Andrew Burstein. Philadelphia: U of Pennsylvania P, 2003. 187–203.

Corrigan, Timothy. *A Short Guide to Writing about Film*. New York: Longman, 2001.

Cortázar, Julio. *"We Love Glenda So Much" and Other Tales*. Trans. Gregory Rabassa. New York: Knopf, 1983.

Creepy. No. 67. New York: Warren, 1974.

Cullen, Jim. *The American Dream: A Short History of an Idea That Shaped a Nation*. New York: Oxford UP, 2003.

Cunliffe, W. Gordon. "The Cask of Amontillado." *Insight I: Analyses of American Literature*. Ed. John Hagopian et al. Frankfurt: Hirschgrabenverlag, 1979. 203–07.

Curl, James Stevens. *The Victorian Celebration of Death*. Detroit: Partridge, 1972.

Dain, Bruce. *A Hideous Monster of the Mind: American Race Theory in the Early Republic*. Cambridge: Harvard UP, 2002.

Dameron, J. Lasley. "Poe, Plagiarism, and American Periodicals." *Poe Studies / Dark Romanticism* 30 (1997): 39–47.

Dameron, J. Lasley, and Irby Cauthen, Jr., eds. *Edgar Allan Poe: A Bibliography of Criticism, 1827–1967*. Charlottesville: UP of Virginia, 1974.

Daniels, George H. *American Science in the Age of Jackson*. New York: Columbia UP, 1968.

Davidson, Cathy. *Revolution and the Word: The Rise of the Novel in America*. New York: Oxford UP, 1984.

Davidson, Edward H. *Poe: A Critical Study*. Cambridge: Belknap–Harvard UP, 1957.

Davidson, Michael, and Tobin Siebers. "Introduction to the Conference on Disability Studies and the University." *PMLA* 120 (2005): 498–501.

Davis, Lennard J. *Enforcing Normalcy: Disability, Deafness, and the Body*. London: Verso, 1995.

Day, William Patrick. *In the Circles of Fear and Desire: A Study of Gothic Fantasy*. Chicago: U of Chicago P, 1985.

Dayan, Joan. "Amorous Bondage: Poe, Ladies, and Slaves." *American Literature* 66.2 (1994): 239–73

———. "Poe, Persons, and Property." Kennedy and Weissberg 106–26.

———. "Romance and Race." *The Columbia History of the American Novel*. Ed. Emory Elliot. New York: Columbia UP, 1991. 89–109.

The Dead Zone. Dir. David Cronenberg. Lorimar, 1983.

Deas, Michael J. *The Portraits and Daguerreotypes of Edgar Allan Poe*. Charlottesville: UP of Virginia, 1989.

Denning, Michael. *Mechanic Accents: Dime Novels and Working-Class Culture in America*. New York: Verso, 1998.

Deutsch, Leonard. "The Satire on Transcendentalism in Poe's 'Ligeia.'" *Bulletin of the West Virginia Association of College English Teachers* 3 (1976): 19–22.

Dobie, Ann B. "Cultural Studies: New Historicism." *Theory into Practice: An Introduction to Literary Criticism*. Boston: Heinle, 2002. 161–84.

Dolmage, Jay. "Between the Valley and the Field: Metaphor and Disability." *Prose Studies* 27 (2005): 108–19.

Donovan, Tim, A. Samuel Kimball, and Jillian Smith. "The Remains of the Dead: Mourning, McNamara, and *The Fog of War*." *Journal of Postmodern Culture* 16.1, forthcoming.

Dwight, Thomas, and David K. Jackson. *The Poe Log: A Documentary Life of Edgar Allan Poe, 1809–1849*. Boston: Hall, 1987.

Edgar Allan Poe: Terror of the Soul. American Masters. PBS. 22 Mar. 1995.

Edgar Allan Poe: "The Raven." Edgar Allan Poe Society of Baltimore. 2 Jan. 2008. 16 Jan. 2008 <http://www.eapoe.org/works/info/pp073.htm>.

"Editorial Introduction." *Southern Literary Messenger* 1.10 (1835): 533. *Making of America*. 2005. U of Michigan Digital Lib. Text Collections. 15 June 2005 <http://name.umdl.umich.edu/acf2679.0001.010>.

Edmundson, Mark. *Nightmare on Main Street: Angels, Sadomasochism, and the Culture of Gothic*. Cambridge: Harvard UP, 1997.

Edwards, Justin D. *Gothic Passages: Racial Ambiguity and the American Gothic*. Iowa City: U of Iowa P, 2003.

Eisner, Will. *Comics and Sequential Art*. Tamarac: Poorhouse, 1995.

Eliot, T. S. "From Poe to Valery." *Hudson Review* 2 (1949): 327–42.

Elmer, Jonathan. "Poe, Plagiarism, and the Prescriptive Rights of the Mob." *Discovering Difference: Contemporary Essays in American Culture*. Ed. Christoph K. Lohman. Bloomington: Indiana UP, 1993. 65–87.

———. *Reading at the Social Limit: Affect, Mass Culture, and Edgar Allan Poe*. Stanford: Stanford UP, 1995.

Emerson, Ralph Waldo. "Circles." Emerson, *"Nature" and Selected Essays* 225–38.

———. *Essays and Lectures*. Ed. Joel Porte. New York: Lib. of Amer., 1983.

———. "Nature." Emerson, *Essays* 5–49.

———. "Nature." Emerson, *"Nature" and Selected Essays* 35–83.

———. *"Nature" and Selected Essays*. Ed. Larzer Ziff. New York: Penguin, 2003.

———. "Self-Reliance." Emerson, *Essays* 259–82.

English, Thomas Dunn. "Our Bookshelves no. 8." *Aristidean* 1 (1845): 399–403. Rpt. in Walker 230–35.

Feldstein, Richard, Bruce Fink, and Maire Jaanus, eds. *Reading Seminar I and II: Lacan's Return to Freud: Seminar I, Freud's Papers on Technique; Seminar II: The Ego in Freud's Theory and the Technique of Psychoanalysis*. Albany: State U of New York P, 1996.

Fiedler, Leslie. *Love and Death in the American Novel*. New York: Anchor, 1960.

Fisher, Benjamin Franklin, ed. *Essential Tales and Poems of Edgar Allan Poe*. New York: Barnes, 2004.

———. "That 'Daughter of Old Time': Science in the Writings of Edgar Allan Poe." *Publications of the Arkansas Philological Association* 9 (1983): 36–41.

Fitting, Peter. Introduction. "John Cleves Symmes Jr. and *Symzonia* (1820)." *Subterranean Worlds: A Critical Anthology*. Ed. Fitting Middletown: Wesleyan UP, 2004. 95–106.

Fitzgerald, F. Scott. *The Great Gatsby*. New York: Scribner's, 1995.

Fitzhugh, George. *Cannibals All! or, Slaves without Masters*. Ed. C. Vann Woodward. Cambridge: Harvard UP, 1960.

———. *Sociology for the South; or, The Failure of Free Society*. 1854. New York: Franklin, 1965.

"Footprints." *Qrisse's Poe Pages*. <http://www.poedecoder.com/Qrisse>.

Foucault, Michel. "What Is an Author?" *The Foucault Reader*. Ed. Paul Rabinow. New York: Pantheon, 1984. 101–20.

Frank, Frederick S., and Anthony Magistrale. *The Poe Encyclopedia*. Westport: Greenwood, 1997.

Freud, Sigmund. *The Freud Reader.* Ed. Peter Gay. New York: Norton, 1995.

———. *The Interpretation of Dreams*. Freud, *Freud Reader* 129–41.

———. "The Paths to the Formation of Symptoms." *Introductory Lectures on Psychoanalysis*. By Freud. Ed. James Strachey. New York: Norton, 1989. 445–68.

———. "A Special Type of Choice of Object Made by Men." Freud, *Reader* 387–94.

Fuller, Margaret. *Woman in the Nineteenth Century*. 1845. Ed. Larry J. Reynolds. New York: Norton, 1998.

Fuqua, Jonathon Scott, Steven Parke, and Stephen John Phillips. *In the Shadow of Edgar Allan Poe*. New York: DC Comics-Vertigo, 2002.

Gargano, James W. "The Question of Poe's Narrators." *College English* 25 (1963): 177–81. Rpt. in Regan 164–71.

Geary, Rick. *The Mystery of Mary Rogers*. New York: NBM Comics Lit., 2001.

Geary, Robert F. *The Supernatural in Gothic Fiction: Horror, Belief, and Literary Change*. Lewiston: Mellon, 1992.

George, Norman. *Edgar Allan Poe's Greatest Hits*. 2001.

Ginsberg, Lesley. "Slavery and the Gothic Horror of Poe's 'The Black Cat.' " *American Gothic: New Intervention in a National Narrative*. Ed. Robert K. Martin and Eric Savoy. Iowa City: U of Iowa P, 1998. 99–128.

Godden, Richard. "Poe and the Poetics of Opacity; or, Another Way of Looking at That Black Bird." *ELH* 67 (2000): 993–1009.

Goddu, Teresa. *Gothic America: Narrative, History, and Nation*. New York: Columbia UP, 1997.

———. "Poe, Sensationalism, and Slavery." Hayes 92–112.

Goffman, Erving. *Stigma: Notes on the Management of Spoiled Identity*. Engelwood Cliffs: Prentice, 1963.

Graffam, Ben. "Constructivism and Understanding: Implementing the Teaching for Understanding Framework." *Journal of Secondary Gifted Education* 15.1 (2003): 13–25.

Graphic Classics: Edgar Allan Poe. 2001. Mount Horeb: Eureka, 2004.

Grauerholz, Liz. "Teaching Holistically to Achieve Deep Learning." *College Teaching* 49.2 (2001): 44–50.

Gray, Richard. *Southern Aberrations: Writers of the American South and the Problem of Regionalism*. Baton Rouge: Louisiana State UP, 2000.

Gray, Thomas R. Introduction. *The Confessions of Nat Turner*. 1831. *The Southampton Slave Revolt of 1831: A Compilation of Source Material*. Comp. Henry Irving Tragle. Amherst: U of Massachusetts P, 1971. 303–05.

Greenberg, Clement. "Avant-Garde and Kitsch." *Partisan Review* 6 (1939): 34–49.

Gross, Louis S. *Redefining the American Gothic: From* Wieland *to* Day of the Dead. Ann Arbor: UMI Research P, 1989.

Grosz, Elizabeth. "Intolerable Ambiguity: Freaks as/at the Limit." *Freakery: Cultural*

Spectacles of the Extraordinary Body. Ed. Rosemarie Garland Thomson. New York: New York UP, 1996. 55–68.

Guillory, John. *Cultural Capital: The Problem of Literary Canon Formation*. Chicago: U of Chicago P, 1993.

Halttunen, Karen. *Confidence Men and Painted Women: A Study of Middle-Class Culture in America, 1830–1870*. New Haven: Yale UP, 1982.

Haraway, Donna J. *Simians, Cyborgs, and Women*. New York: Routledge, 1991.

Harris, Thomas. *Red Dragon*. New York: Putnam's, 1981.

———. *The Silence of the Lambs*. New York: St. Martin's, 1988.

Hayes, Kevin J., ed. *The Cambridge Companion to Edgar Allan Poe*. New York: Cambridge UP, 2002.

Hitchcock, Alfred. "Why I Am Afraid of the Dark." *Hitchcock on Hitchcock: Selected Writings and Interviews*. Ed. Sidney Gottlieb. Berkeley: U of California P, 1995. 142–45.

Histoires extraordinaires. Dir. Federico Fellini, Louis Malle, and Roger Vadim. Perf. Brigitte Bardot, Jane Fonda, Peter Fonda. 1968.

Hochman, Barbara. "*Uncle Tom's Cabin* in the *National Era*: An Essay in Generic Norms and the Contexts of Reading." *Book History* 7 (2004): 143–69.

Hoffman, Daniel. *Poe Poe Poe Poe Poe Poe Poe*. Garden City: Doubleday, 1972.

House of Usher. Dir. Roger Corman. Perf. Vincent Price. Alta Vista, 1960.

Howells, William Dean. *Literary Friends and Acquaintances: A Personal Retrospect of American Authorship*. 1900. New York: Harper, 1911.

Hull, Richard. " 'The Purloined Letter': Poe's Detective Story vs. Panoptic Foucauldian Theory." *Style* 24.2 (1990): 201–14.

Hulsey, Dallas. "Plagiarizing the Plagiarists: Poe's Critique of Exploration Narratives." *Poe Studies Association Newsletter* 3.2 (2002): 28–36.

Inge, M. Thomas. *The Incredible Mr. Poe: Comic Book Adaptations of the Works of Edgar Allan Poe, 1943–2007*. Richmond: Edgar Allan Poe Museum, 2008.

Ingraham, Joseph Holt. *The South-West, by A Yankee*. 1835. 2 vols. Ann Arbor: U Microfilms, 1966.

Irwin, John T. *American Hieroglyphics: The Symbol of the Egyptian Hieroglyphics in the American Renaissance*. Baltimore: Johns Hopkins UP, 1980.

———. *The Mystery to a Solution: Poe, Borges, and the Analytic Detective Story*. Baltimore: Johns Hopkins UP, 1994.

Jackson, Leon. " 'Behold Our Literary Mohawk, Poe': Literary Nationalism and the 'Indianation' of Antebellum American Culture." *ESQ* 48 (2002): 97–133.

———. " 'The Italics Are Mine': Edgar Allan Poe and the Semiotics of Print." *Illuminating Letters: Typography and Literary Interpretation*. Ed. Megan Benton and Paul Gutjahr. Amherst: U of Massachusetts P, 2001. 139–61.

Jacobs, Robert D. *Poe: Journalist and Critic*. Baton Rouge: Louisiana State UP, 1969.

James, Henry. "Charles Baudelaire." *Nation* 27 Apr. 1876: 280.

Jones, David Pryce. *Graham Greene*. Edinburgh: Oliver, 1963.

Jones, Paul Christian. "The Danger of Sympathy: Edgar Allan Poe's 'Hop-Frog' and the Abolitionist Rhetoric of Pathos." *Journal of American Studies* 35.2 (2001): 239–54.

Jones, William B., Jr. *Classics Illustrated: A Cultural History, with Illustrations.* Jefferson: McFarland, 2002.

Jordan, Cynthia S. "Poe's Re-vision: The Recovery of the Second Story." *American Literature* 59 (1987): 1–19.

Jordan, Winthrop D. *White over Black. American Attitudes toward the Negro, 1550–1812.* Chapel Hill: U of North Carolina P, 1968.

Kafton-Minkel, Walter. *Subterranean Worlds: 100,000 Years of Dragons, Dwarfs, the Dead, Lost Races, and UFOs from Inside the Earth.* Port Townsend: Loompanics, 1989.

Kammen, Michael. *American Culture, American Tastes: Social Change and the Twentieth Century.* New York: Basic, 2000.

Kennedy, J. Gerald, ed. Arthur Gordon Pym *and Related Tales.* New York: Oxford UP, 1998.

———, ed. *A Historical Guide to Edgar Allan Poe.* Oxford: Oxford UP, 2001.

———. " 'A Mania for Composition': Poe's 'Annus Mirabilis and the Violence of Nation-Building." *American Literary History* 17 (2005): 1–35.

———. *Poe, Death, and the Life of Writing.* New Haven: Yale UP, 1987.

———. " 'Trust No Man': Poe, Douglass, and the Culture of Slavery." Kennedy and Weissberg 225–28.

Kennedy, J. Gerald, and Liliane Weissberg, eds. *Romancing the Shadow: Poe and Race.* Oxford: Oxford UP, 2001.

Kennedy, X. J., and Dana Gioia, eds. *Literature: An Introduction to Fiction, Poetry, and Drama.* 9th ed. New York: Longman, 2005.

Kete, Mary Louise. *Sentimental Collaborations: Mourning and Middle-Class Identity in Nineteenth-Century America.* Durham: Duke UP, 2000.

Kimball, A. Samuel. "D-Ciphering Dupin's Fac-simile Signature: The Infanticidal Implications of a 'Dessein si Funeste.' " *Edgar Allan Poe Review* 6.1 (2005): 20–36.

King, Stephen. *Bare Bones: Conversations on Terror with Stephen King.* Ed. Tim Underwood and Chuck Miller. New York: McGraw, 1988.

———. *Carrie.* 1974. New York: New Amer. Lib., 1975.

———. *The Dark Half.* New York: Viking, 1989.

———. *The Dead Zone.* New York: Viking, 1979.

———. "Dolan's Cadillac." *Nightmares and Dreamscapes.* By King. New York: Viking, 1993. 11–66.

———. *Gerald's Game.* New York: Viking, 1992.

———. *The Girl Who Loved Tom Gordon.* New York: Scribner's, 1999.

———. *Needful Things.* New York: Viking, 1991.

———. *'Salem's Lot.* New York: New Amer. Lib., 1975.

———. *The Shining.* New York: Viking, 1977.

Kopley, Richard. *Edgar Allan Poe and the* Philadelphia Saturday News. Baltimore: Enoch Pratt Free Lib., The Edgar Allan Poe Soc., and the Lib. of the U of Baltimore, 1991.

———, ed. *Poe's* Pym: *Critical Explorations.* Durham: Duke UP, 1992.

Kristeva, Julia. *The Kristeva Reader*. Ed. Toril Moi. New York: Columbia UP, 1986.

Lacan, Jacques. "Seminar on 'The Purloined Letter.'" *The Seminar of Jacques Lacan. Book II: The Ego in Freud's Theory and in the Technique of Psychoanalysis, 1954–1955*. Ed. Jacques-Alain Miller. Trans. Sylvana Tomaselli. New York: Norton, 1991. 191–205.

———. "Seminar on 'The Purloined Letter.'" Trans. Jeffrey Mehlman. *The Purloined Poe: Lacan, Derrida, and Psychoanalytic Reading*. Ed. John P. Miller and William J. Richardson. Baltimore: Johns Hopkins UP, 1988. 28–54. Rpt. of "Seminar on 'The Purloined Letter.'" Trans. Mehlman. *French Freud: Structural Studies in Psychoanalysis*. Spec. issue of *Yale French Studies* 48 (1972): 39–72.

Laderman, Gary. *The Sacred Remains: American Attitudes toward Death, 1799–1883*. New Haven: Yale UP, 1996.

Lauter, Paul, et al., eds. *The Heath Anthology of American Literature*. 4th ed. 2 vols. Boston: Houghton, 2002.

Lawrence, D. H. *Studies in Classical American Literature*. New York: Seltzer, 1923.

Lee, Maurice S. "Absolute Poe: His System of Transcendental Racism." *American Literature* 75.4 (2003): 751–81.

Lehan, Richard. "The Grotesque End Product of the American Dream." *Readings on The Great Gatsby*. Ed. Katie De Koster. San Diego: Greenhaven, 1998. 104–10.

Lenz, William E. "Poe's *Arthur Gordon Pym* and the Narrative Techniques of the Antarctic Gothic." *CEA Critic* 53.3 (1991): 30–38.

Leverenz, David. "Poe and the Gentry Virginia." Rosenheim and Rachman 210–36.

Levin, Harry. *The Power of Blackness: Hawthorne, Poe, Melville*. New York: Vintage, 1960.

Levine, Lawrence W. *Highbrow/Lowbrow: The Emergence of Cultural Hierarchy in America*. Cambridge: Harvard UP, 1990.

Levine, Susan F., and Stuart Levine. "Poe in Spanish America." Vines, *Poe Abroad* 121–29.

———, eds. *The Short Fiction of Edgar Allan Poe: An Annotated Edition*. Urbana: U of Illinois P, 1990.

Ljungquist, Kent P. "The 'Little War' and Longfellow's Dilemma: New Documents in the Plagiarism Controversy of 1845." *Resources for American Literary Study* 23.1 (1997): 28–57.

Lloyd, Rosemary, ed. *Selected Letters of Baudelaire: The Conquest of Solitude*. Chicago: U of Chicago P, 1986.

Locke, Richard Adams. "Great Astronomical Discoveries Lately Made by Sir John Herschel, L.L.D., F.R.S, &c. at The Cape of Good Hope." *The Museum of Hoaxes*. Ed. Alex Boese. 2002. 15 June 2005 <http:// www.museumofhoaxes .com/moonhoax1.html>.

Lolita. Dir. Adrian Lyne. Perf. Jeremy Irons, Dominique Swain, Melanie Griffith, and Frank Langella. Lion's Gate, 1997.

Lolita. 8 Jul 2008. <http://www.pathe-lolita.com/>. Path: Director and Actors.

Longmore, Paul K. *"Why I Burned My Book" and Other Essays on Disability*. Philadelphia: Temple UP, 2003.

Lovecraft, H. P. *Supernatural Horror in Literature*. New York: Abramson, 1945.

Loving, Jerome. *Lost in the Customhouse: Authorship in the American Renaissance*. Iowa City: U of Iowa P, 1993.

Lowell, James Russell. "A Fable for Critics." *American Poetry: The Nineteenth Century*. Ed. John Hollander. New York: Lib. of Amer., 1996: 315–16.

Mabbott, Thomas Ollive, ed. *Collected Works of Edgar Allan Poe*. 3 vols. Cambridge: Belknap–Harvard UP, 1969.

———, ed. *Complete Poems*. By Edgar Allan Poe. Cambridge: Harvard UP, 1969; Urbana: U of Illinois P, 2000.

Magistrale, Tony. *Student Companion to Edgar Allan Poe*. Westport: Greenwood, 2001.

Marvin, Thomas F. " 'These Days of Double Dealing': Edgar Allan Poe and the Business of Magazine Publishing." *American Periodicals* 11 (2001): 81–94.

Masur, Louis. *1831: Year of Eclipse*. New York: Hill, 2001.

Matthiessen, F. O. *American Renaissance: Art and Expression in the Age of Emerson and Whitman*. New York: Oxford UP, 1941.

May, Charles E. *Edgar Allan Poe: A Study of the Short Fiction*. New York: Twayne, 1991.

McCloud, Scott. *Understanding Comics*. Northampton: Tundra, 1993.

McGann, Jerome. *Radiant Textuality: Literature after the World Wide Web*. New York: Palgrave, 2001.

———. *The Textual Condition*. Princeton: Princeton UP, 1991.

McGill, Meredith L. *American Literature and the Culture of Reprinting, 1834–1853*. Philadelphia: U of Pennsylvania P, 2003.

———. "Poe, Literary Nationalism, and Authorial Identity." Rosenheim and Rachman 271–304.

Mead, Joan Tyler. "Poe's 'Manual of Seamanship.' " Kopley, *Poe's Pym* 20–32.

Mehlman, Jeffrey. "Poe Pourri: Lacan's Purloined Letter." *Semiotexte* 1.3 (1975): 51–58.

Meyers, Jeffrey. "Poe Heavily Influenced Other Writers." *Readings on Edgar Allan Poe*. Ed. Bonnie Szumski and Carol Prime. San Diego: Greenhaven, 1998. 49–56.

Meyers, Marvin. *The Jacksonian Persuasion: Politics and Belief*. Stanford: Stanford UP, 1957.

Miller, John Carl. *John Henry Ingram's Poe Collection at the University of Virginia*. Charlottesville: U of Virginia Lib., 1994.

Miller, Perry. *The Raven and the Whale: The War of Words and Wits in the Era of Poe and Melville*. New York: Harcourt, 1956.

———, ed. *The Transcendentalists: An Anthology*. Cambridge: Harvard UP, 1950.

Miner, Madonne M. "Lady No Longer Sings the Blues: Rape, Madness, and Silence in *The Bluest Eye*." *Toni Morrison*. Ed. Harold Bloom. *Modern Critical Views*. New York: Chelsea, 1990. 85–99.

Moldenhauer, Joseph J. "*Pym*, the Dighton Rock, and the Matter of Vineland." Kopley, *Poe's Pym* 75–94.

Morrison, Toni. *The Bluest Eye*. New York: Penguin, 1994.

————. *Playing in the Dark: Whiteness and the Literary Imagination*. Cambridge: Harvard UP, 1992.

Morton, Donald E. *Vladimir Nabokov*. New York: Unger, 1974.

Moss, Sidney P. *Poe's Literary Battles: The Critic in the Context of His Literary Milieu*. Carbondale: Southern Illinois UP, 1963.

Mott, Frank Luther. *A History of American Magazines: 1741–1850*. Cambridge: Harvard UP, 1930.

Muller, John. "Negation in 'The Purloined Letter': Hegel, Poe, and Lacan." Muller and Richardson 343–68.

Muller, John P., and William J. Richardson, eds. *The Purloined Poe: Lacan, Derrida, and Psychoanalytic Reading*. Baltimore: Johns Hopkins UP, 1988.

Myerson, Joel, ed. *Emerson and Thoreau: The Contemporary Reviews*. Cambridge: Cambridge UP, 1992.

Nabokov, Peter. *Native American Testimony: A Chronicle of Indian-White Relations from Prophecy to the Present, 1492–2000*. Rev. ed. New York: Penguin, 1999.

Nabokov, Vladimir. *The Annotated* Lolita. 1970. New York: Vintage, 1991.

Rev. of *Nature, Addresses and Lectures*, by Ralph Waldo Emerson. *Literary World* 3 Nov. 1849: 374–76.

Neimeyer, Mark. "Poe and Popular Culture." Hayes 205–24.

Nelson, Dana. *The Word in Black and White: Reading "Race" in American Literature, 1638–1867*. New York: Oxford UP, 1992.

Nutall, Christine. *Teaching Reading Skills in a Foreign Language*. London: Heinemann, 1982.

Oates, Joyce Carol. *Haunted: Tales of the Grotesque*. New York: Dutton, 1994.

————. "Martyrdom." Oates, *Haunted* 284–302.

————. "The Premonition." Oates, *Haunted* 172–87.

————. "Where Are You Going, Where Have You Been?" *Selected Early Stories of Joyce Carol Oates*. New York: Ontario Rev., 1993. 118–36.

————. "The White Cat." Oates, *Haunted* 72–96.

O'Brien, Frank M. *Story of the Sun*. New York: Doran, 1918.

O'Brien, Ian. "Straying from the American Dream." Unpublished essay, 27 May 2005.

Ostrom, John Ward, ed. *The Letters of Edgar Allan Poe*. New York: Gordian, 1948.

Pahl, Dennis. "Recovering Byron: Poe's 'The Assignation.'" *Criticism* 26.3 (1984): 211–29.

Parini, Jay, ed. *The Complete Poems of Edgar Allan Poe*. New York: Signet, 1996.

Parkin-Gounelas, Ruth. *Literature and Psychoanalysis: Intertextual Readings*. New York: Palgrave, 2001.

Paulding, J[ames] K[irke]. *Slavery in the United States*. 1836. New York: Negro UP, 1968.

Pease, Donald. "Marginal Politics and 'The Purloined Letter': A Review Essay." *Poe Studies* 16.1 (1983): 18–23.

————. *Visionary Compacts: American Renaissance Writings in Cultural Context*. Madison: U of Wisconsin P, 1987.

Pedersen, Susan, and Doug Williams. "A Comparison of Assessment Practices and the Effects on Learning." *Journal of Educational Multimedia and Hypermedia* 13.3 (2004): 283–307.

Peeples, Scott. *The Afterlife of Edgar Allan Poe*. Rochester: Camden, 2004.

———. " 'The *Mere* Man of Letters Must Ever Be a Cipher': Poe and N. P. Willis." *ESQ* 46 (2000): 125–47.

Perry, Dennis. *Hitchcock and Poe: The Legacy of Delight and Terror*. Lanham: Scarecrow, 2003.

Petrie, William. "To the Editor of the Literary Gazette." *Literary Gazette* 14 Mar. 1846: 237–38. Rpt. in I. Walker 257–59.

Pike, Martha, and Janice Armstrong, eds. *A Time to Mourn: Expressions of Grief in Nineteenth-Century America*. Stony Brook: Museums at Stony Brook, 1980.

Poe, Edgar Allan. "Annabel Lee." Poe, *Poetry* 102–03.

———. "The Assignation." Poe, *Poetry* 200–11.

———. Rev. of *Ballads and Other Poems*, by Henry Wadsworth Longfellow. Thompson, *Edgar Allan Poe* 679–83.

———. "The Balloon-Hoax." Poe, *Poetry* 643–55.

———. "Berenice." Poe, *Poetry* 225–33.

———. "The Black Cat." Poe, *Poetry* 597–606.

———. "The Cask of Amontillado." Poe, *Poetry* 848–54.

———. "The Colloquy of Monos and Una." Poe, *Poetry* 449–57.

———. *The Complete Works of Edgar Allan Poe*. Ed. James Harrison. Vol. 16. New York: AMS, 1965.

———. Rev. of *Conti the Discarded*, by Henry F. Chorley. Thompson, *Edgar Allan Poe* 164–67.

———. Rev. of *A Fable for the Critics*, by James Russell Lowell. Thompson, *Edgar Allan Poe* 814–22.

———. "The Fall of the House of Usher." Poe, *Poetry* 317–36.

———. "Fifty Suggestions." Thompson, *Edgar Allan Poe* 1297–308.

———. "Hop-Frog." Poe, *Poetry* 899–908.

———. "How to Write a Blackwood Article." Poe, *Poetry* 278–97.

———. "The Imp of the Perverse." Poe, *Poetry* 826–32.

———. "Lenore." Poe, *Poetry* 68–69.

———. *The Letters of Edgar Allan Poe*. 1948. Ed. John Ward Ostrom. 2 vols. New York: Gordian, 1966.

———. "Letter to B——." Poe, *Poetry* 1365–72.

———. Letter to John P. Kennedy. 11 Sept. 1835. Poe, *Letters* 1: 73–74.

———. "Letter to Mr. —— ——." Poe, *Poetry* 10–17.

———. "Ligeia." Poe, *Poetry* 262–77.

———. "The Literati of New York City." Thompson, *Edgar Allan Poe* 1118–22.

———. "The Man That Was Used Up." Poe, *Poetry* 307–16.

———. "Marginalia." 1844. Thompson, *Edgar Allan Poe* 1354.

———. "The Masque of the Red Death." Poe, *Poetry* 485–90.

———. "Morella." Poe, *Poetry* 234–39.

———. "Morning on the Wissahiccon." Poe, *Poetry* 937–44.

———. "The Murders in the Rue Morgue." Poe, *Poetry* 397–431.

———. *The Narrative of Arthur Gordon Pym of Nantucket*. Poe, *Poetry* 1003–182.

———. "Never Bet the Devil Your Head." Poe, *Poetry* 458–67.

———. "The Oval Portrait." Poe, *Poetry* 481–84.

———. "The Philosophy of Composition." Poe, *Poetry* 1373–85.

———. "The Pit and the Pendulum." Poe, *Poetry* 491–505.

———. "The Poetic Principle." Poe, *Poetry* 1431–54.

———. *Poetry, Tales, and Selected Essays*. Notes by Patrick F. Quinn and G. R. Thompson. New York: Lib. of Amer., 1996.

———. Preface. *Tales of the Grotesque and Arabesque*. 1840. Poe, *Poetry* 129–30.

———. "The Premature Burial." Poe, *Poetry* 666–79.

———. "The Purloined Letter." Poe, *Poetry* 680–98.

———. "The Raven." Poe, *Poetry* 81–85.

———. *"The Raven" and Other Favorite Poems*. Dover Thrift Mineola: Dover, 1991.

———. "The Sleeper." Poe, *Poetry* 64–65.

———. "Some Secrets from the Magazine Prison-House." Thompson, *Edgar Allan Poe* 1036–38.

———. "Some Words with a Mummy." Poe, *Poetry* 805–21.

———. "Sonnet—To Science." Poe, *Poetry* 38.

———. "The South-West." *Southern Literary Messenger* Jan. 1836: 122–23. *Making of America*. 20 June 2005 <http://quod.lib.umich.edu/m/moagrp>. <www.hti.umich .edu>.

———. "The System of Doctor Tarr and Professor Fether." Poe, *Poetry* 699–716.

———. *Tales of Terror and Detection*. Dover Thrift ed. Mineola: Dover, 1995.

———. "The Tell-Tale Heart." Poe, *Poetry* 555–60.

———. Rev. of *Twice-Told Tales* and *Mosses from an Old Manse*, by Nathaniel Hawthorne. Thompson, *Edgar Allan Poe* 577–88.

———. "Ulalume—A Ballad." Poe, *Poetry* 89–90.

———. "The Unparalleled Adventure of One Hans Pfaall." Poe, *Poetry* 951–1001.

———. "The Visionary (The Assignation)." Mabbott 2: 148–69.

———. "William Wilson." Poe, *Poetry* 337–57.

"Poe and Griswold." 12 Sept. 1999. *Edgar Allan Poe Society of Baltimore*. 28 June 2005 <http://www.eapoe.org/geninfo/poegrisw.htm>.

"Poe's Problematic Biography." *Edgar Allan Poe Society of Baltimore* 7 Apr. 2007. 2 July 2007 <http://www.eapoe.org>. Path: General Topics about Edgar Allan Poe; Poe's Problematic Biography.

Pollin, Burton R. ed. *The Collected Writings of Edgar Allan Poe*. Boston: Twayne, 1981–1997. Vol. 1: *The Imaginary Voyages: Pym, Hans Pfall, Julius Rodman*; Vol. 2: *The Brevities:* Pinakidia, *Marginalia, and Other Works*; Vol. 3: *Writings in the* Broadway Journal, *Non-fictional Prose, Part I: The Text*; Vol. 4: *The* Broadway Journal, *Non-fictional Prose, Part II: Annotations*; Vol. 5: *Writings in the* Southern Literary Messenger. 5 Vols.

———. *Images of Poe's Works: A Comprehensive Descriptive Catalogue of Illustrations.* Westport: Greenwood, 1989.

———. Introduction. *The Narrative of Arthur Gordon Pym.* Pollin, *Collected Writings* 1: 4–52.

———. "Music and Edgar Allan Poe: A Second Annotated Checklist." *Poe Studies / Dark Romanticism* 15 (1982): 7–13.

———. "Poe's Life Reflected through the Sources of *Pym.*" Kopley, *Poe's* Pym 95–106.

Polonsky, Rachel. "Poe's Aesthetic Theory." Hayes 42–56.

Pop, Iggy. "The Tell-Tale Heart." *Closed on Account of Rabies: Poems and Tales of Edgar Allan Poe.* Mercury, 1997.

Porter, Dennis. "Of Poets, Politicians, Policemen, and the Power of Analysis." *New Literary History* 19.3 (1988): 501–19.

Prucha, Francis Paul. *The Great Father: The United States Government and the American Indians.* Abr. ed. Lincoln: U of Nebraska P, 1986.

Psycho. Dir. Alfred Hitchcock. Perf. Anthony Perkins, Janet Leigh. Paramount, 1960.

Quinn, Arthur Hobson. *Edgar Allan Poe: A Critical Biography.* New York: Appleton-Century, 1941.

Quinn, Patrick, and G. R. Thompson, eds. *Edgar Allan Poe: Poetry, Tales, and Selected Essays.* New York: Lib. of Amer., 1984.

Race, William H. *Classical Genres and English Poetry.* London: Helm, 1988.

Rachman, Stephen. " 'Es lässt sich nicht schreiben': Plagiarism and 'The Man of the Crowd.' " *The American Face of Edgar Allan Poe.* Ed. Shawn Rosenheim and Stephan Rachman. Baltimore: Johns Hopkins UP, 1995. 49–90.

Railton, Stephen, ed. Uncle Tom's Cabin *and American Culture: A Multimedia Archive.* 1998–2007. 29 June 2007 <www.iath.virginia.edu/utc/>.

Rajan, Gita. "A Feminist Rereading of Poe's 'The Tell-Tale Heart.' " *Papers on Language and Literature* 24.3 (1988): 283–300.

Rapatzikou, Tatiana, and David Galloway, eds. The Fall of the House of Usher *and Other Writings: Poems, Tales, Essays, and Reviews.* New York: Penguin, 2003.

Reed, Lou. *The Raven.* Sire, 2004.

Reese, Jim. "Creating a Place for Lesbian and Gay Readings in Secondary English Classrooms." *Lesbian and Gay Studies and the Teaching of English: Positions, Pedagogies, and Cultural Politics.* Ed. William J. Spurlin. Urbana: NCTE, 2000.

Regan, Robert, ed. *Poe: A Collection of Critical Essays.* Englewood Cliffs: Prentice, 1967.

Renza, Louis A. " 'Ut Pictura Poe': Literary Politics in 'The Island of the Fay' and 'Morning on the Wissahiccon.' " Rosenheim and Rachman 305–29.

Reynolds, David. *Beneath the American Renaissance: The Subversive Imagination in the Age of Emerson and Melville.* New York: Knopf, 1988.

Richard, Claude. "Destin, Design, Dasein: Lacan, Derrida, and 'The Purloined Letter.' " *Iowa Review* 12.4 (1981): 1–11.

————. "The Heart of Poe and the Rhythmics of the Poems." Carlson, *Critical Essays* 195–206.

Richards, Eliza. *Gender and the Poetics of Reception in Poe's Circle*. Cambridge: Cambridge UP, 2004.

Riddell, Joseph. "The Crypt of Edgar Allan Poe." *Boundary 2* 7.3 (1979): 117–44.

Ringe, Donald. *American Gothic: Imagination and Reason in Nineteenth-Century Fiction*. Lexington: UP of Kentucky, 1982.

Rorty, Richard. *The Linguistic Turn: Essays in Philosophical Method*. Chicago: U of Chicago P, 1967.

Rosenheim, Shawn. "Detective Fiction, Psychoanalysis, and the Analytic Sublime." Rosenheim and Rachman 153–78.

Rosenheim, Shawn, and Stephen Rachman, eds. *The American Face of Edgar Allan Poe*. Baltimore: Johns Hopkins UP, 1995.

Rowe, John Carlos. "Edgar Allan Poe's Imperial Fantasy and the American Frontier." Kennedy and Weissberg 75–105.

————. "Poe, Antebellum Slavery, and Modern Criticism." Kopley, *Poe's* Pym 117–40.

Samuels, Shirley, ed. *The Culture of Sentiment: Race, Gender, and Sentimentality in Nineteenth-Century America*. New York: Oxford UP, 1992.

Saum, Louis O. "Death in the Popular Mind of Pre–Civil War America." *Death in America*. Ed. David E. Stannard. Philadelphia: U of Pennsylvania P, 1975. 30–49.

Sawyer, Michael. "Albert Lewis Kanter and the Classics: The Man behind the Gilberton Company." *Journal of Popular Culture* 20.4 (1987): 1–18.

Schiff, Stephen. *Lolita: The Book of the Film*. New York: Applause, 1998.

Scudera, Domenick. *Poe on Poe*. Unpub. ms.

Sears, John F. *Sacred Places: American Tourist Attractions in the Nineteenth Century*. New York: Oxford UP, 1989.

Sellers, Charles. *The Market Revolution: Jacksonian America, 1815–1846*. New York: Oxford UP, 1991.

Seltzer, Mark. *Serial Killers: Death and Life in America's Wound Culture*. New York: Routledge, 1998.

Sigourney, Lydia. "Death of an Infant." *The Heath Anthology of American Literature*. Ed. Paul Lauter. Concise ed. New York: Houghton, 2004. 687–88.

Silsbee, William. "The Transcendental Doctrine of Self-Reliance." *Christian Examiner and Religious Miscellany* 1844: 331–49.

Silverman, Kenneth. *Edgar A. Poe: Mournful and Never-ending Remembrance*. New York: Harper, 1991.

————. Introduction. Silverman, *New Essays* 1–26.

————, ed. *New Essays on Poe's Major Tales*. New York: Cambridge UP, 1993.

Simpson, Philip L. *Psycho Paths: Tracking the Serial Killer through Contemporary Film and Fiction*. Carbondale: Southern Illinois UP, 2000.

Smith, Don G. *The Poe Cinema: A Critical Filmography of Theatrical Releases Based on the Works of Edgar Allan Poe*. Jefferson: McFarland, 1999.

Spiegelman, Art. *Maus*. New York: Pantheon, 1986.

Stanton, Elizabeth Cady, and Lucretia Mott. "Declaration of Sentiments." 1848. *Antebellum American Culture: An Interpretive Anthology*. Ed. David Brion Davis. Lexington: Heath, 1979. 91–93.

Stanton, William. *The Great United States Exploring Expedition of 1838–1842*. Berkeley: U of California P, 1975.

Stavola, Thomas J. *Scott Fitzgerald: Crisis in an American Identity*. New York: Harper, 1979.

Steele, Jeffrey. *The Representation of the Self in the American Renaissance*. Chapel Hill: U of North Carolina P, 1987.

Stern, Jane, and Michael Stern. *The Encyclopedia of Bad Taste*. New York: Harper, 1990.

Stern, Philip van Doren, ed. *The Portable Edgar Allan Poe*. New York: Penguin, 1977.

Stolar, Arieh. "Sensations from Behind Glass: Another Tale a la Blackwood." Unpublished essay, 2004.

Stowe, Harriet Beecher. "Concluding Remarks [to *Uncle Tom's Cabin*]." *National Era* 1 Apr. 1852: 1.

———. *Uncle Tom's Cabin; or, Life among the Lowly*. Illus. ed. Boston: Jewett, 1853. Uncle Tom's Cabin *and American Culture: A Multimedia Archive*. Ed. Stephen Railton. U of Virginia, 2007. <http://www.iath.virginia.edu/utc/uncletom/illustra/53illf.html>.

Straub, Peter. *The Blue Rose*. San Francisco: Underwood, 1985.

———. *Mystery*. New York: Dutton, 1990.

Streeby, Shelley. *American Sensations: Class, Empire, and the Production of Popular Culture*. Berkeley: U of California P, 2002.

Sundquist, Eric. *Home as Found: Authority and Genealogy in Nineteenth-Century American Literature*. Baltimore: Johns Hopkins UP, 1979.

———. *To Wake the Nations: Race in the Making of American Literature*. Cambridge: Harvard UP, 1993.

Sutherland, Kathryn, ed. *Electronic Text: Investigations in Method and Theory*. Oxford: Clarendon, 1997.

———. Introduction. Sutherland, *Electronic Text* 1–18.

Tate, Allen. "The Angelic Imagination." *Essays of Four Decades*. By Tate. Wilmington: Intercollegiate Studies Inst., 1999. 401–23.

———. "Our Cousin, Mr. Poe." 1949. *Collected Essays*. Denver: Swallow, 1959. 38–50.

The Tell-Tale Heart. Dir. Art Babbitt and Ted Parmalee. Narr. James Mason. 1953.

Telotte, J. P. "Faith and Idolatry in the Horror Film." *Literature/Film Quarterly* 8 (1980): 143–55.

Thompson, G. R. "Edgar Allan Poe and the Writers of the Old South." *Columbia Literary History of the United States*. Ed. Emory Elliot. New York: Columbia UP, 1988. 262–77.

———, ed. *Edgar Allan Poe: Essays and Reviews*. New York: Lib. of Amer., 1984.

———. Introduction. *Great Short Works of Edgar Allan Poe: Poems, Tales, Criticism*. Ed. Thompson. 1–48.

———. *Poe's Fiction: Romantic Irony in the Gothic Tales*. Madison: U of Wisconsin P, 1973.

———, ed. *The Selected Writings of Edgar Allan Poe*. Norton Critical ed. New York: Norton, 2004.

Thoreau, Henry David. *Collected Poems of Henry Thoreau*. Ed. Carl Bode. Chicago: Packard, 1943.

———. *Walden; or, Life in the Woods*. Baym B: 1807–1981.

———. *Walden*. Walden *and "Resistance to Civil Government."* 2nd ed. Ed. William Rossi. New York: Norton, 1992. 1–223.

Tissera, Graciela E. "Jorge Luis Borges." Vines, *Poe Abroad* 221–26.

Tocqueville, Alexis de. *Democracy in America*. Trans. Harvey C. Mansfield and Delba Winthrop. Chicago: U of Chicago P, 2000.

Tom Petty and the Heartbreakers. "Mary Jane's Last Dance." *Mary Jane's Last Dance*. MCA, 1993. Music video. Dir. Keir McFarlane. MTV, 1995.

Tomc, Sandra M. "Poe and His Circle." Hayes 21–41.

Tompkins, Jane. *Sensational Designs: The Cultural Work of American Fiction, 1790–1860*. New York: Oxford UP, 1985.

Trafton, Scott. *Egypt Land: Race and Nineteenth-Century American Egyptomania*. Durham: Duke UP, 2004.

"Treehouse of Horror." *The Simpsons*. 24 Oct. 1990.

United States. Dept. of Defense. "DoD News Briefing—Secretary Rumsfeld and Gen. Myers." 12 Feb. 2002. 19 Oct. 2007 <www.defenselink.mil/transcripts/transcript .aspx?transcriptid=2636>.

Valéry, Paul. *The Evening with Monsieur Teste*. Trans. Jackson Mathews. Princeton: Princeton UP, 1972.

———. "The Place of Baudelaire." *Leonardo Poe Mallarmé*. Trans. Malcolm Cowley and James R. Lawler. Princeton: Princeton UP, 1972.

Varner, Cornelia. "Notes on Poe's Use of Contemporary Materials in Certain of His Stories." *Journal of English and Germanic Philology* 32 (1933): 77–80.

Verne, Jules. *Five Weeks in a Balloon*. 18 Dec. 2007 <http://www.readbookonline.net/ read/1154/11190>.

———. *The Sphinx of Ice*. *Works of Jules Verne*. Trans. Charles F. Horne. Vol. 14. New York: Park, 1911.

Vertigo. Dir. Alfred Hitchcock. Paramount, 1958.

Vines, Lois Davis, ed. *Poe Abroad: Influence, Reputation, Affinities*. Iowa City: U of Iowa P, 1999.

———. "Poe in France." Vines, *Poe Abroad* 9–18.

———. *Valéry and Poe: A Literary Legacy*. New York: New York UP, 1992.

Wagenknecht, Edward. *Edgar Allan Poe: The Man behind the Legend*. New York: Oxford UP, 1963.

Walker, David. *Appeal to the Coloured Citizens of the World*. 1829. Ed. Sean Wilentz. New York: Hill, 1995.

Walker, I. M., ed. *Edgar Allan Poe: The Critical Heritage*. Critical Heritage Ser. New York: Routledge, 1986.

Ware, Chris. *Jimmy Corrigan: The Smartest Kid on Earth*. New York: Knopf, 2000.

Weber, Jean-Paul. "Edgar Poe; or, The Theme of the Clock." Regan 79–97.

Weld, Theodore Dwight. *American Slavery As It Is: Testimony of a Thousand Witnesses*. 1839. New York: Arno, 1968.

Weskamp, Ralf. *Fachdidaktik: Grundlagen und Konzepte*. Berlin: Cornelsen, 2001.

Wetherill, Peter M. "Edgar Poe and Madame Sabatier." *Modern Language Quarterly* 20.4 (1959): 344–54.

Whalen, Terence. "Average Racism: Poe, Slavery, and the Wages of Literary Nationalism." Kennedy and Weissberg 3–40.

———. *Edgar Allan Poe and the Masses: The Political Economy of Literature in Antebellum America*. Princeton: Princeton UP, 1999.

Whitman, Walt. *"Leaves of Grass" and Other Writings*. 2nd ed. Ed. Michael Moon. New York: Norton, 2002.

Widmer, Ted. *Martin Van Buren*. New York: Times, 2005.

Wiggins, Grant, and Jay McTighe. *Understanding by Design*. Upper Saddle River: Merrill, 2001.

Wilbur, Richard. "The House of Poe." Regan 99–120.

Wilentz, Sean. *Chants Democratic: New York City and the Rise of the American Working Class, 1788–1850*. New York: Oxford UP, 1984.

Williams, Linda R. *Critical Desire: Psychoanalysis and the Literary Subject*. New York: St. Martin's, 1995.

Williams, Raymond. *Keywords: A Vocabulary of Culture and Society*. New York: Oxford UP, 1983.

Winters, Yvor. "Edgar Allan Poe: A Crisis in the History of American Obscurantism." *On Poe: The Best from American Literature*. Ed. Louis J. Budd and Edwin Cady. Durham: Duke UP, 1993. 55–77.

Wood, Robin. *Hitchcock's Films Revisited*. New York: Columbia UP, 1989.

Woodward, Servanne. "Lacan and Derrida on 'The Purloined Letter.' " *Comparative Literature Studies* 26.1 (1989): 39–49.

Wright American Fiction, 1851–75. Indiana University. <www.letrs.indiana.edu/cgi/t/text/text-idx?c=wright2;cc=wright2;sid=407a3d9c56416348ee1b27c11a6bbd1b;tpl=home.tpl>.

Zackodnik, Teresa. "Fixing the Color Line: The Mulatto, Southern Courts, and Racial Identity." *American Quarterly* 53.3 (2001): 420–72.

Zboray, Ronald. *A Fictive People: Antebellum Economic Development and the American Reading Public*. Oxford: Oxford UP, 1993.

Zochert, Donald. "Science and the Common Man in Ante-bellum America." *Science in America since 1820*. Ed. Nathan Reingold. New York: Science History Pub., 1976. 7–32.

Zola, Irving K. *Missing Pieces: A Chronicle of Living with a Disability*. Philadelphia: Temple UP, 1982.

INDEX OF NAMES

INDEX OF WORKS BY POE

Modern Language Association of America
Approaches to Teaching World Literature
Joseph Gibaldi, series editor

Achebe's Things Fall Apart. Ed. Bernth Lindfors. 1991.
Arthurian Tradition. Ed. Maureen Fries and Jeanie Watson. 1992.
Atwood's The Handmaid's Tale *and Other Works*. Ed. Sharon R. Wilson,
    Thomas B. Friedman, and Shannon Hengen. 1996.
Austen's Emma. Ed. Marcia McClintock Folsom. 2004.
Austen's Pride and Prejudice. Ed. Marcia McClintock Folsom. 1993.
Balzac's Old Goriot. Ed. Michal Peled Ginsburg. 2000.
Baudelaire's Flowers of Evil. Ed. Laurence M. Porter. 2000.
Beckett's Waiting for Godot. Ed. June Schlueter and Enoch Brater. 1991.
Beowulf. Ed. Jess B. Bessinger, Jr., and Robert F. Yeager. 1984.
Blake's Songs of Innocence and of Experience. Ed. Robert F. Gleckner and
    Mark L. Greenberg. 1989.
Boccaccio's Decameron. Ed. James H. McGregor. 2000.
British Women Poets of the Romantic Period. Ed. Stephen C. Behrendt and
    Harriet Kramer Linkin. 1997.
Charlotte Brontë's Jane Eyre. Ed. Diane Long Hoeveler and Beth Lau. 1993.
Emily Brontë's Wuthering Heights. Ed. Sue Lonoff and Terri A. Hasseler. 2006.
Byron's Poetry. Ed. Frederick W. Shilstone. 1991.
Camus's The Plague. Ed. Steven G. Kellman. 1985.
Writings of Bartolomé de Las Casas. Ed. Santa Arias and Eyda M. Merediz. 2008.
Cather's My Ántonia. Ed. Susan J. Rosowski. 1989.
Cervantes' Don Quixote. Ed. Richard Bjornson. 1984.
Chaucer's Canterbury Tales. Ed. Joseph Gibaldi. 1980.
Chaucer's Troilus and Criseyde *and the Shorter Poems*. Ed. Tison Pugh and
    Angela Jane Weisl. 2006.
Chopin's The Awakening. Ed. Bernard Koloski. 1988.
Coleridge's Poetry and Prose. Ed. Richard E. Matlak. 1991.
Collodi's Pinocchio *and Its Adaptations*. Ed. Michael Sherberg. 2006.
Conrad's "Heart of Darkness" and "The Secret Sharer." Ed. Hunt Hawkins and
    Brian W. Shaffer. 2002.
Dante's Divine Comedy. Ed. Carole Slade. 1982.
Defoe's Robinson Crusoe. Ed. Maximillian E. Novak and Carl Fisher. 2005.
DeLillo's White Noise. Ed. Tim Engles and John N. Duvall. 2006.
Dickens's Bleak House. Ed. John O. Jordan and Gordon Bigelow. 2009.
Dickens's David Copperfield. Ed. Richard J. Dunn. 1984.
Dickinson's Poetry. Ed. Robin Riley Fast and Christine Mack Gordon. 1989.
Narrative of the Life of Frederick Douglass. Ed. James C. Hall. 1999.
Early Modern Spanish Drama. Ed. Laura R. Bass and Margaret R. Greer. 2006

Eliot's Middlemarch. Ed. Kathleen Blake. 1990.

Eliot's Poetry and Plays. Ed. Jewel Spears Brooker. 1988.

Shorter Elizabethan Poetry. Ed. Patrick Cheney and Anne Lake Prescott. 2000.

Ellison's Invisible Man. Ed. Susan Resneck Parr and Pancho Savery. 1989.

English Renaissance Drama. Ed. Karen Bamford and Alexander Leggatt. 2002.

Works of Louise Erdrich. Ed. Gregg Sarris, Connie A. Jacobs, and
   James R. Giles. 2004.

Dramas of Euripides. Ed. Robin Mitchell-Boyask. 2002.

Faulkner's The Sound and the Fury. Ed. Stephen Hahn and Arthur F. Kinney. 1996.

Flaubert's Madame Bovary. Ed. Laurence M. Porter and Eugene F. Gray. 1995.

García Márquez's One Hundred Years of Solitude. Ed. María Elena de Valdés
   and Mario J. Valdés. 1990.

Gilman's "The Yellow Wall-Paper" *and* Herland. Ed. Denise D. Knight and
   Cynthia J. Davis. 2003.

Goethe's Faust. Ed. Douglas J. McMillan. 1987.

Gothic Fiction: The British and American Traditions. Ed. Diane Long Hoeveler
   and Tamar Heller. 2003.

Grass's The Tin Drum. Ed. Monika Shafi. 2008.

Hebrew Bible as Literature in Translation. Ed. Barry N. Olshen and
   Yael S. Feldman. 1989.

Homer's Iliad *and* Odyssey. Ed. Kostas Myrsiades. 1987.

Ibsen's A Doll House. Ed. Yvonne Shafer. 1985.

Henry James's Daisy Miller *and* The Turn of the Screw. Ed. Kimberly C. Reed
   and Peter G. Beidler. 2005.

Works of Samuel Johnson. Ed. David R. Anderson and Gwin J. Kolb. 1993.

Joyce's Ulysses. Ed. Kathleen McCormick and Erwin R. Steinberg. 1993.

Works of Sor Juana Inés de la Cruz. Ed. Emilie L. Bergmann and Stacey Schlau.
   2007.

Kafka's Short Fiction. Ed. Richard T. Gray. 1995.

Keats's Poetry. Ed. Walter H. Evert and Jack W. Rhodes. 1991.

Kingston's The Woman Warrior. Ed. Shirley Geok-lin Lim. 1991.

Lafayette's The Princess of Clèves. Ed. Faith E. Beasley and
   Katharine Ann Jensen. 1998.

Works of D. H. Lawrence. Ed. M. Elizabeth Sargent and Garry Watson. 2001.

Lazarillo de Tormes *and the Picaresque Tradition.* Ed. Anne J. Cruz. 2009.

Lessing's The Golden Notebook. Ed. Carey Kaplan and Ellen Cronan Rose. 1989.

Mann's Death in Venice *and Other Short Fiction.* Ed. Jeffrey B. Berlin. 1992.

Marguerite de Navarre's Heptameron. Ed. Colette H. Winn. 2007.

Medieval English Drama. Ed. Richard K. Emmerson. 1990.

Melville's Moby-Dick. Ed. Martin Bickman. 1985.

Metaphysical Poets. Ed. Sidney Gottlieb. 1990.

Miller's Death of a Salesman. Ed. Matthew C. Roudané. 1995.

Milton's Paradise Lost. Ed. Galbraith M. Crump. 1986.

Milton's Shorter Poetry and Prose. Ed. Peter C. Herman. 2007.

Molière's Tartuffe *and Other Plays*. Ed. James F. Gaines and
    Michael S. Koppisch. 1995.

Momaday's The Way to Rainy Mountain. Ed. Kenneth M. Roemer. 1988.

Montaigne's Essays. Ed. Patrick Henry. 1994.

Novels of Toni Morrison. Ed. Nellie Y. McKay and Kathryn Earle. 1997.

Murasaki Shikibu's The Tale of Genji. Ed. Edward Kamens. 1993.

Nabokov's Lolita. Ed. Zoran Kuzmanovich and Galya Diment. 2008.

Poe's Prose and Poetry. Ed. Jeffrey Andrew Weinstock and Tony Magistrale. 2008.

Pope's Poetry. Ed. Wallace Jackson and R. Paul Yoder. 1993.

Proust's Fiction and Criticism. Ed. Elyane Dezon-Jones and
    Inge Crosman Wimmers. 2003.

Puig's Kiss of the Spider Woman. Ed. Daniel Balderston and Francine Masiello.
    2007.

Pynchon's The Crying of Lot 49 *and Other Works*. Ed. Thomas H. Schaub. 2008.

Novels of Samuel Richardson. Ed. Lisa Zunshine and Jocelyn Harris. 2006.

Rousseau's Confessions *and* Reveries of the Solitary Walker. Ed. John C. O'Neal
    and Ourida Mostefai. 2003.

Shakespeare's Hamlet. Ed. Bernice W. Kliman. 2001.

Shakespeare's King Lear. Ed. Robert H. Ray. 1986.

Shakespeare's Othello. Ed. Peter Erickson and Maurice Hunt. 2005.

Shakespeare's Romeo and Juliet. Ed. Maurice Hunt. 2000.

Shakespeare's The Tempest *and Other Late Romances*. Ed. Maurice Hunt. 1992.

Shelley's Frankenstein. Ed. Stephen C. Behrendt. 1990.

Shelley's Poetry. Ed. Spencer Hall. 1990.

Sir Gawain and the Green Knight. Ed. Miriam Youngerman Miller and
    Jane Chance. 1986.

Song of Roland. Ed. William W. Kibler and Leslie Zarker Morgan. 2006.

Spenser's Faerie Queene. Ed. David Lee Miller and Alexander Dunlop. 1994.

Stendhal's The Red and the Black. Ed. Dean de la Motte and Stirling Haig. 1999.

Sterne's Tristram Shandy. Ed. Melvyn New. 1989.

Stowe's Uncle Tom's Cabin. Ed. Elizabeth Ammons and Susan Belasco. 2000.

Swift's Gulliver's Travels. Ed. Edward J. Rielly. 1988.

Thoreau's Walden *and Other Works*. Ed. Richard J. Schneider. 1996.

Tolstoy's Anna Karenina. Ed. Liza Knapp and Amy Mandelker. 2003.

Vergil's Aeneid. Ed. William S. Anderson and Lorina N. Quartarone. 2002.

Voltaire's Candide. Ed. Renée Waldinger. 1987.

Whitman's Leaves of Grass. Ed. Donald D. Kummings. 1990.

Wiesel's Night. Ed. Alan Rosen. 2007.

Works of Oscar Wilde. Ed. Philip E. Smith II. 2008.

Woolf's To the Lighthouse. Ed. Beth Rigel Daugherty and Mary Beth Pringle. 2001.

Wordsworth's Poetry. Ed. Spencer Hall, with Jonathan Ramsey. 1986.

Wright's Native Son. Ed. James A. Miller. 1997.